THE AFROCENTRIC PRAXIS OF TEACHING *FOR* FREEDOM

A great book! Carefully thought out and developed. It will be easy for teachers to follow and to learn.

Carl A. Grant, *University of Wisconsin–Madison, USA*

An important and foundational piece in the field, this book is impressive, timely, engaging, and much needed. It is at once "deep" and understandable, advancing both theoretical and practical understandings of Afrocentric praxis. I am smiling as I write this and activated to use and build on this brilliant work.

Gloria Swindler Boutte, *University of South Carolina, USA*

King and Swartz demonstrate how to teach content based on Afrocentric theory and African worldviews in ways that result in a more holistic and historically accurate presentation of people of African descent and related events. This will not only reconnect African American children to their heritage knowledge, but will elevate and deepen all students' understanding of people of African descent.

Sandra Winn Tutwiler, *Washburn University, USA*

This book shows how an African worldview, as a platform for culture-based teaching and learning, helps educators to retrieve African heritage and cultural knowledge which have been historically discounted and decoupled from teaching and learning. It exemplifies how the emancipatory pedagogies it delineates and demonstrates are supported by African worldview concepts and parallel knowledge and values. Making African Diasporan cultural connections visible in the curriculum, the book provides teachers with content drawn from Africa's legacy to humanity as a model for locating all students—and the cultures and groups they represent—as subjects in the curriculum and pedagogy of schooling.

Joyce E. King holds the Benjamin E. Mays Endowed Chair for Urban Teaching, Learning and Leadership at Georgia State University, USA.

Ellen E. Swartz is an independent scholar and education consultant in curriculum development and the construction of culturally informed instructional materials for K-12 teachers and students.

THE AFROCENTRIC PRAXIS OF TEACHING *FOR* FREEDOM

Connecting Culture to Learning

Joyce E. King and Ellen E. Swartz

Routledge
Taylor & Francis Group

NEW YORK AND LONDON

First published 2016
by Routledge
711 Third Avenue, New York, NY 10017

and by Routledge
2 Park Square, Milton Park, Abingdon, Oxon OX14 4RN

Routledge is an imprint of the Taylor & Francis Group, an informa business

© 2016 Taylor & Francis

The right of Joyce E. King and Ellen E. Swartz to be identified as the
authors of this work has been asserted by them in accordance with
sections 77 and 78 of the Copyright, Designs and Patents Act 1988.

Library of Congress Cataloging-in-Publication Data
King, Joyce Elaine, 1947-
The Afrocentric praxis of teaching for freedom : connecting culture to
learning / Joyce E. King, Ellen E. Swartz.
    pages cm
    Includes bibliographical references and index.
    1. African Americans–Education. 2. African American schools–
Curricula. 3. Afrocentrism–Study and teaching–United States.
    4. African American teachers–Training of. I. Swartz, Ellen. II. Title.
    LC2771.K55 2016
    371.829'96073–dc23   2015009015

ISBN: 978-1-138-90493-4 (hbk)
ISBN: 978-1-138-90494-1 (pbk)
ISBN: 978-1-315-69612-6 (ebk)

Typeset in Bembo
by Wearset Ltd, Boldon, Tyne and Wear

Printed and bound in the United States of America by Publishers Graphics,
LLC on sustainably sourced paper.

YBP Library Services

KING, JOYCE ELAINE, 1947-

AFROCENTRIC PRAXIS OF TEACHING FOR FREEDOM:
CONNECTING CULTURE TO LEARNING.
                              Paper   167 P.
NEW YORK: ROUTLEDGE, 2016

AUTH: GEORGIA STATE UNIVERSITY.

  LCCN 2015009015
  ISBN 1138904945   **Library PO#** FIRM ORDERS

                                  List   49.95   USD
  8395 NATIONAL UNIVERSITY LIBRAR **Disc**   5.0%
  App. Date   2/17/16   SOE-K12   8214-08 **Net**   47.45   USD

SUBJ: 1. AFRICAN AMERICANS--EDUC. 2. AFROCENTRISM
--STUDY & TEACH.--U.S.

CLASS LC2771   DEWEY# 371.82996073 LEVEL ADV-AC

This book is dedicated to our grandchildren and their children's children, and to the teachers who assist them in pursuing academic and cultural excellence, in coming to know that knowledge is inseparable from wisdom, and that gaining knowledge is for the purpose of bringing good into the world.

CONTENTS

A NOTE ABOUT THE COVER IMAGE

The symbol on the cover is an Adinkra symbol called *Nsaa*. Adinkra is an indigenous Akan (West African) script whose many symbols are epistemic expressions of Akan philosophy, cosmology, values, and cultural concepts. *Nsaa* is a symbol of excellence, genuineness, and authenticity. Chapter 2 provides more information about the origin and meaning of this and other Adinkra symbols and their relationship to emancipatory pedagogy.

FOREWORD

The freedom referred to in the title of this rich piece on pedagogy is available to those in bondage and it is equally relevant to those who cling tenaciously to their thinly disguised philosophical idiom. This group needing freedom has as their role practitioners of bondage. The fetters of superiority and the myriad of manifestations of its power have crippled both groups and have inhibited humanities' possibilities.

If there is truly the deep desire to alter and modify pedagogical practice and enhance its richness, this volume makes it possible, practical, and it is within our grasp. But is the cost too high? The fundamental question is: With all this research and documentation, why is it that educational reformation is so emphatically resisted? Why are educational systems so tenacious in resisting the inclusion of undisputable truths that would liberate the oppressed groups in whose intellectual development educators express such an interest? I know of no accredited scholar who has refuted the details of this volume, nor of the books and articles noted in its references, and index. The Afrocentric praxis of Teaching *for* Freedom needs no explanation, defense, or enhancement. It is impressive, persuasive, and lucid. It is for me to ponder the why.

Will it be read, received, and set aside as not universal in scope and applicability and therefore dispensable to educators? Will it be marginalized or obscured and ignored in the conversations as educational policy makers prepare their agendas? Is the seminal question: How to humanize and actualize the process of education or is the agenda the perpetuation of the myths and obscurities of writers who seek to maintain their premise of superiority and entitlement? Is the agenda also, while including some bits of accuracy of historical events, to minimize the specific instances of cruelty and vicious indignities under which African Americans have suffered, and are suffering, and sometimes paralyzed? It is this exact specificity that gives clarity and meaning to the horrific experiences that must be faced and revisited with their current residue. The effort to protect the historical oppressor and to obscure the identity of his progeny is an issue. It allows a soft and more palpable existence to those who benefited from the past and seek to disassociate themselves from its most blatant acts of inequity.

The New York State Board of Regents chose not to vote on the state-sponsored documents on a "curriculum of inclusion" not because it was inaccurate and sought to correct a damaging curriculum that promoted school failure among four groups of children in the state. The members of the Board of Regents set the document aside because the language was harsh and might expose culpable groups. It was a self-serving decision. The children's academic acumen was secondary to the suppression of the comfort of the policy makers. This is not a singular example of the duality between the needs of the children and the protection of the oppressors. The repertoire of African American pedagogy is replete with similarities and frames too many experiences.

Let us not succumb. While the richness of the scholarship, the logical analysis, the beauty of the African-centered pedagogy, and its healing possibilities is extraordinarily appealing, let us not minimize the abundance of examples of why these findings are not at the core of educational dialogue when decisions, publications, and professional requirements are being decided. *Teaching for Freedom* promises a freedom that is universal and inclusive. It may liberate the oppressor as well as determined African American scholars. Willingness to recognize the value, the art, the fabric, the artifacts, the cogent beauty, and the pithy examples of intelligence are not enough. We must be receptive to examining why the viciousness, ancient and continuous, of the various methods to liberate and free people is not the primary agenda. We must not purify and weaken the specific examples that will give us the ability to recognize their constant existence.

Dr. Adelaide L. Hines Sanford
Philadelphia, Pennsylvania
March 1, 2015

PREFACE AS PREQUEL

In early discussions related to this volume, we were thinking of it as a sequel to our earlier publication, *"Re-membering" History in Student and Teacher Learning: An Afrocentric Culturally Informed Praxis* (King & Swartz, 2014). After all, this new work follows and expands upon the first volume's treatment of emancipatory pedagogy and the connection between cultural concepts and school practices. However, as this volume began to take shape, we realized that the "story" it tells actually precedes the earlier work—that the Afrocentric praxis of Teaching *for* Freedom described herein existed long before *"Re-membering" History in Student and Teacher Learning* was written. In fact, it *had* to.

In order to write about Teaching *for* Freedom, we *had* to observe—and in some cases read about—PK-12 teachers and teacher educators who demonstrated elements of this model. Likewise, we *had* to experience teachers who engaged in historical recovery in their classrooms prior to writing about a praxis of historical recovery and a process of "re-membering" (King & Swartz, 2014). It is the work of these highly effective teachers that is the prequel to both volumes. They had already eschewed standard eurocratic instructional materials and assessments, found or written their own materials, reconnected the multiple knowledge bases and experiences that shaped the past, centered students culturally and individually, invited parents to participate in curriculum and assessment, and regularly engaged—both formally and informally—in critically examining the outcomes of their practices (Bigelow, 1996, 2001; Campbell, 2014; Dean, 2008; Goodwin, 1996, 1998, 2004; Gutstein, 2001; Mbatha, 2012; Secret, 1998; Shakes, 1993, 2004; Smith, 1996, 2004, 2009).

What we have done in both volumes is use Afrocentric theory and culturally informed principles to frame and write about our observations of these highly effective teachers. Thus, we have written about improved student engagement and performance related to the use of culturally informed instructional materials, because we observed it; we have written about the use of emancipatory pedagogies—what they are, the African cultural platforms that support them, and what they can accomplish—because we observed teachers using these pedagogies in classrooms; and we have written about teachers engaging parents in curriculum and assessment, because we have observed how the presence of family members—and the community standards and cultural ideals they embody—results in enthusiastic responses from students and more authentic curriculum and assessment (Campbell, 2014; King, Goss, & McArthur, 2014). In other words, it is PK-12 teachers who have consistently demonstrated these emancipatory practices that we have later named and described as praxis, process, and model.

In the current volume, we explain how the Afrocentric praxis of Teaching *for* Freedom educates children as a shared responsibility to enhance community well-being and belonging. Our share of this responsibility is to make connections between practice and theory (in that order)—between the effective practices we observe in classrooms and what scholars of the Black intellectual tradition have written about African Diasporan worldview, culture, and history (Asante, 1987/1998, 2007a & b, 2011; Boykin, 1983, 1994; Dixon, 1971; Du Bois, 1924, 1945; Franklin, 1992, 1995; Hilliard, 1997, 2003; Karenga, 1999, 2006a & b; King, 2006a & b; Lee, 1993, 2007; Nobles, 1985, 1991, 2006; Perry, 2003; Smitherman, 1994, 2000; Woodson, 1919, 1928, 1933/1990; Wynter, 1992, 2006; Wynter & McKittrick, 2015). Within an African Diasporan worldview—and from the perspective of its cultural concepts—freedom is understood as inherent and as a shared human entitlement (Bennett, 1975; Franklin, 1992; Gyekye, 1997; Harding, 1990; Ikuenobe, 2006; Karenga, 2006b). Thus, to Teach *for* Freedom means that classroom teachers identify and implement those cultural concepts, culturally informed principles, and African-informed emancipatory pedagogies that support the continuation of freedom defined as the knowledge, consciousness, agency, and self-determination to create and sustain communal well-being and belonging and goodness in the world through just and right action (Abímbólá, 1976; Anyanwu, 1981; Gyekye, 1987; Nkulu-N'Sengha, 2005; Waghid, 2014). In so doing, the teachers we have observed, and in some instances with whom we have collaborated, model how to create community, encourage inquiry and agency, produce academic and cultural excellence, and sustain cultural continuity—all instructional practices and outcomes that support the continuation of freedom understood as a collective experience of well-being and belonging. What we add is the epistemic authority that comes from theory-framing and naming our observations, establishing an historical context with examples, and re-creating demonstrations of emancipatory practices that already exist in classrooms. If our epistemic authority is authentic, and we believe it is, this work will expand the ranks of practitioners who Teach *for* Freedom.

For pre-service teachers, in-service teachers, and teacher educators who join us and become practitioners of Teaching *for* Freedom, this model will assist you to: (1) expand your heritage or cultural knowledge about the worldview, experiences, and cultural productions of African Diasporan Peoples; (2) select content and pedagogies that can strengthen your relationships with all students and families; (3) transform the way you present topics and academic disciplines to be more reflective of the cultures that inform them; (4) avoid omissions and distortions about Africa and African and Indigenous Peoples that have historically been embedded in school knowledge at all levels; (5) widen the cultural field by using cultural concepts from beyond the Anglosphere; (6) use democratized content and emancipatory pedagogies that sustain cultural continuity across time and place; and (7) consider how people's differing worldviews and their attendant cultural concepts shape school policies and practices. In these ways, PK-12 teachers and teacher educators share in the responsibility of developing the knowledge, facilitating consciousness, supporting agency, and enabling the self-determination students need to participate in sustaining the inherency of freedom for themselves, their families, and communities. This is a pathway to human freedom in the larger world. Teachers who were already engaged in these practices that we later bundled and described as Teaching *for* Freedom have been our guides. Their work is without doubt the prequel to what we have written in both volumes.

References

Abímbólá, W. (1976). *Ifá: An exposition of the Ifá literary corpus*. Ibadan, Nigeria: Oxford University Press Nigeria.

Anyanwu, K. C. (1981). The African world-view and theory knowledge. In E. A. Ruch & K. C. Anyanwu (Authors), *African philosophy: An introduction to the main philosophical trends in contemporary Africa* (pp. 77–99). Rome: Catholic Book Agency.

Asante, M. K. (1987/1998). *The Afrocentric idea*. Philadelphia, PA: Temple University Press.

Asante, M. K. (2007a). *An Afrocentric manifesto*. Malden, MA: Polity Press.

Asante, M. K. (2007b). *The history of Africa: The quest for eternal harmony*. New York, NY: Routledge.

Asante, M. K. (2011). *Maat and human communication: Supporting identity, culture, and history without global domination*. Retrieved from www.asante.net/articles/47/maat-and-human-communication-supporting-identity-culture-and-history-without-global-domination/.

Bennett, L. Jr. (1975). *The shaping of Black America*. Chicago, IL: Johnson Publishing Company.

Bigelow, B. (1996). Inside the classroom: Social vision and critical pedagogy. In W. Ayers & P. Ford (Eds.), *City kids, city teachers, reports from the front row* (pp. 292–304). New York, NY: The New Press.

Bigelow, B. (2001). The human lives behind the labels. In B. Bigelow, B. Harvey, S. Karp, & L. Miller (Eds.), *Rethinking our classrooms, Vol. 2* (pp. 91–99). Williston, VT: Rethinking Schools.

Boykin, A. W. (1983). The academic performance of Afro-American children. In J. Spence (Ed.), *Achievement and achievement motives* (pp. 321–371). San Francisco, CA: W. Freeman.

Boykin, A. W. (1994). Afrocultural expression and its implications for schooling. In E. R. Hollins, J. E. King, & W. C. Hayman (Eds.), *Teaching diverse populations: Formulating a knowledge base* (pp. 243–273). Albany, NY: State University of New York Press.

Campbell, L. (2014). Austin Steward: "Home-style teaching, planning, and assessment". In J. E. King & E. E. Swartz (Authors), *"Re-membering" history in student and teacher learning: An Afrocentric culturally informed praxis* (pp. 105–120). New York, NY: Routledge.

Dean, J. (2008). Textbook scripts, student lives: A math teacher goes beyond the standardized curriculum. *Rethinking Schools, 22*(3), 37–40.

Dixon, V. J. (1971). African-oriented and Euro-American-oriented world views: Research methodologies and economics. *The Review of Black Political Economy, 7*(2), 119–156.

Du Bois, W. E. B. (1924). *The gift of Black folk, the Negroes in the making of America.* Boston, MA: The Stratford Company.

Du Bois, W. E. B. (1945). *Color and democracy.* New York, NY: Harcourt Brace and Company.

Franklin, V. P. (1992). *Black self-determination: A cultural history of African American resistance.* Chicago, IL: Lawrence Hill Books.

Franklin, V. P. (1995). *Living our stories, telling our truths.* New York, NY: Oxford University Press.

Goodwin, S. (1996). Teaching students of color. *Raising Standards: Journal of the Rochester Teachers Association, 4*(1), 23–35.

Goodwin, S. (1998). Sankofan education and emancipatory practices. *Raising Standards: Journal of the Rochester Teachers Association, 6*(1), 20–30.

Goodwin, S. (2004). Emancipatory pedagogy. In S. Goodwin & E. E. Swartz (Eds.), *Teaching children of color: Seven constructs of effective teaching in urban schools* (pp. 37–48). Rochester, NY: RTA Press.

Gutstein, E. (2001). Math, maps, and misrepresentation. *Rethinking Schools, 15*(3), 6–7.

Gyekye, K. (1987). *An essay on African philosophical thought: The Akan conceptual scheme.* Cambridge, MA: Cambridge University Press.

Gyekye, K.(1997). *Tradition and modernity: Philosophical reflections on the African experience.* New York, NY: Oxford University Press.

Harding, V. (1990). *Hope and history.* New York, NY: Orbis Books.

Hilliard, A. G. III (1997). *SBA: The reawakening of the African mind.* Gainesville, FL: Makare Publishing Company.

Hilliard, A. G. III (2003). No mystery: Closing the achievement gap between Africans and excellence. In T. Perry, C. Steele, & A. Hilliard, III (Eds.), *Young, gifted, and Black: Promoting high achievement among African American students* (pp. 131–165). Boston, MA: Beacon Press.

Ikuenobe, P. (2006). *Philosophical perspectives on communalism and morality in African traditions.* Lanham, MD: Lexington Books.

Karenga, M. (1999). *Odù Ifá: The ethical teachings.* Los Angeles, CA: University of Sankore Press.

Karenga, M. (2006a). *Maat, the moral ideal of ancient Egypt: A study in classical African ethics.* New York, NY: Routledge.

Karenga, M. (2006b). Philosophy in the African tradition of resistance: Issues of human freedom and human flourishing. In L. R. Gordon & J. A. Gordon (Eds.), *Not only the master's tools: African American studies in theory and practice* (pp. 243–271). Boulder, CO: Paradigm Publishers.

King, J. E. (2006a). "If justice is our objective": Diaspora literacy, heritage knowledge and the praxis of critical studyin' for human freedom. *Yearbook of the National Society for the Study of Education, 105*(2), 337–360.

King, J. E. (2006b). Perceiving reality in a new way: Rethinking the Black/White duality of our times. In A. Bogues (Ed.), *Caribbean reasonings. After Man toward the human. Critical essays on Sylvia Wynter* (pp. 25–56). Kingston, Jamaica: Ian Randle Publishers.

King, J. E., Goss, A. C., & McArthur, S. A. (2014). Recovering history and the "parent piece" for cultural well-being and belonging. In J. E. King and E. E. Swartz (Authors), *"Re–membering" history in student and teacher learning: An Afrocentric culturally informed praxis* (pp. 155–188). New York, NY: Routledge.

King, J. E., Swartz, E. E., with Campbell, L., Lemons-Smith, S., & López, E. (2014). *"Re-membering" history in student and teacher learning: An Afrocentric culturally informed praxis.* New York, NY: Routledge.

Lee, C. D. (1993). *Signifying as a scaffold for literary interpretation: The pedagogical implications of an African American discourse genre.* Urban, IL: National Council of Teachers of English.

Lee, C. D. (2007). *Culture, literacy, and learning: Taking bloom in the midst of the whirlwind.* New York, NY: Teachers College Press.

Mbatha, W. (2012). "My family's not from Africa—we come from North Carolina!": Teaching slavery in context. *Rethinking Schools, 27*(1), 37–41.

Nkulu-N'Sengha, M. (2005). African epistemology. In M. K. Asante & A. Mazama (Eds.), *Encyclopedia of Black studies* (pp. 39–44). Thousand Oaks, CA: Sage Publications.

Nobles, W. W. (1985). *Africanity and the Black family: The development of a theoretical model.* Oakland, CA: Institute for the Advanced Study of Black Family Life and Culture.

Nobles, W. W. (1991). African philosophy: Foundations for Black psychology. In R. Jones (Ed.), *Black psychology* (3rd ed., pp. 47–63). Berkeley, CA: Cobb and Henry.

Nobles, W. W. (2006). *Seeking the Sakhu: Foundational writing for an African psychology.* Chicago, IL: Third World Press.

Perry, T. (2003). Up from the parched earth: Toward a theory of African American achievement. In T. Perry, C. Steele, & A. Hilliard III (Eds.), *Young, gifted, and Black, promoting high achievement among African American students* (pp. 1–108). Boston, MA: Beacon Press.

Secret, C. (1998). Embracing Ebonics and teaching standard English: An interview with Oakland teacher Carrie Secret. In T. Perry & L. Delpit (Eds.), *The real Ebonics debate: Power, language, and the education of African American children* (pp. 79–88). Boston, MA: Beacon Press, in collaboration with Rethinking Schools, Ltd.

Shakes, G. R. (1993). Reader response as emancipatory pedagogy. *Raising Standards: Journal of the Rochester Teachers Association, 1*(1), 10–17.

Shakes, G. (2004). Student experience. In S. Goodwin & E. E. Swartz (Eds.), *Teaching children of color: Seven constructs of effective teaching in urban schools* (pp. 97–105). Rochester, NY: RTA Press.

Smith, F. (1996). Student voice and classroom practice. *Raising Standards: Journal of the Rochester Teachers Association, 4*(1), 13–17.

Smith, F. (2004). Classroom environment. In S. Goodwin & E. E. Swartz (Eds.), *Teaching children of color: Seven constructs of effective teaching in urban schools* (pp. 83–90). Rochester, NY: RTA Press.

Smith, F. (2009). *Teacher Guide, Journeys to freedom: Self-determination, abolition, and the Underground Railroad*. Rochester, NY: RTA Press.

Smitherman, G. (1994). *Black talk*. Boston, MA: Houghton Mifflin Company.

Smitherman, G. (2000). *Talkin that talk: Language, culture, and education in African America*. New York, NY: Routledge.

Waghid, Y. (2014). *African philosophy of education reconsidered: On being human*. New York, NY: Routledge.

Woodson, C. G. (1919). Negro life and history as presented in the schools. *The Journal of Negro History, IV*, 273–280.

Woodson, C. G. (1928). *Negro makers of history: The story of the Negro retold*. Washington, DC: The Associated Publishers.

Woodson, C. G. (1933/1990). *The mis-education of the Negro*. Trenton, NJ: Africa World Press.

Wynter, S. (1992). *Do not call us "Negroes": How multicultural textbooks perpetuate racism*. San Francisco, CA: Aspire Books.

Wynter, S. (2006). On how we mistook the map for the territory, and re-imprisoned ourselves in our unbearable wrongness of being, of Désêtre: Black studies toward the human project. In L. R. Gordon & J. A. Gordon (Eds.), *Not only the master's tools: African American studies in theory and practice* (pp. 107–169). Boulder, CO: Paradigm Publishers.

Wynter, S., & McKittrick, K. (2015). Unparalleled catastrophe for our species? Or, to give humanness a different future: Conversations. In K. McKittrick (Ed.), *Sylvia Wynter: On being human as praxis* (pp. 9–89). Durham, NC: Duke University Press.

ACKNOWLEDGMENTS

We acknowledge all those scholars, activists, and wisdom keepers whose work has had a profound effect on our thinking over several decades. These women and men have blazoned intellectual realms intimately tied to the pursuit of freedom and to the identification and preservation of cultural integrity and sovereignty. In particular, we wish to acknowledge Anna Julia Cooper, who understood and embodied the relationship between women and freedom; Asa Hilliard III, who demonstrated the role of historical knowledge in rethinking hegemonic conceptions of African people; John Henrik Clarke, who taught us the importance of Heritage Teaching as a way of passing on the African legacy that makes a feeling of belonging to one's people possible and essential; Adelaide L. Hines Sanford, whose courageous and wise ways of struggle on behalf of all children and families in general and African American children and families in particular will stand the test of time; Molefi Kete Asante, who persists in the refinement of the culturally centered ideas and practices of Afrocentricity upon which our work is based; Susan Goodwin, whose deep understanding of the connection between culture and learning informs the professional development of teachers learning to teach for liberation, which in turn offers us opportunities to observe such teaching; and Sylvia Wynter, whose analysis of the praxis of being human throughout history points us toward non-complicity with the limited bodies of knowledge—epistemes—that attempt to define us.

We thank James D. Anderson at the University of Illinois, Urbana–Champaign and Randall K. Burkett and Pellom McDaniels III, Curators of African American Collections at Emory University's Manuscript, Archives, & Rare Books Library—for assistance with research sources on Carter G. Woodson, in particular. We also thank the staff of the Patron Services Interlibrary Loan Section at the University of Rochester Libraries for their extraordinary efforts in providing requested research materials. Finally, we acknowledge teachers and students whose work precedes and guides what we do, families and communities who are essential to refashioning the eurocratic model of education we seek to change, and the Routledge editorial and production staff, whose consistent support throughout the process of preparing, finalizing, and publishing this manuscript has carried us to our destination once again.

1

INTRODUCTION

"Re-membering" More

...the good of all determines the good of each. Seek the good of the community and you seek your own good. Seek your own good and you seek your own destruction.

Kwame Gyekye, *An Essay on African Philosophical Thought:
The Akan Conceptual Scheme*, 1987, p. 20

One arrives at an understanding and rapprochement by accepting the agency of the African person as the basic unit of analysis of social situations involving African-descended people.

Molefi Kete Asante, *An African Manifesto*, 2007, p. 105

In a previous volume, *"Re-membering" History in Student and Teacher Learning: An Afrocentric Culturally Informed Praxis* (King & Swartz, 2014), we presented an approach to recovering historical content that entails "re-membering" or reconnecting knowledge of the past that has been silenced or distorted. In the current volume, we broaden this approach to include emancipatory pedagogy in an expanded Afrocentric praxis called Teaching *for* Freedom. Developed within the Black intellectual tradition, this freedom praxis combines "re-membered" (democratized) historical content with emancipatory pedagogy that has been "re-membered" or put back together with African worldview and the cosmologies, philosophies, and cultural concepts and practices of African and Diasporan Peoples (Abímbólá, 1976; Anyanwu, 1981; Karenga, 1999, 2005a & b, 2006a; Gyekye, 1987). By locating pedagogy within an African cultural context, Teaching *for* Freedom views educating children as a shared responsibility to enhance community well-being and belonging (King, Goss, & McArthur, 2014). To explore this concept of shared responsibility, we begin with African worldview—a framework that maintains the concepts, ethical teachings, and cultural continuities upon which Teaching *for* Freedom is built.

African Worldview

Worldview is a cultural framework shaped by specific ontological and epistemological orientations, axiological commitments, virtues, and principles that endure across time, with each of these elements bearing influence on all phenomena that people who share a cultural heritage produce. Culture—which is an integrated pattern of knowledge, values, assumptions, and social practices—is situational, and differences exist among diverse African peoples—then and now, including the Diaspora. However, the frequency of common concepts, values, assumptions, and practices reflects the underlying unity among these groups and suggests how cohesive cultural factors appear and have been retained across time and geographical location (Anyanwu, 1981; Gyekye, 1987, 1997; Hazzard-Donald, 2012; Idowu, 1973; Konadu, 2010; Mbiti, 1990; Nyang, 1980; Obenga, 1989; Tedla, 1995). Thus, African Diasporan philosophies, cosmologies, and cultural concepts and practices that shape the Afrocentric praxis of Teaching *for* Freedom are outcomes produced by people who share an African worldview. For example, *sharing responsibility for communal well-being and belonging*—as a cultural concept of educating children—is one of these outcomes. The five elements of this African cultural framework are shown below in Figure 1.1, with the following descriptions of each element.

1   Ontology is the study of being, of what existence and human relationships look like in particular cultural contexts. In African ontology, the nature of existence includes Collectivity (the well-being of the group supersedes the needs of individuals who benefit *because* the group benefits), Cooperation, Collective Responsibility (everyone contributes to the well-being of the group), Wholeness (all life viewed as one interconnected phenomenon), Harmony (a natural rhythm and movement that exists among all living things), and Interdependence that together speak to the interconnectedness of all forms of life as seen in commitments to human welfare and social, spiritual, and planetary equilibrium (Anyanwu, 1981; Deng, 1973; Dixon, 1971; Karenga, 2006b; Myers, 2003; Nobles, 1985, 1991, 2006; Waghid, 2014).

2   Epistemology is the study of ways of knowing and conceptions of the nature of knowledge that also vary across cultural contexts. Along with authority, empiricism, logic, and revelation, African epistemology includes relational knowing (learning from reciprocal interactions), empathy, intuition-reasoning (learning from heart-mind knowledge, which are linked not separate), divination (a learned discipline of decision making based on integrated knowledge from the spiritual, scientific, and unseen worlds), and symbolic imagery

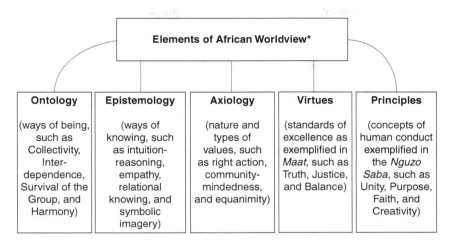

FIGURE 1.1 Elements of African Worldview.

Note
* Throughout this volume, ontological orientations, *Maatian* Virtues, and *Nguzo Saba* Principles are capitalized, but epistemologies and values are not. The former have been identified by scholars cited herein as "the" elements of specific sets of ontological orientations, virtues, and principles; the latter are selected by the authors among many possible examples of epistemologies and values.

(use of proverbs, gestures, rhythms, metaphors, and affect) (Abímbólá, 1976; Dixon, 1971, 1976; Gyekye, 1987; Ikuenobe, 2006; Nkulu-N'Sengha, 2005). Several of these epistemologies are seen in Diasporan expressions as described in Wade Boykin's (1983, 1994) African American Cultural Dimensions (e.g., Spirituality, Orality, Verve, Movement, Communalism). In these epistemologically informed cultural continuities, speaking and listening are experienced as performance, cognitive and affective expressions are linked, and sharing and lively interactions and interrelatedness characterize knowing and being with others (Anyanwu, 1981; Boykin, 1983; King & Goodwin, 2006; Nkulu-N'Sengha, 2005; Senghor, 1964).

3 Axiology is the study of the nature and types of values—especially in ethics—that also vary across cultural contexts. As seen in African and Diasporan oral and written literature, African axiology reflects commitments to community mindedness, service to others, human welfare, right action, equanimity, and the sacredness of both the spiritual and the material (Anyanwu, 1981; Foster, 1997; Gyekye, 1987; Karenga, 1980, 2006b; King et al., 2014; Sindima, 1995; Tedla, 1995).

4 Virtues refer to standards of excellence as exemplified by those found in the Kemetic spiritual and ethical practice of *Maat* in which disciplined thought of the heart-mind leads to right relations that bring good to family, community, and self through living by its Seven Cardinal Virtues of Truth,

Justice, Harmony, Balance, Order, Reciprocity, and Propriety (Asante, 2011; Ashanti, 2008; Karenga, 2006b).

5   Principles refer to comprehensive concepts and practices of human conduct, such as those expressed in the *Nguzo Saba* or Kwanzaa Principles (Unity, Self-Determination, Collective Work and Responsibility, Cooperative Economics, Purpose, Creativity, and Faith). This body of Principles, which are celebrated in the African American holiday Kwanzaa, were drawn from consistent patterns of African thought and practice to affirm and guide the development of African families and communities throughout the world (Asante, 2009; Karenga, 1998, 2005a).

Heritage Knowledge and Cultural Knowledge

Heritage knowledge refers to group memory, a repository or heritable legacy that makes a feeling of belonging to one's people possible (Clarke, 1994; King, 2006). All cultures have heritage knowledge, which "holds" the cultural legacies and patterns produced by worldview that inform what is taught and how it is taught. For African Americans, this birthright is embodied in knowledge of shared African Diasporan cultural continuities, such as mutuality, spirituality, service to others, justice, and reciprocity. These cultural continuities can be seen in past and present forms of community building that include, for example, adaptive familial structures, mutual aid societies, churches, economic coopera- tives, social movements, Freedom schools, and Kwanzaa; and in the relentless collective pursuit of human freedom understood as inherent and present even though denied (King & Goodwin, 2006; King & Swartz, 2014). The Afrocen- tric praxis of Teaching *for* Freedom makes it possible for all students to experi- ence belonging in continuity with their ancestral heritage by creating instructional opportunities for them to build on and expand their heritage knowledge. For students of African ancestry, this means that they can use African Diasporan cultural continuities, such as communal responsibility and service to others as contexts for learning.

Cultural knowledge is knowledge gained about the cultural legacies and pat- terns in cultures other than one's own. When teachers learn and use cultural knowledge to plan and teach lessons in the social studies and other disciplines, the content and pedagogies they select center students by drawing upon the history and heritage of all students in general and the students they are teaching in particular. For example, we show in Chapter 3 how Harriet Tubman's African understanding of freedom was at the core of her response to enslave- ment. When teachers have this cultural knowledge, they can preserve the cul- tural continuity that is typically severed when figures like Tubman are lifted out of the context of their communities and cultures as special individuals who did extraordinary things. Of course Harriet Tubman was special, but keeping Tubman anchored in her cultural heritage *and what it taught her* explains so much more about who she was and why she acted as she did. All students benefit from this contextualized presentation of Tubman, and her story is a platform on which students of African ancestry can stand to experience the continuity of their African Diasporan legacy. In terms of pedagogy, when teachers know about the communal values and ways of being and knowing that African people such as Tubman retained in the Diaspora, they understand the logic of building a classroom community and authentic relationships with students and parents, providing opportunities for collaboration and for oral and affective expression, and building on what students know. In these ways, all students can benefit from teachers' access to cultural knowledge—from content and pedagogy that permit them to learn about diverse histories, legacies, and the worldviews that shape people's assumptions, ideas, and actions. Both heritage knowledge *and* cultural knowledge position students as subjects with agency at the center of teaching and learning.

By using content and pedagogy that draw upon heritage knowledge—and the worldviews students' heritages reflect—we can provide comprehensive instruction *and* locate students culturally. This is especially important for students of African ancestry, since over several centuries a massive cultural assault due to the *Maafa* (European enslavement of African people), colonialism, neo-colonialism, and white supremacy racism, has denigrated all things African. This denigration has occurred to such an extent that Africa's cultural legacy and African American students' heritage knowledge must be identified and recuperated, even if they exist and operate unconsciously (Akbar, 1984; Dixon, 1971; Nkulu-N'Sengha, 2005). This is especially urgent today when the African continent remains marginalized geopolitically, Africa's cultural legacy is omitted in school knowledge, and only crises such as war, famine, drought, and disease in Africa appear to be newsworthy.

It is important to emphasize here that this is a call for teachers at all levels to learn about African worldview and incorporate their heritage knowledge or cultural knowledge through accurate scholarship. In pre-colonial African societies, abundant evidence of Africa's cultural legacy existed in oral, written, and material forms, some of which we provide in this volume. Scholarship in the Black intellectual tradition continues to recover this legacy, thereby helping educators to design and implement schools and liberating educational interventions in service to students and parents of African ancestry and their communities (Goodwin, 2003; King, 2006, 2008; Lee, 1993, 2007; Madhubuti & Madhubuti, 1994; Maïga, 1995, 2005). The praxis of Teaching *for* Freedom models the use of this scholarship to identify African heritage knowledge, develop cultural knowledge, and consciously locate all students at the center of the learning experience as actors who have the knowledge, skills, and agency to produce academic and cultural excellence, develop good character, and bring just and right action into the world (Karenga, 1999, 2006a & b; King, 2006; Tedla, 1995). In this model, teachers and students are unfettered by coercive pedagogies and limited knowledge that omit or distort diverse ways of knowing and being; and they have opportunities to experience and implement African-informed values, virtues, and principles, such as community mindedness, right action, Reciprocity, and Collective Work and Responsibility.

Worldview and Freedom

The historical record provides further insight into the relationship between African worldview and practices of freedom that undergird the Afrocentric praxis of Teaching *for* Freedom. This relationship is seen in the experiences of freedom, justice, and social responsibility practiced in Indigenous African Nations—a relationship that African people have continued in the Diaspora. (See King & Swartz, 2014, p. 53 for a detailed explanation of the use and capping of "Nations" and "Peoples.") From East to West Africa, justice, rightness, and ethical consciousness have been guiding principles that define[d] and demonstrate[d] unity among philosophies as exemplified in Ancient Kemet and in the Songhoy, Yoruba, Dogon, Bambara, and Akan Nations to name only a few (Diop, 1959/1990, 1974; Obenga, 1989). The Kemetic practices of *Maat*, a spiritual and ethical ideal and way of life, view humans as inherently and equally worthy and responsible for demonstrating good character and excellence through action (Karenga, 2006b). In the Songhoy Empire (*Gandawey*), there were practices of public accountability and shared responsibility for decision making; the freedom to practice more than one religion; an administrative office for the benefit of foreigners; and leaders who were evaluated based on their just, fair, and caring treatment of people (Maïga, 2010; Sissoko, 1984). Akan philosophy views humans as free and responsible for their actions—for enacting "the good" through behaviors that are truthful, just, compassionate, generous, and peaceable—which create harmony in human relations and lead to the well-being of the community (Gyekye, 1987). And there are the ethical teachings in the *Odù Ifá*—the sacred wisdom text of the Yoruba people that parallels sacred texts in ancient Kemet (Karenga, 1999, 2006b). This text, composed of 256 *Odù* (chapters) and many *ese* (verses) of poems, proverbs, stories, chants, and ethical narratives, is used in a divination system based on the principles of a well-ordered universe able to provide insights into every human action (Abímbólá, 1976, 1997; Karenga, 2005c).

The African worldview elements evident in the *Odù Ifá* are representative of the ways of being and knowing, values, principles, and virtues that African people brought with them to the Americas (Hazzard-Donald, 2012). For example, *Odù* 202:1 refers to "the principle of grouping together" that defines how all forms of life are gathered in groups "[s]o that the goodness of together-ness could come forth at once. Indeed all goodness took the form of a gathering together in harmony" (Karenga, 1999, p. 361, 364). In Maulana Karenga's (2006a) commentary on this *Odù*, he explains that "great goods" such as freedom and justice are real when they are shared. He states:

the great goods of freedom, justice, love, family, friendship, sisterhood, brotherhood, a life of peace, a life of dignity and decency, and the world itself, are all shared goods. And they are not real if only some people are deemed worthy of them or worthier than others.

(pp. 269–270)

Notice the ontological and epistemological orientations of Collectivity, Harmony, Interdependence, relational knowing, and empathy (feeling *with*) that shape Yoruba thinking about how the universe is ordered and how sharing is the greatest good that results from the experience of "gathering together in harmony." The values of service to others, right action, and equanimity; the virtues of Reciprocity and Justice; and the principles of Unity and Self-Determination—which all consider the needs of the collective—are present throughout the *Odù Ifá*—a cosmology and lived philosophy that Yoruba people brought with them to the Americas. Likewise, African people who were taken from the Kôngo, Songhoy, Akan, Dogon, Bambara, Baluba, Fulani, and other Nations brought with them knowledge of their cosmologies, philosophic traditions, oral and/or written texts, and cultural concepts and practices, which are the material and spiritual expressions of their worldview.

People of African ancestry in the Americas continue to share a common cultural legacy in which freedom, justice, and love are to be shared by all, as are dignity and decency; and people are responsible to develop harmonious relationships and foster the well-being of the community through respect for knowledge, wisdom, and the inherent worth of all humans (Hazzard-Donald, 2012; Karenga, 1999, 2005c; Sublette, 2008). This has been apparent for centuries. For example, when Africans in 18th century North America petitioned legislatures and courts for freedom, they often wrote that they had never given up their natural right to be free (Aptheker, 1951/1969; Bennett, 1975; Hart, 1985/2002; Kaplan, 1973). They came here—both peasants and nobles alike—with the experience of freedom and with ways of being and knowing that produced ethical traditions of speaking truth and doing justice, sharing responsibility for community welfare, and having value for the dignity and equal worth of all people (Karenga, 2006a). And while freedom for the enslaved was literally taken away, Africans in North America often spoke and wrote that they had never given it up. They understood freedom as inherent and shared, that all humans were worthy and responsible to live and act in ways that were just and right—to be of good character and to bring good into the world. Listen to Amoyi Awodele as he describes his father's Yoruba teachings that were passed on to him.

VIGNETTE 1.1

Amoyi Awodele Speaks

I took my freedom from the plantation of Miguel Fortier in Louisiana and carefully made my way north to Philadelphia in 1841.* I was called Francois on the plantation, but my real name is Amoyi Awodele. My first name means "the one who knows the way." I am Yoruba and my family is from *Ilé-Ifè*. My father's real first name is Abiye, meaning "born to stay alive," which is certainly true of my father, since he managed, unlike many others, to live through the brutal passage from our homeland to this country. His name reflects his chosen destiny. My mother was sold away by the time I was two years old. Her first name is Jumoke, which means "everybody loves the child," and from the stories I have heard about her, this was certainly true.

My father has passed on; his body is no longer among us, but his soul or *ori* lives on among the ancestors. In this life he did everything he could—of course in secret—to teach me about my family, including my ancestors, and about the lives they led before being enslaved. My parents—along with other Yoruba, Fon, Hausa, and Edo men, women, and children—were kidnapped, shackled, and put in the hold of a ship bound for New Orleans around 1815. They were captured during a trip to visit relatives in the city of Akure.

It is now 1848. I have established a small business in Philadelphia and have recently married. Every day I think about the teachings my father passed on to me. In Ilé-Ifè he was a Babalawo or Priest of the Ifa religion and spent years studying the Yoruba sacred wisdom texts called the *Odù Ifá*. He never forgot what he learned as a Babalawo and how to speak Yoruba, but if we spoke our language or practiced our religion we were severely beaten and even mutilated. So, in his efforts to protect me, I only know a few Yoruba words and phrases. My father used stories to pass on many Yoruba teachings—about honoring elders, caring for and living in harmony with others, and about freedom and justice.

Among enslaved and free Africans in this country, the Yoruba are not alone in knowing that freedom and the worth of each person is something you are born with. That is why I began to work with Mr. W. S—after he arrived in Philadelphia a few years ago. We are part of a network that conducts "passengers" on the Underground Railroad to safety here and further north. I also have signed several petitions advocating for the freedom of my brothers and sisters who are still enslaved.

The *Odù* teaches that there is goodness in coming together in harmony. Yoruba and other African Peoples brought ideas like this with them to this country. However, most of us have been separated from our People and from our languages, so it has been very difficult to pass on knowledge to our children. But I have noticed that, even without this direct knowledge, African people living here still value African ideals like respecting elders and ancestors, being of good character, caring for others, being generous, bringing good into the world, being kind to guests and strangers, being responsible community members, and valuing goodness and justice for everyone. These ideals I will teach to my children, and more importantly they will see them practiced in what I do.

★ This vignette is based on historical records about Yoruba ethical teachings, the system of slavery, African Peoples in Louisiana, and individual historical figures. Amoyi Awodele and his family are created in order to convey African People's cultural retentions—a topic about which there are few historical records during this period. Using the convention of the time, only initials refer to Africans involved in abolition work. Mr. W. S refers to William Still, who in 1872 wrote a book titled *The Underground Railroad: Authentic narratives and first-hand accounts*, which documents his abolition work in Philadelphia. See also Abímbólá (1976), Dopamu (2006), Karenga (1999), and Hall (2005).

Additional evidence of this African conceptualization and experience of freedom as an inherent right can also be seen in early and ongoing revolts and the establishment of hidden communities throughout the Americas in which men and women chose liberation over enslavement and the freedom to maintain their own culture, which they viewed as a common right and responsibility, even though denied by enslavement (Gomez, 2004; Hart, 1985/2002; Hilliard, 1995). In fact, the centuries-long pursuit of freedom *never given up* by African people has been so intense and pervasive that it has wrenched the U.S. Constitution from its conception as an oxymoronic document of stated freedom but practiced exclusion to an amended document that, over time, has become more inclusive.

Our exploration of the relationship between worldview and related African and Diasporan practices of freedom emanates from an Afrocentric theoretical framework that locates African people at the center not the periphery of phenomena. It is to this theoretical framework that we now turn to discuss "re-membered" (democratized) content and emancipatory pedagogies, and to introduce how these pedagogies—whose cultural base is shaped by the worldview, ethical teachings, and cultural concepts of African Diasporan Peoples—are used to teach this content.

Afrocentricity

Almost a century ago, Carter G. Woodson (1919)—a seminal figure in the Black intellectual tradition—understood the value of locating African people at the center of phenomena when he explained the role that school curricula play in the denigration of Africa and the disregard of African and Diasporan achieve-ments in diverse disciplines. His analysis of school knowledge in the early 20th century explained how systemic distortions have resulted from omissions and misrepresentations of African descent people—a people located in thousands of years of historical accomplishments and cultural excellence. By so doing, Woodson foreshadowed Afrocentricity as developed in the work of scholars such as Molefi Kete Asante (1980/1988, 1987/1998, 2007), Ama Mazama (2003a & b), Danjuma Sinue Modupe (2003), Maulana Karenga (1980, 2003), Linda James Myers (1988/1993, 2003), and Clovis E. Semmes (1981) that locates people of African descent as historical agents who speak for and name themselves. These and many other African-centered scholars provide theoretical and conceptual frameworks for the type of research needed to recover Contin-ental and Diasporan African knowledge that has either been hidden, distorted, or appropriated by white supremacist conceptualizations of African Peoples (Carruthers, 1999; Clarke, 1991, 1993; Diop, 1967, 1974; Dixon, 1976; Hilliard, 1997; King, 2005; Nobles, 1993, 2006; Obenga, 1989).

Afrocentricity is a paradigm or philosophical framework located within the discipline of Africology that examines knowledge in all other academic disci-plines and fields through an African worldview and analytical stance (Asante, 2008; Kershaw, 1992; Mazama, 2003a). Because it is interdisciplinary, Africol-ogy provides multiple theoretical frameworks. Related to the discipline of history, and useful in the wide-ranging field of education, one of these theories posits that by locating Africa and African people at the center of phenomena, not on the periphery to be described and defined by others, the universalized knowledge of the hierarchal European episteme can be replaced with democra-tized knowledge (Asante, 1980/1988, 2003a & b, 2007; Karenga, 2003; Mazama 2003a & b). With the concept of locating people as normative subjects at the center of the sociopolitical, economic, and cultural phenomena of their time, this Afrocentric theory is a human-centric theory of representation with the potential to turn about the distortions that have been embedded in school knowledge related to African as well as all other groups of people (Asante 2007, 1991; Karenga, 2003).

As seen in Figure 1.2, we begin with an African worldview in the praxis of Teaching *for* Freedom. This worldview—made visible through the philosophies, cosmologies, and cultural concepts and practices that African Peoples produced over time—is the cultural ground from which an Afrocentric theoretical frame-work has emerged. This framework includes Afrocentric concepts and culturally informed principles that 1) "re-member" (democratize) or bring back together knowledge of those cultures and groups that have shaped the past and 2) identify and "re-member" emancipatory pedagogies with their African-informed sources (discussed more fully in Chapter 2). These pedagogies (described in Table 1.2 later in this chapter) include Eldering, Locating Students, Multiple Ways of Knowing, Question-Driven Pedagogy, Culturally Authentic Assessment, and

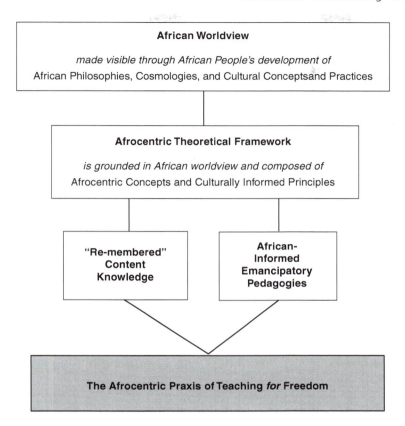

FIGURE 1.2 Afrocentric Praxis of Teaching *for* Freedom.

Communal Responsibility. Together, "re-membered" content and "re-membered" emancipatory pedagogies shape the Afrocentric praxis of Teaching *for* Freedom. When used in the classroom, this praxis is designed to produce group (and therefore individual) academic and cultural excellence, expand students' heritage and cultural knowledge, teach agency, and create a shared commitment to group well-being and belonging through just and right action.

The Afrocentric praxis of Teaching *for* Freedom is an alternative to the omnipresent euro-pedagogical continuum that runs the gamut from management-driven transmission pedagogy at one end to "best practices" at the other (Daniels, Bizar, & Zemelman, 2001; Kliebard, 1986; Tomlinson & Edison, 2003; Zemelman, Daniels, & Hyde, 1998). (In this volume we use the term "euro" in the construction of words, rather than the general term "Eurocentric," in order to identify and locate specific practices and outcomes of a European episteme.) While transmission pedagogy remains standard in schools today, especially with the preponderance of test-driven scripted curriculum (Au, 2009; Karp, 2013–2014; Kumashiro, 2008; Ravitch, 2010, 2013), "best practices" (e.g., collaboration, student centering, experiential learning, differentiated instruction, social interaction, and drawing upon students' pre-existing knowledge) are arguably the "best" of euro-framed thinking about how to educate children to critically think rather than follow scripts. Yet, these "best practices" fail to acknowledge what Molefi Kete Asante (1980/1988) calls the "cultural platform" on which stand the principles, values, traditions, and ways of knowing (epistemology) and being (ontology) in any culture across time.

In the case of these "best practices," such as collaboration, experiential learning, and drawing upon students' pre-existing knowledge, their unacknowledged cultural platform is actually African. These "best" practices depend upon building relationships and dialogic interactions, which run counter to European ontological orientations such as Individualism, Competition, and Survival of the Fittest (Dixon, 1971; Nobles, 1976). Likewise, practices that require Interdependence and Reciprocity—such as social interaction, student centering, and differentiated instruction—also run counter to a European worldview that values individual mindedness (the rugged individual) and the "I" as more important than the "We." These values restrict interaction and view learning as primarily an individual experience. Collaboration, social interaction, and meeting the needs of each child are excellent goals, but without Interdependence, mutuality, community mindedness, and Reciprocity—which come from an African (not European) worldview and cultural platform—these goals are difficult to realize.

While some teachers resonate with "best practices," such as those identified above, and use them effectively in their classrooms, content and pedagogical practices in most schools in the United States are shaped by a European worldview that provides little or no support for these "best" practices. This discussion of what is "best" and why exemplifies the need for the praxis of Teaching *for* Freedom that models how to recover African Diasporan knowledge and expand learning opportunities. Not knowing about and/or failing to acknowledge the African cultural platform as the foundation of these "best practices" compromises them even further by separating them from centuries of culturally grounded philosophical tenets, ethical teachings, and worldview characteristics. We have all been so disconnected from a positive identification with Africa and its cultural legacy—which includes thousands of years of educational excellence—that it has become the norm for African-derived content, concepts, and practices to be appropriated and presented as culturally denuded (corporate-driven) "best" knowledge and "best" pedagogical practices. Educators are thus denied a human/cultural connection to significant African sources of learning regarding "what works" and why. It is in this context that Afrocentric concepts and the worldview from which they come can help us to retrieve African Diasporan knowledge and culturally informed pedagogy that have been discounted, decoupled, and stripped from teaching and learning.

Afrocentric Concepts and Worldview

Bringing back together the multiple and shared knowledge bases and experiences that shaped the past connects the cultural platforms of those who were present in any context; and using Afrocentric theory, concepts, and culturally informed principles to frame, write, and teach more accurate historical accounts, liberates subject-area content and pedagogy from the agreed-upon and incomplete versions that have become standard in school knowledge. There are several concepts that define the emancipatory intent and character of Afrocentric theory, and can be used in the construction of democratized social studies knowledge, knowledge in other disciplines, and pedagogical knowledge (Asante, 1987/1998; Bethel, 2003; Cokely, 2003; Goodwin, 2004; Karenga, 2006a; King & Swartz, 2014; Mazama, 2003b; Modupe, 2003; Nobles, 2005). Table 1.1 below defines each of these Afrocentric concepts (left side of Table 1.1) and shows how each one is shaped by the elements of an African worldview (right side of Table 1.1).

TABLE 1.1 Afrocentric Theoretical Concepts and Worldview Elements

Afrocentric Theoretical Concepts	*African Worldview Elements*
This side of the table is reprinted from *"Re-membering" History in Student and Teacher Learning: An Afrocentric Culturally Informed Praxis* (King & Swartz, 2014, p. 38).	This side of the table describes how each Afrocentric theoretical concept is shaped by various elements of an African worldview.
Collective Consciousness—This epistemology refers to the "retention of ancestral sensibilities" within and across generations (Nobles, 2005, p. 199). This way of knowing conveys the historic continuity of African essence, energy, and excellence; is sustained through relationships within the collective African family that make awareness, knowledge, and meaning possible; and elicits value for the human collective.	As an epistemology, **Collective Consciousness** is a relational way of knowing that is part of heritage knowledge. Across time this heritable knowledge has retained that which is excellent within the collective African family as shaped by mutuality, equanimity, and the sacredness of both the spiritual and the material (African values); Reciprocity and Harmony (*Maatian* Virtues); and Unity and Self-Determination (*Nguzo Saba* Principles). These African worldview elements are revealed in cultural continuities across time and location.
Collective Responsibility—There are reciprocal and interconnected relationships among African people that together make and are made by the "best" practices within African culture. These practices are emancipatory in that their collaborative enactment increases justice and right action for African people and the whole of humanity.	**Collective Responsibility** is also an ontological orientation, along with Harmony and Interdependence that describe African ways of being. Together with relational and group-based ways of knowing and empathy (epistemologies); and community mindedness, service to others, and right action (values), these elements of an African worldview have shaped this concept that represents a commitment to human interconnectedness.

continued

TABLE 1.1 Continued

Centrality/Location—Placing Africa and African people and experiences at the center of phenomena means that African knowledge, cultural ideals, values, and ways of knowing and being are a location or standing place from which the past and present can be viewed and understood.

The concept of **Centrality/Location** is shaped by intuition-reasoning (epistemology), which combines heart knowledge and mind knowledge, and an ethical dialog between the two. Together with Truth and Justice (*Maatian* Virtues), it is reasonable and right to center every cultural group as a location from which to know about the past and present.

Self-Determination—African individuals make decisions and control their lives within the context of considering the collective needs and interests of African people and maintaining the sovereignty of African and other cultures.

Self-Determination is also a principle of the *Nguzo Saba*. It is shaped by Collectivity (ontology); right action and community mindedness (values); Reciprocity (*Maatian* Virtue); and Unity and Purpose (*Nguzo Saba*). These African worldview elements move this concept beyond the individual level to mutuality and the needs of the collective.

Subjects with Agency—African people and ideas are subjects when and where they are present. They have the will and capacity to act in and on the world—not only as individuals, but as members of their cultural group.

Subjects with Agency is a concept shaped by relational knowing (epistemology); Reciprocity (*Maatian* Virtue); and Self-Determination and Purpose (*Nguzo Saba* Principles). These African worldview elements support the voicing of ideas and community-minded right action by subjects who act collectively in social contexts.

Reclamation of Cultural Heritage— The conscious recovery of African history, culture, and identity that is grounded in knowledge of African cosmology, ontology, epistemology, and axiology and presented with a culturally authentic lexicon is a model for reclaiming the heritage of diverse cultures and groups.

Reclamation of Cultural Heritage is a concept that is shaped by Collective Responsibility (ontology); intuition-reasoning (epistemology); right action (values); Truth and Order (*Maatian* Virtues); and Creativity (*Nguzo Saba* Principle). Together, these African worldview elements support the recovery of heritage that has been hidden or distorted.

Anteriority of Classical African Civilizations—Ancient Kemet and prior African civilizations developed and exhibited the earliest demonstrations of excellence in foundational disciplines such as philosophy, mathematics, science, medicine, the arts, and architecture.

Anteriority of Classical African Civilizations is shaped by right action (value) as well as Truth and Order (*Maatian* Virtues). Since this anteriority has been denied for centuries, these elements of an African worldview support the scholarship needed to document and validate the accomplishments of Classical African civilizations.

Understanding how Afrocentric concepts are shaped by the elements of an African worldview is a way to experience African Diasporan cultural continuity, since a recent theoretical framework such as Afrocentricity is informed by enduring worldview elements or cultural characteristics that are centuries old. (The concept of cultural continuity is further developed in later chapters.)

Culturally Informed Principles and Emancipatory Pedagogy

We use the six culturally informed principles listed in Table 1.2 to "write" Afrocentric concepts into instructional materials, and to connect this "re-membered" content with emancipatory pedagogy. These principles connect content and pedagogy by locating the individuals and groups being studied as normative subjects at the center of the sociopolitical, economic, and cultural phenomena of their time; and by locating students as the subjects of instruction (Asante, 2007; Goodwin & Swartz, 2008; King & Swartz, 2014). In other words, the six principles shape both content and pedagogy, which means that students and teachers experience each principle through content *and* during instruction. These principles were drawn from numerous analyses, guidelines, and criteria found in the scholarship of the Black intellectual tradition dating from the 19th century. This scholarship is the foundation from which evolved 20th century theories and practices, such as intercultural and multicultural education, the modern Black Studies movement, culturally congruent/relevant/responsive education, and Afrocentricity (ANKN, 1999; Banks, 1988, 1996, 2004; Cajete, 1994; CIBC, 1977; Gay, 2000, 2004; Grande, 2004; Karenga, 2003; King, 1994, 2004; Ladson-Billings, 1994, 2004; Mazama, 2003b). We have refined and used these six culturally informed principles in empirical research, in the critique of instructional materials, in the development of social studies texts and professional development materials, and in professional development sessions with PK-12 teachers (Goodwin & Swartz, 2004, 2009; RTC, 2007; Swartz, 2009, 2010, 2012, 2013; Swartz & Bakari, 2005). More recently, we have identified how these culturally informed principles are related to specific pedagogies. Table 1.2 below defines each culturally informed principle as it is applied to both content and pedagogy. As you review this table, ask yourself, "What is the value of having both the content and the pedagogies I use shaped by the same culturally informed principles?"

As part of the Afrocentric praxis of historical recovery, the six culturally informed principles in Table 1.2 "re-member" or reconnect knowledge about the past that has been torn apart by eurocratic narratives. These narratives are hierarchal, since they *always* take the lead in standard school knowledge, solipsistically positioning Europeans and their descendants as having produced most of the knowledge worth knowing in every subject area. As a remedy, writing "re-membered" content framed by Afrocentric concepts and written with culturally informed principles produces heterarchal accounts in which there is a shifting

TABLE 1.2 Culturally Informed Principles: Content and Pedagogy

Content	Pedagogy*
Inclusion—This principle refers to including all cultures and groups as the subjects of their own accounts, not as objects of others' accounts about them. Inclusion asserts that, when all cultures and groups are understood as substantive participants in human development, their presence is necessary, not expedient or token.	Students experience inclusion when they are in right relationship with their teachers through the emancipatory pedagogy called **Eldering**. Students feel dignity and respect when teachers exhibit authentic authority based on knowledge, wisdom, and expertise—qualities that lead to building upon what students know and who they are, asking critical questions, and co-creating curriculum with students. **Eldering** views knowledge as a communal experience; everyone has something to contribute.
Representation—This principle refers to comprehensive portrayals that provide enough content and context about individuals and groups to avoid distortions and stereotypes. Individuals and groups remain connected to their ancestral cultures and communities as normative subjects of their own experience. Representation asserts that, when the cultural characteristics of individuals or groups are taught, more authentic portrayals are possible.	Students experience Representation when instruction is designed using their normative cultural characteristics in the emancipatory pedagogy called **Locating Students**. For example, if oral interactions in group settings are normative for some or all of your students, you can locate or center students by providing opportunities for learning in collective and interdependent settings where students can exchange ideas and learn together.
Accurate Scholarship—This principle refers to avoiding errors and omissions. It asserts that, when relevant knowledge is present and when errors or omissions are avoided, curricular content becomes a reflection of the past rather than an appropriation of it. While what is considered accurate can change based on new information, accuracy is identifiable when knowledge is examined with integrity (Karenga, 2006a).	Students experience Accurate Scholarship when teachers use the emancipatory pedagogy called **Multiple Ways of Knowing**, which taps into the heritage or cultural knowledge teachers have about their students. For example, relational knowing and empathy are ways to know and learn things in relationships. If you have studied the scholarship about these epistemologies and/or observed them being used by your students, you would organize activities that allow students to learn with and from each other.
Indigenous Voice—This principle refers to the curricular portrayal of *all* cultures and groups through the experiences of their members and historical events through the voices and actions of those who were present. Indigenous Voice asserts that, when cultures and groups speak for, name, and define themselves, their textual presence as historical agents mirrors their agency in life.	Students experience Indigenous Voice when teachers use the emancipatory pedagogy called **Question-Driven Pedagogy**. Teachers ask students thought-provoking questions that build on what they know. When teaching and learning is a reciprocal experience based on inquiry, students demonstrate agency by defining themselves and their ideas during instruction.

Content	*Pedagogy**
Critical Thinking—This principle refers to instructional materials and curricula that provide broad and typically omitted and/or distorted content. Critical Thinking asserts that, when content is broad, students question, see connections and patterns, evaluate and synthesize information, identify areas of significance, and produce knowledge, rather than only recalling and restating it.	Students experience Critical Thinking informed by African worldview when teachers use the emancipatory pedagogy called **Culturally Authentic Assessment** to 1) guide students to produce knowledge and arrive at solutions through demonstration rather than being asked to give predetermined "right" answers; and 2) assess students' learning using community-informed standards and expectations. Students, teachers, and parents work together to complete and assess projects and performances that reflect imagination and bring benefit to the classroom and community.
A Collective Humanity—This principle refers to the oneness of all humanity, meaning that all groups of people equally belong to the human collective. A Collective Humanity asserts that, when there is equity in the presentation of knowledge across all cultures and groups, there is no hierarchy of human worth that places some groups above others. For example, content that presents freedom and justice as human entitlements—rather than legal rights that depend upon who is in power in a particular time and place—models this principle, since freedom and justice are the inherent rights of all people in any time and place.	Students experience a Collective Humanity when teachers use the emancipatory pedagogy called **Communal Responsibility**. This pedagogy fosters group belonging, working together, reciprocity, right action, and being responsible for each other. Individuals are valued for what they contribute to the group during cooperative learning, collaborative projects, and group-based assessments. For example, engaging students in collective decision making is a way for them to experience unity or oneness in a group, since everyone participates, and by participating, decisions can be made that reflect the interests of the class as a whole, not only some or a majority of individuals.

Note

* We acknowledge Dr. Beverly Gordon (1986, 1990) and Dr. Susan Goodwin (1996, 1998, 2004) for their conceptualization and exemplifications of emancipatory pedagogy.

order of leadership based on knowledge, expertise, and location (standing place) (Lincoln & Guba, 1985; Schwartz & Ogilvy, 1980; Swartz, 2009). Heterarchal narratives are more accurate and complete, since all voices are represented and leadership in the telling of the narrative depends upon which group has the knowledge, expertise, and location to bring all group narratives into a coherent whole. For example, in a "re-membered" account of Reconstruction, Afrocentric concepts (e.g., Collective Responsibility, Centrality/Location, Self-Determination, and Subjects with Agency) and culturally informed principles (e.g., Inclusion,

Accurate Scholarship, Critical Thinking, and a Collective Humanity) frame and write the group narratives of Black and White people from the North and South (Swartz, 2007). The leadership in connecting these narratives comes from the group whose ideas and actions were congruent with the inclusive aims of Reconstruction. It was people of African ancestry who—with the support of some White politicians and advocates of freedom and justice—defined and pursued an inclusive democracy that advanced the country closer to freedom during Reconstruction. Thus, the African American narrative leads in weaving together diverse accounts on this topic, with *all* accounts being written using culturally informed principles. (See King & Swartz, 2014, for a full discussion and exemplification of the process of "re-membering," including the role of heterarchal macro narratives.)

As stated above and seen in Table 1.2, the principles that write "re-membered" (democratized) content also inform emancipatory pedagogies so that students and teachers can experience each principle through content as well as during instruction. In the next chapter, we suggest ways to use these pedagogies in teaching a "re-membered" student text that was framed with Afrocentric concepts and written with culturally informed principles. Importantly, we include specific examples from oral and written African and Diasporan literature that provide a cultural platform for each of the six emancipatory pedagogies described in Table 1.2. These "re-membered" accounts and emancipatory pedagogies are the substance of the praxis called Teaching *for* Freedom.

Journeying Toward Freedom

Schools and classrooms can be communal spaces in which teachers, students, and families learn not only content and skills, but also how to engage collectively and responsibly in just and right action. The praxis of Teaching *for* Freedom fosters such communal spaces in which subject-area knowledge is gained through content and pedagogical practices that also teach students about freedom and justice, that is, how to live and act based on beliefs and values that bring shared good into the world of which all are worthy (Karenga, 2006a). In this way, Teaching *for* Freedom models how to connect learning in various disciplines to a larger purpose of realizing a communal vision of well-being and belonging that is congruent with students' ancestral heritage. As educators, we can contribute to realizing this vision by affirming the heritage knowledge of all students while expanding our cultural knowledge. All children are born into communities (families), and even for those children whose cultures engage in limited communal and relational practices, there is a need to belong—to be a part of the group (S. Goodwin, *personal communication*, May 15, 2009). This need echoes all of our earliest experiences in family life and suggests why communal practices resonate with and are valuable for all children.

In this first chapter, we have introduced the Afrocentric praxis of Teaching *for* Freedom. A legacy of the Black intellectual tradition, this praxis uses Afrocentric theory and culturally informed principles to "re-member" or put back together curricular content, and to "re-member" emancipatory pedagogies (e.g., Eldering, Question-Driven Pedagogy, Locating Students, Culturally Authentic Assessment) with their African-informed sources. We describe the elements of an African worldview or cultural framework and introduce the idea that this framework is observable in the philosophies, cosmologies, and cultural concepts developed over time by African Peoples and seen in African heritage knowledge and in practices of freedom in Africa and the Diaspora. With its capacity to produce democratized knowledge in the form of "re-membered" accounts and emancipatory pedagogies, Teaching *for* Freedom emerges from an African worldview that values students' heritage knowledge, making it possible for all students to experience belonging in continuity with their ancestral heritage.

Chapter 2, "Culture Connects," applies the Afrocentric praxis of Teaching *for* Freedom presented in Chapter 1 to a student text entitled *Black Community Building: The African Tradition of Collective Work and Responsibility* (Swartz, 2013). This text is written for grades 5–7, but can be used with younger students as a read aloud and with older students as an introduction leading to more in-depth study. Two highly effective teachers model how to teach this text using emancipatory pedagogies that are connected to an African worldview and the cultural platforms it has produced. These cultural platforms provide examples from various African cultures to support all six emancipatory pedagogies, which are described as: (1) cultural practices, meaning that they are supported and shaped within cultural contexts; and (2) emancipatory practices in that they produce belonging, agency, and excellence, with an ethical focus on relationship building, communal well-being, and right action. Importantly, this chapter demonstrates how the praxis of Teaching *for* Freedom accesses and builds upon African heritage knowledge, and in so doing, maintains cultural continuity across generations.

Chapter 3, "Harriet Tubman: 'Re-membering' Cultural Continuities," presents two approaches to teaching about Harriet Tubman—one that disregards culture and one that shows African Diasporan cultural continuities her life and work represent. Although she is now regularly included in social studies materials, Tubman is still presented through the grand narrative of slavery that isolates her from other free and enslaved African people who also resisted enslavement. By ignoring scholarship that could result in greater accuracy and a more complete account—including the African cultural context of these accomplishments—this presentation of Tubman replicates the intended dehumanizing, objectifying nature of enslavement and cloaks this institution's white supremacist assumption of the right to dominate. In contrast, we use Afrocentric theory and culturally informed principles to frame and write a "re-membered" student text about Harriet Tubman that locates her at the center of her story as an African woman who embodies the African understanding that for anyone to be free, everyone has to be free—that freedom is a shared responsibility and inherent right that she and millions of others had never given up.

Chapter 4, "'Re-membering' the Jeanes Teachers," examines a much ignored aspect of the Black intellectual tradition, the pedagogical practices of the Jeanes teachers. In the context of Black education, Jeanes teachers exemplify the Afrocentric praxis of Teaching *for* Freedom in their demonstration of shared responsibility or collective agency for community well-being. In the early 1900s, these determined educators of African ancestry—mostly women and a few men—were sent throughout the South to support rural Black teachers and to improve public health and living conditions for students, families, and communities. Jeanes teachers, funded by Anna T. Jeanes, not only demonstrated emancipatory approaches to teaching, but they taught how to meet the educational needs of students in cross-age classrooms, advocated for resources from local (racist) school boards, and raised money from the communities in which they worked to improve, and in some cases build, rural Black schools. These teachers worked with limited material resources to bring the good of public education to disenfranchised African Americans whose educational and other social, political, and economic needs and interests were disregarded and/or obstructed in the Jim Crow South. Under these conditions, their recorded accomplishments are outstanding. How was this possible? What ways of being and knowing, values, virtues, and principles are consistently found in their work? And how does an African worldview guide us to "read" the African Diasporan cultural continuity of these Jeanes teachers as an example of the praxis of Teaching *for* Freedom?

Chapter 5, "'Re-membering' Cultural Concepts," explains how the Afrocentric praxis of Teaching *for* Freedom engages students, teachers, and families with democratized content and emancipatory pedagogies that recognize culture as the medium of exchange that has been absent in the school experience for all students. This absence is due to the disconnection of content and pedagogical practices from the cultural concepts and worldviews they represent—as if content and pedagogy were conceived outside of culture. When teachers ask students to gain knowledge through the lens of cultural concepts, which endure across time and place, they can guide students not only to learn about past events, but to use the cultural concepts that inform those events to act in the present. In contrast with mainstream content and pedagogy—and the invisible yet ubiquitous European worldview and cultural concepts that shape and maintain them—the praxis of Teaching *for* Freedom brings knowledge and examples of African as well as other People's worldview and heritage knowledge into the school experience. In so doing, this praxis models how "re-membering" African cultural concepts with democratized content and emancipatory pedagogies can create cultural continuity for all groups of students, their families, and communities.

Chapter 6, "Practicing Cultural Concepts and Continuity," presents several African Diasporan topics, identifies the cultural concepts that informed these topics, and shows how two practitioners of Teaching *for* Freedom use these concepts to shape their presentation of content and selection of pedagogies. Their teaching occurs within the context of culture by engaging with the meaning of past events as a way to maintain continuity between Africa and the Diaspora. In addition to the content, pedagogies, and concepts they select, these and other practitioners of Teaching *for* Freedom know that creating multiple opportunities for families to be part of instruction also strengthens cultural continuity. They understand that families "hold" and convey heritage knowledge (group memory), including worldview and cultural concepts that maintain the continuity of diverse cultural legacies. The chapter ends with an activity that helps to clarify many of the concepts, principles, and pedagogies presented in this volume. We invite our readers to be practitioners of Teaching *for* Freedom—to build upon and expand students' heritage knowledge and support students in gaining cultural knowledge by learning about the cultures of others. In so doing, they can guide their students in using knowledge of the past to act with agency in the present.

References

Abímbólá, W. (1976). *Ifá: An exposition of the Ifá literary corpus.* Ibadan, Nigeria: Oxford University Press Nigeria.

Abímbólá, W. (1997). *Ifá will mend our broken world: Thoughts on Yoruba religion and culture in Africa and the Diaspora.* Roxbury, MA: Aim Books.

Akbar, N. (1984). Africentric social sciences for human liberation. *Journal of Black Studies, 14*(4), 395–414.

ANKN (Alaska Native Knowledge Network) (1999). *Guidelines for preparing culturally responsive teachers for Alaska's schools.* Retrieved from www.ankn.uaf.edu/publications/teachers.html.

Anyanwu, K. C. (1981). The African world-view and theory knowledge. In E. A. Ruch & K. C. Anyanwu (Authors), *African philosophy: An introduction to the main philosophical trends in contemporary Africa* (pp. 77–99). Rome: Catholic Book Agency.

Aptheker, H. (1951/1969). *A documentary history of the Negro people in the United States: From colonial times through the Civil War* (Vol. I). New York, NY: The Citadel Press.

Asante, M. K. (1980/1988). *Afrocentricity.* Trenton, NJ: Africa World Press.

Asante, M. K. (1987/1998). *The Afrocentric idea.* Philadelphia, PA: Temple University Press.

Asante, M. K. (1991). The Afrocentric idea in education. *Journal of Negro Education, 60*(2), 170–180.

Asante, M. K. (2003a). Locating a text: Implications of Afrocentric theory. In A. Mazama (Ed.), *The Afrocentric paradigm* (pp. 235–244). Trenton, NJ: Africa World Press.

Asante, M. K. (2003b). African American studies: The future of the discipline. In A. Mazama (Ed.), *The Afrocentric paradigm* (pp. 97–108). Trenton, NJ: Africa World Press.

Asante, M. K. (2007). *An Afrocentric manifesto.* Malden, MA: Polity Press.

Asante, M. K. (2008). Africology: Making a long story short in the age of intellectual confusion. *International Journal of Africana Studies, 14*(2), 352–369.

Asante, M. K. (2009). *Maulana Karenga: An intellectual portrait.* Malden, MA: Polity Press.

Asante, M. K. (2011). *Maat and human communication: Supporting identity, culture, and history without global domination*. Retrieved from www.asante.net/articles/47/maat-and-human-communication-supporting-identity-culture-and-history-without-global-domination/.

Ashanti, K. O. (2008). Maat in the classroom: A comparative analysis of the thought(s) of W. E. B. Du Bois and C. A. Diop. *Africological Perspectives, 5*(1), 45–65.

Au, W. (2009). *Unequal by design: High-stakes testing and the standardization of inequality.* New York, NY: Routledge.

Banks, J. A. (1988). *Multiethnic education, theory and practice.* Newton, MA: Allyn and Bacon.

Banks, J. A. (1996). The African American roots of multicultural education. In J. A. Banks (Ed.), *Multicultural education, transformative knowledge, and action: Historical and contemporary perspectives* (pp. 30–45). New York, NY: Teachers College Press.

Banks, J. A. (2004). Multicultural education: Historical development, dimension, and practice. In J. A. Banks & Cherry A. McGee Banks (Eds.), *Handbook of research on multicultural education* (2nd ed., pp. 3–29). San Francisco, CA: Jossey-Bass.

Bennett, L., Jr. (1975). *The shaping of Black America.* Chicago, IL: Johnson Publishing Company.

Bethel, K. E. (2003). Afrocentricity and the arrangement of knowledge. In J. L. Conyers, Jr. (Ed.), *Afrocentricity and the academy: Essays on theory and practice* (pp. 50–65). Jefferson, NC: McFarland & Company Publishers.

Boykin, A. W. (1983). The academic performance of Afro-American children. In J. Spence (Ed.), *Achievement and achievement motives* (pp. 321–371). San Francisco, CA: W. Freeman.

Boykin, A. W. (1994). Afrocultural expression and its implications for schooling. In E. R. Hollins, J. E. King, & W. C. Hayman (Eds.), *Teaching diverse populations: Formulating a knowledge base* (pp. 243–273). Albany, NY: State University of New York Press.

Cajete, G. (1994). *Look to the mountain: An ecology of Indigenous education.* Durango, CO: Kivaki Press.

Carruthers, J. H. (1999). *Intellectual warfare.* Chicago, IL: Third World Press.

CIBC (The Council on Interracial Books for Children) (1977). *Stereotypes, distortions, and omissions in U.S. history textbooks.* New York, NY: CIBC.

Clarke, J. H. (1991). *Africans at the crossroads: Notes for an African world revolution.* Trenton, NJ: Africa World Press.

Clarke, J. H. (1993). *African people in world history.* Baltimore, MD: Black Classic Press.

Clarke, J. H. (1994). *Christopher Columbus and the Afrikan holocaust: Slavery and the rise of European capitalism.* Brooklyn, NY: A & B Publishers Group.

Cokely, K. (2003). Afrocentricity and African psychology. In J. L. Conyers, Jr. (Ed.), *Afrocentricity and the academy: Essays on theory and practice* (pp. 141–162). Jefferson, NC: McFarland & Company Publishers.

Daniels, H., Bizar, M., & Zemelman, S. (2001). *Rethinking high school: Best practice in teaching, learning, and leadership.* Portsmouth, NH: Heinemann.

Deng, F. M. (1973). *The Dinka and their songs.* London: Oxford University Press.

Diop, C. A. (1959/1990). *The cultural unity of Black Africa.* Chicago, IL: Third World Press.

Diop, C. A. (1967). *Anteriority of Negro civilizations.* Paris: Presence Africaine.

Diop, C. A. (1974). *The African origins of civilization: Myth or reality?* (M. Cook, Trans.). Westport, CT: Lawrence Hill Company.

Dixon, V. J. (1971). African-oriented and Euro-American-oriented world views: Research methodologies and economics. *The Review of Black Political Economy, 7*(2), 119–156.

Dixon, V. J. (1976). World views and research methodology. In L. M. King, V. J. Dixon, and W. W. Nobles (Eds.), *African philosophy: Assumptions and paradigms for research on Black persons* (pp. 51–102). Los Angeles, CA: Fanon Research and Development Center.

Dopamu, A. P. (2006). *Change and continuity: The Yoruba belief in life after death.* Retrieved from www.obafemio.com/uploads/5/1/4/2/5142021/dopamu-lifeafter_death.pdf.

Foster, M. (1997). *Black teachers on teaching.* New York, NY: The New Press.

Gay, G. (2000). *Culturally responsive teaching: Theory, research, and practice.* New York, NY: Teachers College Press.

Gay, G. (2004). Curriculum theory and multicultural education. In J. A. Banks & C. A. McGee Banks (Eds.), *Handbook of research on multicultural education* (2nd ed., pp. 30–49). San Francisco, CA: Jossey-Bass.

Gomez, M. (2004). *Reversing sail: A history of the African Diaspora.* New York, NY: Cambridge University Press.

Goodwin, S. (1996). Teaching students of color. *Raising Standards: Journal of the Rochester Teachers Association, 4*(1), 23–35.

Goodwin, S. (1998). Sankofan education and emancipatory practices. *Raising Standards: Journal of the Rochester Teachers Association, 6*(1), 20–30.

Goodwin, S. (2003). African life is art. *Raising Standards: Journal of the Rochester Teachers Association, 7*(1), 56–62.

Goodwin, S. (2004). Emancipatory pedagogy. In S. Goodwin & E. Swartz (Eds.), *Teaching children of color: Seven constructs of effective teaching in urban schools* (pp. 37–48). Rochester, NY: RTA Press.

Goodwin, S., & Swartz, E. E. (Eds.) (2004). *Teaching children of color: Seven constructs of effective teaching in urban schools.* Rochester, NY: RTA Press.

Goodwin, S., & Swartz, E. E. (2008). *Culturally responsive practice: Lesson planning and construction.* Rochester, NY: RTA Press.

Goodwin, S., & Swartz, E. E. (2009). *Document-based learning: Curriculum and assessment.* Rochester, NY: RTA Press.

Gordon, B. M. (1986). The use of emancipatory pedagogy in teacher education. *Journal of Educational Thought, 20*(2), 59–66.

Gordon, B. M. (1990). The necessity of African-American epistemology for educational theory and practice. *Boston Journal of Education, 172*(3), 88–106.

Grande, S. (2004). *Red pedagogy: Native American social and political thought.* Lanham, MD: Rowman & Littlefield Publishers.

Gyekye, K. (1987). *An essay on African philosophical thought: The Akan conceptual scheme.* Cambridge, MA: Cambridge University Press.

Gyekye, K. (1997). *Tradition and modernity: Philosophical reflections on the African experience.* New York, NY: Oxford University Press.

Hall, G. M. (2005). *Slavery and African ethnicities in the Americas: Restoring the links.* Chapel Hill, NC: University of North Carolina Press.

Hart, R. (1985/2002). *Slaves who abolished slavery: Blacks in rebellion.* Kingston, Jamaica: University of the West Indies Press.

Hazzard-Donald, K. (2012). *Mojo workin': The old African American Hoodoo system.* Chicago, IL: University of Illinois Press.

Hilliard, A. G. III (1995). *The Maroon within us: Selected essays on African American community socialization.* Baltimore, MD: Black Classic Press.

Hilliard, A. G. III (1997). *SBA: The reawakening of the African mind.* Gainesville, FL: Makare Publishing Company.

Idowu, E. B. (1973). *African traditional religion: A definition.* London: SCM Press.

Ikuenobe, P. (2006). *Philosophical perspectives on communalism and morality in African traditions.* Lanham, MD: Lexington Books.

Kaplan, S. (1973). *The Black presence in the era of the American Revolution, 1770–1800.* Greenwich, CT: New York Graphic Society in association with the Smithsonian Institution Press.

Karenga, M. (1980). *Kawaida theory.* Los Angeles, CA: Kawaida Publications.

Karenga, M. (1998). *Kwanzaa: A celebration of family, community, and culture.* Los Angeles, CA: University of Sankore Press.

Karenga, M. (1999). *Odù Ifá: The ethical teachings.* Los Angeles, CA: University of Sankore Press.

Karenga, M. (2003). Afrocentricity and multicultural education: Concept, challenge and contribution. In A. Mazama (Ed.), *The Afrocentric paradigm* (pp. 73–94). Trenton, NJ: Africa World Press.

Karenga, M. (2005a). Kwanzaa. In M. K. Asante & A. Mazama (Eds.), *Encyclopedia of Black studies* (pp. 303–305). Thousand Oaks, CA: Sage Publications.

Karenga, M. (2005b). Maat. In M. K. Asanta & A. Mazama (Eds.), *Encyclopedia of Black studies* (pp. 315–317). Thousand Oaks, CA: Sage Publications.

Karenga, M. (2005c). Odù Ifá. In M. K. Asanta & A. Mazama (Eds.), *Encyclopedia of Black studies* (pp. 388–390). Thousand Oaks, CA: Sage Publications.

Karenga, M. (2006a). Philosophy in the African tradition of resistance: Issues of human freedom and human flourishing. In L. R. Gordon & J. A. Gordon (Eds.), *Not only the master's tools: African American studies in theory and practice* (pp. 243–271). Boulder, CO: Paradigm Publishers.

Karenga, M. (2006b). *Maat, the moral ideal of ancient Egypt: A study in classical African ethics.* New York, NY: Routledge.

Karp, S. (2013–2014). The problems with the Common Core. *Rethinking Schools 28*(2), 10–17.

Kershaw, T. (1992). Afrocentrism and the Afrocentric method. *The Western Journal of Black Studies, 16*(3), 160–168.

King, J. E. (1994). The purpose of schooling for African American children: Including cultural knowledge. In E. R. Hollins, J. E. King, & W. C. Hayman (Eds.), *Teaching diverse populations: Formulating a knowledge base* (pp. 25–56). Albany, NY: State University of New York Press.

King, J. E. (2004). Culture-centered knowledge: Black studies, curriculum transformation, and social action. In J. A. Banks & C. A. McGee Banks (Eds.), *Handbook of research on multicultural education* (2nd ed., pp. 349–378). San Francisco, CA: Jossey-Bass.

King, J. E. (2005). A transformative vision of Black education for human freedom. In J. E. King (Ed.), *Black education: A transformative research and action agenda for the new century* (pp. 3–17). Mahwah, NJ: Lawrence Erlbaum Associates for the American Educational Research Association.

King, J. E. (2006). "If justice is our objective": Diaspora literacy, heritage knowledge and the praxis of critical studyin' for human freedom. *Yearbook of the National Society for the Study of Education, 105*(2), 337–360.

King, J. E. (2008). Critical and qualitative research in teacher education: A Blues epistemology for cultural well-being and a reason for knowing. In M. Cochran-Smith, S. Feiman-Nemser, D. J. McIntyre, & K. E. Demers (Eds.), *Handbook of research on teacher education: Enduring questions in changing contexts* (3rd ed., pp. 1094–1136). New York, NY: Routledge.

King, J. E., & Goodwin, S. (2006). *Criterion standards for contextualized teaching and learning about people of African descent.* Rochester, NY: Authors.

King, J. E., Goss, A. C., & McArthur, S. A. (2014). Recovering history and the "parent piece" for cultural well-being and belonging. In J. E. King and E. E. Swartz (Authors), *"Re–membering" history in student and teacher learning: An Afrocentric culturally informed praxis* (pp. 155–188). New York, NY: Routledge.

King, J. E., Swartz, E. E., with Campbell, L., Lemons-Smith, S., & López, E. (2014). *"Re-membering" history in student and teacher learning: An Afrocentric culturally informed praxis.* New York, NY: Routledge.

Kliebard, H. M. (1986). *The struggle for the American curriculum 1893–1958.* New York, NY: Routledge.

Konadu, K. (2010). *The Akan diaspora in the Americas.* New York, NY: Oxford University Press.

Kumashiro, K. K. (2008). *The seduction of common sense: How the right has framed the debate on America's schools.* New York, NY: Teachers College Press.

Ladson-Billings, G. (1994). *The dreamkeepers: Successful teachers of African American children.* San Francisco, CA: Jossey-Bass.

Ladson-Billings, G. (2004). New directions in multicultural education: Complexities, boundaries, and critical race theory. In J. A. Banks & C. A. McGee Banks (Eds.), *Handbook of research on multicultural education* (2nd ed., pp. 50–65). San Francisco, CA: Jossey-Bass.

Lee, C. D. (1993). *Signifying as a scaffold for literary interpretation: The pedagogical implications of an African American discourse genre.* Urban, IL: National Council of Teachers of English.

Lee, C. D. (2007). *Culture, literacy, and learning: Taking bloom in the midst of the whirlwind.* New York, NY: Teachers College Press.

Lincoln, Y. S., & Guba, E. G. (1985). *Naturalistic inquiry.* Beverly Hills, CA: Sage Publications.

Madhubuti, H., & Madhubuti, S. (1994). *African-centered education: Its value, importance, and necessity in the development of Black children.* Chicago, IL: Third World Press.

Maïga, H. O. (1995). Bridging classroom, curriculum, and community: The Gao School Museum. *Theory Into Practice, 34*(3), 209–215.

Maïga, H. O. (2005). When the language of education is not the language of culture: The epistemology of systems of knowledge and pedagogy. In J. E. King (Ed.), *Black education: A transformative research and action agenda for the new century* (pp. 159–181). Mahwah, NJ and Washington, DC: Lawrence Erlbaum Associates & AERA.

Maïga, H. O. (2010). *Balancing written history with oral tradition: The legacy of the Songhoy people.* New York, NY: Routledge.

Mazama, A. (2003a). The Afrocentric paradigm, an introduction. In A. Mazama (Ed.), *The Afrocentric paradigm* (pp. 3–34). Trenton, NJ: Africa World Press.

Mazama, A. (2003b). *The Afrocentric paradigm.* Trenton, NJ: Africa World Press.

Mbiti, J. S. (1990). *African religions and philosophy,* (2nd ed.). Portsmouth, NH: Heinemann Educational Books.

Modupe, D. S. (2003). The Afrocentric philosophical perspective: A narrative outline. In A. Mazama (Ed.), *The Afrocentric paradigm* (pp. 55–72). Trenton, NJ: Africa World Press.

Myers, L. J. (1988/1993). *Understanding an Afrocentric world view: Introduction to an optimal psychology.* Dubuque, IA: Kendal/Hunt Publishing Company.

Myers, L. J. (2003). The deep structure of culture: The relevance of traditional African culture in contemporary life. In A. Mazama (Ed.), *The Afrocentric paradigm* (pp. 121–130). Trenton, NJ: Africa World Press.

Nkulu-N'Sengha, M. (2005). African epistemology. In M. K. Asante & A. Mazama (Eds.), *Encyclopedia of Black studies* (pp. 39–44). Thousand Oaks, CA: Sage Publications.

Nobles, W. W. (1976). Extended self: Rethinking the so-called Negro self-concept. The *Journal of Black Psychology, 2*(2), 15–24.

Nobles, W. W. (1985). *Africanity and the Black family: The development of a theoretical model.* Oakland, CA: Institute for the Advanced Study of Black Family Life and Culture.

Nobles, W. W. (1991). African philosophy: Foundations for Black psychology. In R. Jones (Ed.), *Black psychology* (3rd ed., pp. 47–63). Berkeley, CA: Cobb and Henry.

Nobles, W. W. (1993). *17th annual conference presentation at the National Conference of Black Studies, Ghana, Africa.* Retrieved from www.youtube.com/watch?v=jL2Jt OgTW9M.

Nobles, W. W. (2005). Consciousness. In M. K. Asante & A. Mazama (Eds.), *Encyclopedia of Black Studies* (pp. 197–200). Thousand Oaks, CA: Sage Publications.

Nobles, W. W. (2006). *Seeking the Sakhu: Foundational writing for an African psychology.* Chicago, IL: Third World Press.

Nyang, S. S. (1980). Reflections on traditional African cosmology. *New Directions: The Howard University Magazine, 7,* 28–32.

Obenga, T. (1989). African philosophy of the Pharaonic period (2780–330 B.C.) (Excerpt from a work in translation). In I. Van Sertima (Ed.), *Egypt revisited* (2nd ed., pp. 286–324). New Brunswick, NJ: Transaction Publishers.

Ravitch, D. (2010). *The death and life of the great American school system: How testing and choice are undermining education.* New York, NY: Basic Books.

Ravitch, D. (2013). *Reign of error: The hoax of the privatization movement and the danger to America's public schools.* New York, NY: Alfred A. Knopf.

RTC (Rochester Teacher Center) (2007). *Cultural learning standards: What students are expected to know, be able to do, and be like.* Rochester, NY: Author.

Schwartz, P., & Ogilvy, J. (1980). *The emergent paradigm: Toward an aesthetics of life.* Paper based on a report written by J. Ogilvy and P. Schwartz and supported by the clients of SRI International's Values and Lifestyles Program; presented by P. Schwartz at the ESOMAR meeting (keynote speech, session IV), Barcelona, Spain in June, 1980.

Semmes, C. E. (1981). Foundations of an Afrocentric social science: Implications for curriculum-building, theory, and research in Black studies. *Journal of Black Studies, 12*(1), 3–17.

Senghor, L. S. (1964). *On African socialism* (Mercer Cook, Trans.). New York, NY: Frederick A. Praeger. (Original work published 1961.)

Sindima, H. (1995). *Africa's agenda: The legacy of liberalism and colonialism in the crisis of African values.* Westport, CT: Greenwood.

Sissoko, S. M. (1984). The Songhoy from 12th to the 16th centuries. In J. Ki-Zerbo & D. T. Niane (Eds.), *UNESCO general history of Africa,* Volume IV (pp. 187–270). Berkeley, CA: University of California Press.

Still, W. (1872). *The Underground Railroad, A record of facts, authentic narratives, letters, etc., narrating the hardships, hair-breadth escapes and death struggles of the slaves in their efforts for freedom.* Philadelphia, PA: Porter & Coates.

Sublette, N. (2008). *The world that made New Orleans: From Spanish silver to Congo Square.* Chicago, IL: Chicago Review Press.

Swartz, E. E. (2007). *Reconstruction: Moving toward democracy.* Rochester, NY: RTA Press.

Swartz, E. E. (2009). Diversity: Gatekeeping knowledge and maintaining inequalities. *Review of Educational Research, 79*(2), 1044–1083.

Swartz, E. E. (2010). *Early African presence in the Americas.* Rochester, NY: African and African American Studies Department of the Rochester City School District and the Rochester Teachers Center.

Swartz, E. E. (2012). *Remembering our ancestors.* Rochester, NY: Rochester City School District.

Swartz, E. E. (2013) *Black community building: The African tradition of collective work and responsibility.* Rochester, NY: RTA Press.

Swartz, E. E., & Bakari, R. (2005). Development of the teaching in urban schools scale. *Teaching and Teacher Education, 21*(7), 829–841.

Tedla, E. (1995). *Sankofa: African thought and education.* New York, NY: Peter Lang.

Tomlinson, C. A., & Edison, C. C. (2003). *Differentiation in practice: A resource guide for differentiating curriculum, grades 5–9.* Alexandria, VA: Association for Supervision and Curriculum Development.

Waghid, Y. (2014). *African philosophy of education reconsidered: On being human.* New York, NY: Routledge.

Woodson, C. G. (1919). *The education of the Negro prior to 1861.* New York, NY: Arno Press.

Zemelman, S., Daniels, H., & Hyde, A. (1998). *Best practice: New standards for teaching and learning in America's schools.* Portsmouth, NH: Heinemann.

2

CULTURE CONNECTS

It should be emphasized here that the specificity of African rationality is to be found in the concept of the thinking heart. In most Bantu languages, the word *heart* (*Mucima* in Kiluba, for example) also stands for thought. A *Muntu wa mucima muyape* is not only a person with a good heart in the sense of being kind, compassionate, and generous but also a person of good thought. The African thinks not only with the head but also with the heart.

Mutombo Nkulu-N'Sengha, "African Epistemology," 2005.
In Asante & Mazama (Eds.), *Encyclopedia of Black Studies*, p. 42

In this chapter, using classroom examples, we show how the praxis of Teaching *for* Freedom connects culture to content and emancipatory pedagogy, and as a result, connects students to learning. This praxis uses the Afrocentric concepts and culturally informed principles presented in Chapter 1 to frame, write, *and* demonstrate how to teach a "re-membered" (democratized) student text entitled *Black Community Building: The African Tradition of Collective Work and Responsibility* (Swartz, 2013). This text is written for grades 5–7, but can be used with younger students as a read aloud and with older students as an introduction leading to more in-depth study. The emancipatory pedagogies demonstrated in this chapter (e.g., Eldering, Question-Driven Pedagogy, Culturally Authentic Assessment) are informed by African worldview, cosmologies, and philosophies that are visible in the practice of cultural concepts such as *sharing responsibility for communal well-being and belonging, knowing as a communal experience in which everyone has something to contribute, pursuing knowledge as inseparable from pursuing wisdom,* and *the authentic authority of eldership.* We should note here that to connect emancipatory pedagogies to African culture(s) is not to suggest the absence of other cultural influences. Making this connection explicit does suggest that there are identifiable cultural platforms that carry African worldview, cosmologies, philosophies, and related cultural concepts and practices drawn from oral and written African literature that support the emancipatory pedagogies used in the praxis of Teaching *for* Freedom, and that these cultural platforms are African. For example, teaching with the intention of modeling a communal vision of freedom and justice—one in which *sharing freedom is a human entitlement*—is a traditional African cultural concept and practice in the context of community (Ikuenobe, 2006; Gyekye, 1997; Karenga, 1999, 2006a). Through the influence of such concepts and practices, emancipatory pedagogies are congruent with "re-membered" texts such as *Black Community Building*, and these pedagogies make it possible for students not only to know about the continuities between Africa and the Diaspora, but also to experience them.

As we discuss how culture, content, and emancipatory pedagogies are connected, you will have an opportunity to observe Ms. Hart teach a unit of study based on *Black Community Building*. Ms. Hart is a highly effective elementary school teacher due to being mentored by Ms. Singleton, who is a veteran teacher at the same school. Through a number of scenarios, you will observe Ms. Hart, her students, and their parents as they engage in using and experiencing the emancipatory pedagogies that fit well with each of the six culturally informed principles described in Table 1.2 in Chapter 1. These scenarios are composites of teachers and teaching that we have observed over the years. Thus, they represent classroom realities and present our vision of the Afrocentric praxis of Teaching *for* Freedom that results in student learning and parent engagement. As you enter Ms. Hart's classroom and listen to the pedagogical advice of Ms. Singleton, think about Ms. Hart's pedagogies, including how she interacts with students, parents, and her colleague and mentor. How might you respond if you were the teacher in this classroom? But first, let's see how *Black Community Building* was framed with Afrocentric concepts and written with those six culturally informed principles discussed in Chapter 1.

Black Community Building and Afrocentricity

Beginning in the late 1870s, thousands of African people migrated to the Midwest due to the brutal acts of white terrorism that took place as Reconstruction was ending in the South (Bennett, 1982; Franklin, 1992; Painter, 1976/1986). Within the theoretical paradigm of Afrocentricity, we use Afrocentric concepts to organize and frame this history and culturally informed principles to write it (see King & Swartz, 2014, for a detailed description of this framing and writing process).

Afrocentric Concepts

The Afrocentric concept of Centrality/Location initially frames *Black Community Building: The African Tradition of Collective Work and Responsibility* by placing

African people at the center of their own story. As this story unfolds, students learn how people of African ancestry established scores of self-governing and self-sufficient towns, such as Nicodemus in Kansas and Langston and Boley in Oklahoma. The Afrocentric concepts of Collective Responsibility, Self-Determination, and Subjects with Agency also frame content about the unity that town members built, the group-based decisions they made, and the actions they took to set up and operate successful businesses and build institutions to meet the needs of residents. (See Table 1.1 in Chapter 1 for descriptions of Afrocentric concepts.) With the use of another Afrocentric concept—the Reclamation of Cultural Heritage—this student text consciously recovers a piece of U.S. history, including the economic and political accomplishments of many Black towns and the responses of White people to Black economic and political influence in the counties and states where these towns were located (Harding, 1981; Painter, 1976/1986; Taylor, 1998; Tolson, 1974). (To inquire about obtaining a copy of *Black Community Building*, contact omnicentricpress@gmail.com.)

Culturally Informed Principles

All six culturally informed principles listed below were used to write the content in *Black Community Building*. (See Table 1.2 in Chapter 1 for descriptions of each principle.)

#1 Inclusion
#2 Representation
#3 Accurate Scholarship
#4 Indigenous Voice
#5 Critical Thinking
#6 A Collective Humanity

While students experience these principles in the "re-membered" content of this text, they can also experience them during instruction that uses emancipatory pedagogies. For example, if "re-membered" content situates all cultures and groups as the subjects of their own accounts, not the objects of others' accounts about them (principle #1, Inclusion), then students can experience being the *subjects of instruction* when they are in right relationship with their teachers as elders whose authority is based on knowledge, expertise, and wisdom. This emancipatory pedagogy called Eldering is a cultural practice that we detail with specific examples below. Our point here is that the emancipatory pedagogies we propose are informed by African worldview and the cosmologies, philosophies, and related cultural concepts that African people have developed and practiced over time.

Principles, Pedagogies, and Cultural Platforms

Each of the six sub-sections below corresponds to one of the six culturally informed principles. In each section we: (1) point out how the featured culturally informed principle is used to write content in *Black Community Building*; (2) demonstrate how teachers can use a related emancipatory pedagogy to enact that culturally informed principle during instruction; and 3) describe the African cultural platform—using examples from oral and written literature—that supports the emancipatory pedagogy discussed in that section. These six sections are a gateway to learning how culture connects content and pedagogy and how teachers using emancipatory pedagogies connect students to learning. While each sub-section is presented in narrative form in the remaining pages of this chapter, Table 2.1 below is a preview of the connections between culturally informed principles, emancipatory pedagogies, and African cultural platforms. To indicate the nature of these platforms, this table includes one example of African Diasporan philosophy, epistemology, cosmology, or cultural dimensions/themes that supports each of the emancipatory pedagogies. Expanded discussion of these and other examples can be found in the narratives that follow this table and in the references cited.

Culturally Informed Principle #1: Inclusion

Inclusion is consistently evident in the content of *Black Community Building*, since the text positions African people who migrated to the Midwest as subjects and substantive participants, not as objects or token figures in the margins of a dominant account of westward movement. There are images and text of numerous men and women who were leaders and participants in this late 19th century migration and in building Black towns and institutions in Kansas and Oklahoma. Working together, they built businesses to service their communities; established schools for children and literary societies for adults; set up newspapers to communicate and promote agreed-upon social behaviors, such as peaceful actions, the setting of moral examples for children, and hard work; created benevolent societies and churches to take care of material and spiritual needs; established banks to assist in economic development; organized town councils to govern themselves; and operated farms to grow and sell food (Crockett, 1979; Hamilton, 1991; O'Dell, 2011; Painter, 1976/1986; Taylor, 1998). These towns were contexts in which people of African ancestry demonstrated what self-reliance, courage, collective work and responsibility, unity, knowledge, and skills can accomplish. By using the principle of Inclusion, *Black Community Building* exemplifies how African people were substantive participants in what Maulana Karenga (1980, 2006a) calls "the forward flow of human history" (p. 107 and p. 246, respectively).

TABLE 2.1 Principles, Pedagogies, and Cultural Platforms

Culturally Informed Principles	Emancipatory Pedagogies	African Cultural Platforms (carries African worldview, philosophies, cosmologies, cultural concepts, and practices)
Inclusion	Eldering	**African philosophy:** • Proverbs that acknowledge the revered position of elders
Representation	Locating Students (centering students culturally)	**African American themes/dimensions:** • Research has identified cultural dimensions such as spirituality, harmony, movement, verve, communalism, and orality in both African and Diasporan contexts.
Accurate Scholarship	Multiple Ways of Knowing	**African epistemology:** • Includes ways of knowing such as symbolic imagery, relational knowing, intuition-reasoning, and empathy.
Indigenous Voice	Question-Driven Pedagogy	**Baluba (of Central Africa) philosophy:** • Proverbs teach that questions are a way to arrive at true knowledge.
Critical Thinking	Culturally Authentic Assessment	**African epistemology:** • The performance of knowledge is a way of knowing through interaction with an audience.
A Collective Humanity	Communal Responsibility	**Bântu-Kôngo (Central Africa) cosmology:** • Proverbs teach that unity, complementary and caring relationships, and right action make communal relations possible.

Eldering—an Emancipatory Pedagogy

During instruction, students can experience the culturally informed principle of Inclusion through the emancipatory pedagogy called Eldering. This pedagogy refers to teacher–student interactions led by teachers' knowledge, expertise, and wisdom, which together represent eldership or authentic authority. In this ethically informed relationship, students experience their "place" or presence as younger/learner with dignity, since teachers' authority is not an attempt to have power *over* them, but to share the power of knowledge *with* them. Teachers who are knowledgeable—not only about a topic, but about the students they are teaching—are confident enough to ask critical questions, build upon cultural characteristics, and co-create curriculum with students. Thus, after teaching about the success of Black towns in the Midwest, a teacher as elder might ask, "How do you think Black towns managed to become self-sufficient in such a short period of time?" (Goodwin, in Swartz, 2013, p. 12). Asking this question, whose answer is not given in the text, assumes that students have ideas, along with text content, to respond to the question; and that the teacher can guide students' responses toward new knowledge and understanding. In Vignette 2.1, we step into Ms. Hart's fifth-grade classroom to see how she demonstrates Eldering, that is, how she uses her knowledge, expertise, and wisdom as the rudder of instruction with her students. In this classroom excerpt, we have included our comments as observers.

VIGNETTE 2.1

Eldering

Ms. Hart
Now that we have read and discussed *Black Community Building*, how do you think Black towns managed to become self-sufficient in such a short period of time?

Kiesha
People were like a group and took care of each other.

Rob
When Black people stick together we get a lot done.

Lerone
Black people were just trying to have a good place to live, so they depended on themselves, not on other people who acted like they didn't care about them.

Observers

One way to view these students' responses is through the presence of heritage knowledge [see Chapter 1]. In this view, Kiesha's cultural memory taps into African ontological orientations (ways of being) such as Cooperation, Collective Responsibility, and Interdependence, along with the epistemology of empathy. Rob's response also reflects heritage knowledge of Collectivity and Cooperation seen when families, friends, or neighbors work together. Lerone's cultural memory links feelings and thoughts (epistemology of intuition-reasoning) to know that it would be reasonable for people in Black towns to depend on themselves, since the hostile actions of White people surrounded them.

Ms. Hart

Yes, I see what you are saying. That reminds me of what happened when the citizens of Langston asked the White county commissioners to provide funds to fix the bridge between Langston and Guthrie. This bridge was needed for safe travel between the two towns, but the commissioners refused to fix the bridge. So what did the residents do?

Kanokwan

They got the materials they needed and built a new bridge themselves.

Ms. Hart

Right! So what does this tell you about how Langston residents thought about their town?

Marcos

They thought that they should have a good bridge.

Ms. Hart

Yes, and what does that tell you, Marcos, about how the residents *felt* about their town?

Marcos

They were proud of their town.

Sharesse

And they wanted it to be a good town so they wanted to keep it up.

Ms. Hart

Yes, I agree with both of you. We call this being community minded. The residents of Langston were community minded, just like their African ancestors. They cared about their town and everyone in it and by thinking together about how to have a good town and working together to make it happen they accomplished a lot in a short period of time.

Observers

By having cultural knowledge, Ms. Hart is able to make a connection between Africa and the Diaspora. Her pedagogical actions suggest her confidence in building on students' ideas to teach about community mindedness—a value that was clearly at work in Langston. Ms. Hart also has expertise with scaffolding and was able to build on what several students knew to create new knowledge for the class (Goodwin & Swartz, 2008). Together, these practices demonstrate Ms. Hart's use of Eldering. Not only has she used the principle of Inclusion through content that substantively includes the ancestral heritage of most of her students and builds cultural knowledge for all students, but her pedagogy of Eldering includes all of her students in right relationship to her. This ethical dimension of her teaching means that students can feel the safety and dignity of being a participating learner in the presence of a knowledgeable elder.

Throughout this chapter, you will see more of Ms. Hart and her use of the other five emancipatory pedagogies. Who is this teacher and how did she develop her pedagogical expertise? Ms. Hart is a mid-30s White teacher with a working class family background. This is her 11th year teaching at Charles Houston Elementary School, a predominately African American elementary school in a mid-size city in the Northeast. This year the school is 78% African American, 19% Latina/o, 2% White, and 1% Southeast Asian. Eighty-eight percent (88%) of its students qualify for federally subsidized breakfast and lunch. In her first year of teaching, Ms. Hart asked for guidance from Ms. Singleton, a veteran African American teacher who also taught fifth grade at her school. Their collegial relationship has continued over the years, with Ms. Hart seeking Ms. Singleton's thoughts and advice on all aspects of teaching, including how to incorporate students' cultures into curriculum and pedagogy. Learning how to make these cultural connections was not part of Ms. Hart's teacher preparation program, and when she began teaching she quickly realized that something was missing.

Ms. Singleton invited Ms. Hart to observe in her classroom, and she was immediately struck by Ms. Singleton's positive and productive relationships with students. They were so engaged and eager to learn in both whole group and small group settings; and there didn't seem to be any need for the classroom management techniques she had just learned in her master's program, since students were typically focused and on task. She was so glad to see this because something about "managing" students with behavior modification techniques didn't feel right to her; and even if rewards and consequences "worked" in the short term, she wondered if they had any lasting effect. It was also striking that parents were a regular part of Ms. Singleton's instructional program. At first Ms. Hart thought that what she was seeing must have something to do with the teacher and most students and their parents being African American, but after several observations she noticed that Ms. Singleton had the same kind of solid connections with her Latina/o, Southeast Asian, and White students and their parents; and that there didn't seem to be any dissention among cultural/racial groups in her classroom. Clearly, something else was going on here.

When Ms. Singleton and Ms. Hart began working together, they talked about their personal and professional goals and approaches and then read and discussed articles and chapters about teaching and learning, including how cultural knowledge and heritage knowledge are linked to curriculum and pedagogy, about the principles used to write "re-membered" or democratized student materials, and how learning has an ethical dimension and involves more than gathering information for the sake of "having it" (Campbell, 2014; Goodwin, 1996, 2004; King, 2006; King & Swartz, 2014; Nkulu-N'Sengha, 2005; Shakes, 2004; Smith, 2004; Swartz, 2012). Ms. Singleton referred to these approaches as Teaching *for* Freedom, which she explained as a way that teachers, families, and communities share the responsibility to teach students how to live and act based on ideals and values that are just and good for self and others. This involves using culturally informed content and emancipatory pedagogies that teach students to think critically and to gain knowledge with the intent of producing the academic and cultural excellence needed to create community well-being and belonging.

Ms. Hart knew that it would take time to absorb and incorporate these new ideas, but they felt right to her. So, she kept reading, asking questions, trying different approaches, and reflecting on the outcomes. Whenever possible, Ms. Singleton observed in Ms. Hart's classroom and gave her feedback. Over the years, Ms. Hart learned from her more experienced colleague how to select culturally informed content, use six overlapping emancipatory pedagogies, build relationships with her students and their families, and continue to grow as a professional. The Ms. Hart you see in this chapter is the result of a willing mind and heart and 11 years of guidance and support.

An African Cultural Platform for Eldering

Each of the six emancipatory pedagogies discussed in this volume is supported by an African cultural platform composed of worldview elements and related philosophies, cosmologies, cultural concepts, and practices. In the case of Eldering, the philosophies in numerous African cultures—which are visible in proverbs, aphorisms, and analyses of traditions—acknowledge the revered position of elders who hold shared authority in communal societies based on their knowledge, experience, and wisdom (Gyeke, 1987; Nkulu-N'Sengha, 2005; Tedla, 1995; Waghid, 2014). Polycarp Ikuenobe (2006) states that elders

> are recognized in the community as reasonable people based on their actions, wealth of experience, knowledge of the tradition and culture, and

their demonstration of such wisdom and knowledge, [and] may be relied on as the source of knowledge and recognized as epistemic authorities.

(p. 178)

As a pedagogy, Eldering refers to the guidance that teachers provide to students through their more advanced knowledge and expertise, which are both informed by wisdom. Teachers as elders are thinkers who are responsible to stand in right relationship with their students. Mutombo Nkulu-N'Sengha (2005) explains that in African societies all knowledge has an ethical dimension and that "the pursuit of knowledge is inseparable from the pursuit of wisdom, for in the African understanding of things, a genuine knowledge necessarily involves wisdom" (pp. 43–44). Eleni Tedla (1998) also references the ethical aspect of eldership in indigenous African education, which we see in Ms. Singleton's guidance of her younger colleague, and both teachers' guidance of their students:

> ... adults are elders to the young, and the old are elders to everyone in the community. Eldership, the pinnacle of human life and the height of indigenous education, is not mere aging. It is the manifestation of the basic values/virtues/morals deemed essential by the community in order to be regarded as a person. Elders are expected to live an exemplary life, to be kind and to be peacemakers, and to provide leadership and guidance.

(p. 35)

In their wisdom, teachers who are elders know that gaining knowledge is a communal experience—it is the outcome of mutual exchanges that assume even the youngest students are knowers who can contribute to everyone's learning. Consider the following Akan proverbs: "One head does not hold a discussion" (Kwame, 1995, p. xxxi); "Wisdom is not in the head of one person" (Gyeke, 1997, p. 131); "All heads are alike, but not all their contents are alike" (Kwame, 1995, p. 83); and "Wisdom is like a baobab tree, a single person's hand cannot embrace it" (Nkulu-N'Sengha, 2005, p. 43). Since each "head" holds different ideas that are valuable, merging and handling these ideas requires more than one head. In communal cultures, people are interdependent—they rely on each other, are community minded, and their interactions are collaborative and relational. As seen in the classroom excerpt in Vignette 2.1, Ms. Hart's use of Eldering involved having this cultural knowledge and viewing knowledge as relational, values driven, and drawn from multiple sources, that is, knowing that everyone has something to contribute to the well-being of the group. In these ways, Eldering, which is the pedagogical application of the principle of Inclusion, connects content and pedagogy, with both standing on an African cultural platform, since gaining knowledge is understood to be a communal and ethical experience, not an individual experience or one of gaining knowledge for knowledge's sake (Gyeke, 1987; Ikuenobe, 2006; Karenga, 2006a; Nkulu-N'Sengha, 2005). By viewing teaching and learning as an experience in which everyone has something to offer, the pedagogy of Eldering is a cultural practice able to connect students to learning in pursuit of academic and cultural excellence.

Culturally Informed Principle #2: Representation

Representation can be seen in the title of the student text—*Black Community Building: An African Tradition of Collective Work and Responsibility*, which names Black community building as an African tradition and portrays Africans in the Americas as located within, not separate from, their ancestral heritage. The principle of Representation continues inside the text where the enduring connection between Black townspeople and the traditions of their African ancestors is described in the collaborative and collectively responsible actions of the men and women who built these towns. They retained and practiced African values, principles, and virtues such as community mindedness, service to others, unity, communal responsibility, participatory/democratic governance, and self-determination, which is evident in the businesses, institutions, and organizations they established (Diop, 1959/1990; Gyeke, 1997; Karenga, 1980, 1996; Painter, 1976/1986; Taylor, 1998; Tedla, 1995).

Locating Students—an Emancipatory Pedagogy

As students in Ms. Hart's classroom moved through a unit of study on *Black Community Building*, they experienced the principle of Representation through the emancipatory pedagogy called Locating Students, which means that students' cultures "hold" information about how to engage them in learning. Ms. Singleton had encouraged Ms. Hart—in her first year of teaching—to observe how her students interacted with each other and what was going on when they seemed to be the most engaged in learning; and she cautioned Ms. Hart not to be too quick to "shut down" interactions that seemed normative for her students. Ms. Hart observed that her students learned effectively in relationships, and that movement and being verbal and expressive were characteristics exhibited by most of her students. Ms. Singleton also introduced Ms. Hart to research by A. Wade Boykin and colleagues (Boykin & Cunningham, 2001; Boykin, Lilja, & Tyler, 2004) that served to confirm Ms. Hart's observations. She soon realized that if she was going to engage her students in learning she had to adjust her ideas about what a classroom "should look like," including her preference for a quieter and less active learning environment. So, she began to structure learning opportunities that involved movement and verbal interaction among students. In every subject area, she regularly asked students to partner or form small groups to discuss and develop responses to the topics they were studying or problems they were trying to solve.

Ms. Hart also had to adjust her ideas about what parent involvement meant. In their early years of working together, Ms. Singleton stressed the importance of involving parents "in a real way." When Ms. Hart asked what she meant by "in a real way," Ms. Singleton said:

> Your relationship with parents and families needs to be a partnership that includes their involvement in instruction. You want parents to come to parent–teacher conferences and be chaperones on field trips, but you and your students need more than that. For example, parents and family members can participate in homework assignments and work on a joint project with their child. They can make a presentation, co-teach a lesson, and be interviewed by students based on their knowledge, skills, and experiences; and they can participate in developing assessments of student work [King, Goss, & McArthur, 2014]. Parents can also participate in action research projects with teachers [Campbell, 2014; Oakes, Rogers, & Lipton, 2006]. When students see you working alongside parents— whether it be their own or others—they know that your classroom is a place where they belong. Most importantly, once you get to know parents, you need to ask them to share their community/cultural expectations for their children's school experience, and then figure out what you need to know to meet those expectations.

Over the years, as Ms. Hart used these suggestions, she began to see the connection between the pedagogy of Locating Students and engaging parents. After all, students carry the cultures of their families into the classroom, so if you are going to locate or center students, you need to acknowledge their families by inviting them—and the cultures they represent—into meaningful participation in classroom learning. For this unit on *Black Community Building*, Ms. Hart invited parents to participate in an interview process related to their knowledge of the *Nguzo Saba* or Kwanzaa Principles and how they were used in her classroom. Students and parents were already familiar with these Principles since Ms. Hart used them as a guide for thinking about how to develop and maintain a classroom community—one of Ms. Singleton's highly effective suggestions. Ms. Hart often referred to various Kwanzaa Principles when they related to what she was teaching (she had a big *Nguzo Saba* poster on the wall); and instead of posting classroom rules, she would regularly ask students which Principle their actions were or were not reflecting. The parent interviews were part of group projects in which students were collaboratively designing and presenting an oral, visual, and/or dramatic demonstration in response to the following assignment: "Select a Kwanzaa Principle and show: (1) how it was used by the residents of Black towns in the Midwest to build their communities; and (2) how the Kwanzaa Principle you selected is used in our classroom, including information gathered from family interviews." Students were encouraged to demonstrate personal expression during the group demonstration in order to enhance the overall group presentation.

Small groups began by identifying and discussing the evidence they could find in the text for the use of *Nguzo Saba* Principles in Black towns. Each group found several, but agreed upon one Principle. They developed a question to ask themselves and a parent or family member about where they saw this Principle used in their classroom and recorded all responses. Students then collaborated about how to combine the text information with what they and their families thought and designed a group presentation that included personal expression. One group did a visual presentation including a mural they painted showing townspeople collaborating, which served as a backdrop for a mime that portrayed how *Ujima* (Collective Work and Responsibility) was visible in the classroom. Another group performed a rap of several rhymed verses that included metaphors and alliteration to demonstrate what the Principle of *Umoja* (Unity) looked like in both Black towns and the classroom. There was a one-act play in which students portrayed how their great-great-grandparents demonstrated *Nia* (Purpose) in a Black town they built and how the Principle was passed on through the generations so that parents could recognize it being used in their classroom. And there was a series of dramatic dialogues, with group members reenacting their preparatory conversations *as* the presentation about *Imani* (Faith). In the first conversation, two students talked about how townspeople believed in each other and in the rightness of being free to build a better life for themselves and their families. In a second conversation, two other students talked about how having faith in their parents and teacher could be seen in their classroom. And in the third conversation, the final two students explored possibilities for a performance about *Imani*. As always, families and friends were invited to be an audience for students' presentations. At the end of the presentations, Ms. Hart proudly pointed out that the seventh *Nguzo Saba* Principle *Kuumba* (Creativity) was fully present in each group's presentation.

An African Cultural Platform for Locating Students

Being connected to one's culture/community (one's lineage) is part of the African cultural platform that supports the emancipatory pedagogy called Locating Students (Akbar, 1984; Gyeke, 1987; Karenga, 1999, 2006a; King, 2006; Maïga, 2010; Nkulu-N'Sengha, 2005). As described in Chapter 1, Afrocentricity recognizes cultural connection as seen in one of its key concepts called Centrality/Location that has helped to identify and recuperate African knowledge, cultural ideals, values, and ways of knowing and being as a location or platform from which the past and present can be viewed and understood (Asante, 1987/1998, 2003; Mazama, 2003). Locating Students is a pedagogical manifestation of this Afrocentric concept, since it views students' cultures/communities as "a place to stand" (Asante, 2003, p. 45); and by so doing, invites teachers to learn about and consider students' cultures as they design instruction. Of course, this locating or centering of students' cultures also includes individuals who are centered because the group is centered, which reflects the African ontological construct, "I am, because we are; and since we are, therefore I am" (Mbiti, 1990, p. 106). In other words, individuals are valued for what they contribute to their cultural community, and it is only in the context of varied relationships within that community that individuals fully experience their identity (Gyeke, 1997; Ikuenobe, 2006).

Diasporan scholars of African ancestry have long recognized the importance of culture and African Diasporan connections (Asante, 1980/1988; Boykin, 1983; Clarke, 1977; Dixon, 1971; Du Bois, 1947; Du Bois & Padamore, 1962; Hilliard, 1986; Karenga, 1980; Nobles, 1972; Turner, 1949; Woodson, 1922/1966). Over 30 years ago, Wade Boykin (1983), an educationally focused experimental psychologist, identified specific connections between African and Diasporan cultures in the interest of providing an alternative to deficit-oriented narratives and approaches that were (and still are) being used to teach students of African ancestry in the United States (King, 1994; King et al., 2014). While U.S. students in general have multiple and overlapping cultural influences, Boykin identified nine distinct cultural themes or dimensions with an African base that exist among African Americans: spirituality, harmony, movement, verve, affect, communalism, expressive individuality, orality, and social time perspective (see Boykin, 1983, pp. 344–346, for a discussion and descriptions of these themes). Even though variations logically exist across time and geographic locations, scholars have independently identified one or more of these themes in African and Diasporan cultures (Anyanwu, 1981a; Dixon, 1971; Goodwin & King, 2006; Karenga, 2006b; Gyeke, 1987, 1997; Mbiti, 1990; Nkulu-N'Sengha, 2005; Nobles, 1976; Nyang, 1980; Senghor, 1964; Smitherman, 1977/1986, 1994; Turner, 1949). Over several decades, Boykin and colleagues have conceptualized and conducted empirical research on a number of these cultural dimensions, such as communalism, verve (energetic intensity), and movement (Allen & Boykin, 1991, 1992; Allen & Butler, 1996; Boykin, 1994; Boykin et al., 2005; Boykin & Bailey, 2000; Boykin & Cunningham, 2001). This school-based research has found that African American and White students perceive and experience the classroom in cultural terms. For example, African American students favor learning environments that are communal, collaborative, and vervistic/high movement compared to White students, who favor individual, competitive, and low-verve/low movement learning environments (Boykin, 2001; Boykin et al., 2005; Boykin et al., 2004; Dill & Boykin, 2000). Collectively, this body of research, echoed by other scholars, suggests that when teaching is culturally informed—when it pedagogically locates students by acknowledging the integrity of their cultural capital and designs instruction around their cultural characteristics—it enhances motivation and learning outcomes (Goodwin, 2004; Yosso, 2005).

As a pedagogical application of the principle of Representation—in which individuals and groups remain connected to their ancestral cultures and communities—Locating Students is a cultural practice that expands teachers' repertoire to actively consider cultural themes/characteristics that exist within groups of students and, in so doing, positions culture as a connector between students and learning. This view of culture as the gluon or medium of exchange that connects students to learning has been operating for students of European ancestry who are well matched with the cultural characteristics of U.S. schools—from their Puritan beginnings to the present (Asante, 1991/1992; Boykin, 1986; Gatto, 2001; Spring, 2011). In these same schools, however, students of African ancestry have experienced and continue to experience extreme dislocation and disconnection due to the absence and denigration and distortion of their culture in subject-area content and pedagogy (Asante, 2007a; King, 1994; Gordon, 1994; Shujaa, 1994). "Re-membered" content and emancipatory pedagogies such as Locating Students are direct curricular responses designed to change schools and classrooms that dysconsciously—that is through an uncritical habit of mind—disregard and disparage the culture of students of African ancestry (see Chapters 3 and 5 for a definition and development of the concept of dysconsciousness) (King, 1991; King & Akua, 2012).

This may be a good time to make note that, in our discussion of culturally informed principles, emancipatory pedagogies, and African cultural platforms we use examples that were outcomes of veteran teachers at Charles Houston Elementary School coming together to study and develop a response to dysconsciousness and the dislocation it causes students. Ms. Singleton is part of this ongoing teacher-led collegial group, along with other experienced teachers at each grade level who have committed to supporting new teachers interested in guidance. As the group studies, gathers student materials, experiments with emancipatory pedagogies, and conducts teacher research, its members share what they have learned and discuss effective approaches with their younger colleagues.

Culturally Informed Principle #3: Accurate Scholarship

Writing *Black Community Building* with the culturally informed principle of Accurate Scholarship produces relevant (and typically omitted) information about Black migration in the late 19th century westward movement in the United States. As explained in an earlier volume (King & Swartz, 2014), all scholarship reflects a particular worldview, standing place, and epistemic order. The principle of Accurate Scholarship guides our consideration of multiple worldviews and cultural orientations, including those of historically liminal identity-groups. To approach accuracy, we place a range of scholarly work on a topic within an Afrocentric theoretical framework. This theory and its human-centric concepts and culturally informed principles represent an epistemic order with the capacity to center *all* cultures and groups, thereby bringing us closer to accurate accounts of the past.

In *Black Community Building*, there are images and text about mass migration of Black people from Southern states and White reactions to this exodus, about promoters of migration such as Henry Adams and Benjamin Singleton, and about early homes and businesses established in Black towns. Students learn about Jenny Smith Fletcher, the first postmistress and school teacher in Nicodemus, Kansas, and Edwin P. McCabe, who was a lawyer, politician, and land speculator in Kansas and then Oklahoma. They not only learn about people and places, but about what people of African ancestry valued about the legacy of community building they carried with them and passed on to future generations. *Black Community Building* presents this significant era in U.S. history with integrity by including knowledge from numerous epistemologies and scholarly sources.

Multiple Ways of Knowing—an Emancipatory Pedagogy

As an emancipatory pedagogy, Multiple Ways of Knowing is a manifestation of a culturally informed principle in student–teacher interactions, meaning that in addition to students experiencing, in this case, Accurate Scholarship in subject-area content, they can experience it during instruction. Ms. Hart's students experience this connection between content and pedagogy when she uses Multiple Ways of Knowing, since this emancipatory pedagogy guides students to use several epistemologies to arrive at rather than accept accounts of historical topics. Ms. Hart uses this pedagogy to teach the first three pages of *Black Community Building*—a section written with the principle of Accurate Scholarship to describe the White assault on Reconstruction, the life-threatening conditions in the South for people of African ancestry, and the growing interest in migration. She frames her teaching of this section with the following questions: "What do you think Black people expected life would be like for them after slavery ended? How do you know?" (Goodwin, in Swartz, 2013, p. 13). She is able to ask these questions and guide students as they respond since she has, over the years, developed cultural knowledge about the backgrounds and experiences of her students. Through her discussions with Ms. Singleton—further informed by recommended readings—Ms. Hart is familiar with the idea that there are multiple epistemologies or ways of learning or coming to know, and she structures contexts in which all students are encouraged to use several epistemologies that reflect both their heritage knowledge (group memory) and their cultural knowledge (learned knowledge about diverse cultural histories and legacies) (Clarke, 1994; Gyekye, 1987; King, 2006; King & Swartz, 2014; Nkulu-N'Sengha, 2005; Senghor, 1964). She has learned that the heritable epistemologies often used by people of African ancestry include relational knowing (interdependent and reciprocal interactions produced in social contexts), group-based knowing (drawing upon the experiences of one's group identities), empathy (caring about and feeling connected to others, past and present, including ancestors), and intuition-reasoning (drawing inferences and constructing responses to questions or problems that use both heart and mind knowledge, with an ethical dialog between the two) (Dixon, 1971; Nkulu-N'Sengha, 2005; Nobles, 1976; Senghor, 1964; Sindima, 1995). Ms. Hart asks students to work in pairs or small groups to produce responses to the question about Black people's expectations of life after slavery, which gives them opportunities to consider the second question (How do you know?). While all students use the authority of the text to make inferences, some use heart-mind knowledge and empathy to answer the question. When combined, these epistemic choices expand the accuracy of knowledge that students create together.

African Cultural Platform for Multiple Ways for Knowing

As a pedagogy, Multiple Ways of Knowing holds assumptions, concepts, and claims in common with African cosmologies and epistemologies. For example, a cosmological assumption about reality that is common in African cultures is that the world has a complementary (not contradictory) quality—that there is no dualism or separation between man and nature, subject and object, matter and spirit (Anyanwu, 1981a; Nobles, 1991). Léopold Sédar Senghor (1964), of Serer and Fulani heritage, was a poet, cultural theorist, and first president of Senegal. He claimed that, compared to the European, the African

> does not draw a line between himself and the object; he does not hold it at a distance, nor does he merely look at it and analyze it. After holding it at a distance, after scanning it without analyzing it, he takes it vibrant in his hands, careful not to kill or fix it. He touches it, feels it, *smells* it ... [he] *sympathizes*, abandons his personality to become identified with the Other, dies to be reborn in the Other. He does not assimilate; he is assimilated. He lives a common life with the Other; he lives in a symbiosis.
>
> (pp. 72–73; italics in original)

This concept of interconnectedness—that all life forces, including the material and spiritual, are linked—expands ways of knowing the world. In accordance with this view, the Nigerian philosopher K. C. Anyanwu (1981a) wrote, "The African culture did not assume that reality could be subordinated to human reason alone. Imagination, intuitive experience, and feelings are also modes of knowing" (p. 89). Thus, African epistemologies and cosmologies assume and understand a world in which nothing is separate and isolated, and nothing is lifeless—where there is unity among all things (Anyanwu, 1981a & b). In the African worldview, heart knowledge (e.g., revelation, relational knowing, empathy, intuitive insight, symbolic imagery) is inseparable from mind knowledge (e.g., authority, empiricism, reason/logic), and all things are interconnected. Similarly, Multiple Ways of Knowing, as a pedagogy, brings together the so-called subjective and objective ways of knowing the world, and in so doing, expands the ways in which students can access knowledge. When teachers view all things as interconnected and complementary rather than separate and discon-nected, they seek content that is interconnected ("re-membered") and ask stu-dents to explore this content by connecting reason, imagination, authority, intuitive experience, thoughts, and feelings. The African cultural platform that offers concepts of interconnectedness exemplifies how culture connects content and pedagogy. When content is written with the principle of Accurate Scholar-ship and taught with Multiple ways of Knowing, teaching and learning experi-ences are more integrated, nuanced, and comprehensive.

Culturally Informed Principle #4: Indigenous Voice

Building Black Communities portrays historic events as told through the voices and actions of those who were present yet typically excluded in standard instructional materials. For example, a range of Black responses to the actions of White terrorist groups like the Ku Klux Klan are included—from petitioning the president of the United States for justice to developing organizations, such as a committee of 500 women of African ancestry that published an address demanding all the rights due to them under the U.S. Constitution to secret meetings to plan emigrating to lands where freedom might be possible. People's actions and voices are heard in quoted and descriptive content in which they speak for, name, and define themselves. Through images and text, students learn about the historical agency and self-sufficiency of Black men and women who established businesses and banks, newspapers, governing councils, schools, churches, and other organizations to enhance community life in the towns they built. For example, the *Langston City Herald* and the *Western Age*—both black newspapers—wrote that the city of Langston was a refuge for Black people where they could enjoy the rights and privileges of any other American citizen (Crockett, 1979; Hamilton, 1991; Taylor, 1998; Tolson, 1974).

Question-Driven Pedagogy—an Emancipatory Pedagogy

During instruction, Ms. Hart's students experience the principle of Indigenous Voice through her use of Question-Driven Pedagogy, which asks students thought-provoking questions that build on what they know. Ms. Hart found Question-Driven Pedagogy difficult to learn at first. In the hands of Ms. Single-ton, this pedagogy was developed to a fine art, so watching her was very helpful. This way of teaching is the antithesis of scripted curriculum, since it involves an improvisational flow between teacher and students who basically create the cur-riculum together. If you ask a critical question, the ensuing interaction depends on how students respond—on what they offer and what you can do with it to extend learning. For example, Ms. Hart began whole-group instruction by restating text content about the abolition of slavery in 1865 with the passage of the 13th Amendment to the U.S. Constitution. She then asked, "If slavery was ended by law, what should have happened as a result of emancipation?" This critical question is an entrance into exploring the contradiction between what a legal document states and what actually occurred. Importantly, all students will have ideas in response to this type of open-ended question. Andrea said, "Since Black people were free by law they should have been able to vote and own land." Miguel said, "Be able to earn enough money to take care of their families." And Latisha said, "We should have been able to go to school." After hearing these responses, Ms. Hart asked, "According to our text, what actually happened?" Students explained that at the beginning of Reconstruction there were improvements, but that White people who did not want any changes in the status of Black people reacted with violence when Black people tried to vote, go to school, or be part of bettering conditions in the South. Northern and Southern White leaders—who had just been enemies in the Civil War—agreed that if the South could continue to provide cheap, almost free labor again they could all continue to make huge profits as they did during slavery. Even the federal government turned its back on Black people when it pulled out federal troops that had been protecting some of the progress made during Reconstruction.

After students shared what they learned in the text, Ms. Hart asked another question: "Why do you think that the 13th Amendment didn't lead to right action and respect for everyone's freedom?" Such a critical question asks students to question (not accept) the contradiction between laws and the absence of right action and respect. Toward the end of the discussion, Ms. Hart asked students to write down at least one question they had about the 13th Amendment and what happened once it was passed, to pair up and ask each other their questions, and to record all responses. Below, Ms. Hart describes her question-driven approach:

> I ask my students questions that get them to think—to go beyond what the text says. I also have them develop their own questions so they can experience agency by defining themselves and their ideas. In this section, I was trying to pedagogically mirror the principles of Accurate Scholarship and Indigenous Voice that provide enough information to give an insider's view of Black people's experiences as Reconstruction was coming to an end. Along with the knowledge students learned from the text, I encouraged them to use other ways of knowing, such as intuition-reasoning, relational knowing, and empathy to respond to a critical question about how laws don't necessarily lead to right action. I want them to make meaning of the past rather than only be limited to what a text—even a "re-membered" text—has to say about a topic.

For homework, Ms. Hart asked students to take home and share a copy of the text, pose the questions they developed to their parents and family members, record their answers, and inform the next day's discussion with the thoughts of their families.

African Cultural Platform for Question-Driven Pedagogy

An example of the African cultural precedent for Question-Driven Pedagogy is found in the epistemology of the Baluba (a Bantu People of Central Africa), which is reflected in the following proverb: "The child who raises questions is the one who will gain knowledge." According to Mutombo Nkulu-N'Sengha (2005), this proverb:

> stipulates the centrality of the question in the path toward knowledge. For the Bantu, knowledge does not stem from a blind repetition of ancestral ways. The Baluba state that in order to know, one has to begin with the "art of unknowing," being carefully aware that everything that shines may not be a "genuine knowledge" (*Bwino ke bwino*). This means that knowledge is not knowledge until it is critically examined and its validity enshrined.
>
> (p. 42)

This Baluba proverb views questions as a way to arrive at knowledge—an approach that is valued over learning to repeat what is already known. True knowledge comes from inquiry, which begins with the acknowledgment of not knowing. Likewise, in Question-Driven Pedagogy, thought-provoking questions lead the exchange of ideas between teachers and students—a process of arriving at answers together, without relinquishing the right relationship between elders and young people. To begin with "unknowing" means that predetermined answers are not a way to gain genuine knowledge. Rather, it is asking questions that leads to knowledge. This relational and interdependent process described in a Baluba proverb shows how an African epistemological concept—when enacted through Question-Driven Pedagogy—connects students to learning.

Culturally Informed Principle #5: Critical Thinking

The principle of Critical Thinking is used to write content broad enough for students to see connections and evaluate and synthesize information. Thus, prior to telling the story of Black migration to the Midwest, *Black Community Building* describes conditions in the South that pressed African families to consider leaving the only homes they had ever known. These common experiences and the features of Black towns—what institutions residents developed and what values they promoted—are patterns that allows students to critically think about what was important to Black people, what they accomplished after migrating, and how their accomplishments represent African Diasporan cultural continuities (Crockett, 1979; Loewen, 2005; O'Dell, 2011; Painter, 1976/1986). With this content, students can evaluate the significance of this mass migration from the standing place of the people who built Black towns, which are a little-known part of the westward movement.

Culturally Authentic Assessment—an Emancipatory Pedagogy

During instruction, students can experience the principle of Critical Thinking through the emancipatory pedagogy called Culturally Authentic Assessment. This pedagogy uses standards elaborated collaboratively with parents to guide students to produce knowledge and arrive at solutions through demonstration rather than being asked to give predetermined "right" answers. Thus, this pedagogy also assesses student learning through community-informed standards and expectations (King et al., 2014). Critical thinking—on the part of teachers, students, and parents—is stimulated when they work together to design, complete, and assess exhibitions, portfolios, demonstrations, or performances that reflect imagination and bring benefit to the classroom and community. For example, Ms. Hart's final unit assessment of *Black Community Building* involves students in problem solving a response to the following end-of-text question: "How is knowing about Black towns in the Midwest valuable to Black communities today?" (Goodwin, in Swartz, 2013, p. 12). Ms. Hart sees this as an opportunity for students to bring learning about the past into the present—a present in which they can see themselves and their ancestors acting with agency and practicing specific principles and ideals.

As Part I of responding to this question, Ms. Hart gave students three questions to discuss in small groups: (1) Do you think it is possible to transfer what was learned and accomplished in the past to the present? (2) What principles, values, and practices in Black towns of the Midwest do you think can be used in Black communities today? (3) What types of values and ideals would your parents and/ or family members like to see practiced in your community? Students took the third question home to ask family members and record their responses. The next day, student groups presented what they learned from their families along with their responses to the other two questions. During and following group presentations, Ms. Hart facilitated class discussion to highlight points that could help students complete the assessment options in Part II of this assessment.

To develop the assessment options for Part II, Ms. Hart had already met with a group of five parents and family members who agreed to participate in developing a final assessment for this unit of study. (Mrs. Hart had sent information home about what students would be learning and doing at the start of the unit and invited interested parents and family members to participate.) They began as a book group, discussing *Black Community Building* in the first meeting. Ms. Hart also shared her interest in having students learn from the past in order to apply their learning to the present, and explained that she needed family input to make that happen. In the second meeting, the teacher–family group discussed the same three questions that students would be answering in Part I of the final assessment; and the third meeting was devoted to developing and refining three assessment options for Part II. During this meeting, Ms. Hart showed and discussed a video of performance-based assessments completed by former students. While parents were impressed with what they saw, a few parents asked how this authentic approach to assessment affected students' performance on standardized tests. Ms. Hart explained that her focus on meaningful projects, rather than test preparation that involves trying to cover a lot of content, meant that she could give students more feedback along the way. This allowed students to participate in assessment and to learn while they were being assessed, which actually resulted in her students' increased motivation and doing better on standardized tests compared to other fifth-grade classrooms in her district. She said she would bring a few articles to the next session that showed how research supported this approach (McTighe, Seif, & Wiggins, 2004; Stiggins, 2002). In the fourth and final meeting, the teacher–family group developed a rubric that the teacher and all parents could use to assess students' projects. After discussing and recording what parents thought should be included in an assessment that was culturally authentic and demonstrated academic excellence, Ms. Hart shared a few rubrics she had used in the past. By combining ideas, the group produced an assessment rubric to evaluate students' final presentations.

After completing Part I, student groups selected one of the following Part II assessment options developed by the teacher–family group: (1) As a group, write and perform a poem, story, song, and/or drama that responds to the statement, "If we did it then, we can do it now!"; (2) Collaborate to (a) produce a mural or group of pictures that depict the accomplishments of 19th century Black towns and what a community that learned from those accomplishments might look like today, and (b) prepare a few questions that can guide a discussion of audience responses to the mural; and (3) Work with parents to (a) develop and conduct a survey of community residents to identify what they see as the most pressing needs in their community, and (b) determine how *Nguzo Saba* Principles identified in 19th century Black towns (through an earlier assignment) can be used today to respond to those needs. As students engaged in creating and completing their projects—building on the knowledge they and their families produced in Part I—Ms. Hart advised, guided, and challenged them to think critically and to consider how the actions they were imagining and visualizing represent right action and positive community building. When the projects were completed, all parents and family members were invited to student performances and were asked to use the rubric developed by the teacher–family group to assess each group performance.

Notice that in the above suggested projects Ms. Hart directed students to consider African Diasporan cultural principles and ideals, cultural practices, and accomplishments as ways to strengthen their cultural communities and the communities in which they live. She has learned that everyone's location or standing place in the world is shaped by the cultural communities in which they were raised. Using Culturally Authentic Assessment pedagogy acknowledges this by positioning culture as the anchor and connector between content and pedagogy and between students and the assessment of their learning. As a cultural practice, this emancipatory pedagogy is a creative teaching and learning context that opens spaces for new ideas that come from the individual and cultural identities of students, teachers, and families. Ideas are drawn from within rather than from the "without" of relying solely on content provided by teachers and texts. When teachers engage with students and families pedagogically in these ways, assessment is also a context in which learning takes place. Instead of assessment being a gatekeeping process, Culturally Authentic Assessment is simultaneously a pedagogical process of assessment *for* learning and community building.

Ms. Hart had invited a friend of hers, Ms. McCormick, and Ms. Singleton to attend the student performances. At the end of the evening, after students and families said their goodbyes and left for home, the three women remained to talk for a while. Ms. McCormick said how impressed she was with students' enthusiastic and knowledgeable performances and parents' high level of participation. She said, "You know … there was such a sense of togetherness in here, like everyone belonged to something special and important. I even felt like I belonged. How did you make all this happen?" "Well, it's all about building real relationships with children and their families," Ms. Hart said, looking at Ms. Singleton and smiling. "I learned from Ms. Singleton to trust that what students and families know is an absolutely essential part of doing my job … so I do a lot of listening and learning." "Yes," said Ms. Singleton, "your desire to learn has been as strong as your desire to be a good teacher, which is why you are getting such good responses from students and parents." As they prepared to leave the classroom, Ms. Singleton asked Ms. Hart if she might be interested in joining the collegial group of veteran teachers at the school. "I know we'll be getting some new fifth-grade teachers next year, and if they show interest, I was hoping that you might be willing to provide some guidance."

An African Cultural Platform for Culturally Authentic Assessment

As an emancipatory pedagogy, Culturally Authentic Assessment mirrors concepts in African worldview, cosmology, philosophy, language, and the arts. For students of African ancestry, this cultural platform of concepts represents continuity with their ancestral heritage; and for students of other cultural backgrounds, these concepts are an opportunity to gain cultural knowledge. For example, several philosophical concepts of the Akan (West Africa), such as the relationship between inquiry and excellence and between knowledge and ethics, are expressed in Adinkra symbols. As an indigenous Akan script, Adinkra symbols are epistemic expressions or visual markers of Akan cosmology, values, and cultural concepts and practices (Arthur, 2001). Used during what the Akan call the "final rites of passage from the world of the living to that of the 'dead'"—Adinkra symbols were stamped on fabric that was made into clothing and worn during funereal services and ceremonies (Willis, 1998, p. 25). In Akan cosmology, death is understood as a transitional passage or stage in life, and specific symbols are used as messages to the person who has passed. Adinkra symbols are still used in this way and are also printed on fabrics for more general attire and on clothing worn during festivals and celebrations such as marriages and naming ceremonies. Today, these symbols are also used in architecture; on pottery, metalwork, woodwork, and sculpture; and as logos for businesses.

Each symbol has specific meaning. Three Adinkra symbols, *Hwehwemudua* (Scheweb-scheweb-meu-doo-ah), *Matemasie* (Mah-tee mah-see-uh), and *Nsaa* (N-sah) are Akan symbols for standards of critical thinking, creativity, and excellence.

#1 (*Hwehwemudua*)

#2 (*Matemasie*)

According to Mutombo Nkulu-N'Sengha (2005), *Hwehwemudua*:

> literally means "search rod" or "measuring rod" and is the symbol for critical examination and excellence. It defines the African concept of critical thinking. *Matemasie* is the symbol of wisdom and insight. It adds an ethical dimension to the epistemology by establishing the connection of knowledge and goodness, harmony, and balance. Thus the purpose of knowledge is to ensure a good life for oneself and the community.
>
> (pp. 41–42)

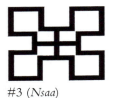

#3 (*Nsaa*)

Nsaa is a symbol of excellence, genuineness, and authenticity. It refers to a type of hand-woven fabric/blanket that is authentic and of excellent quality (Willis, 1998). "*Nsaa* has come to represent excellence, a person or a thing of a very high standard."

(p. 151)

Hwehwemudua, *Matemasie*, and *Nsaa* represent Akan communal standards for creating knowledge and gaining insight that require careful thought. With its ethical dimension, Akan epistemology claims that having knowledge is not for knowledge's sake, but for bringing goodness, harmony, and balance into the world (Gyeke, 1987; Nkulu-N'Sengha, 2005).

Culturally Authentic Assessment pedagogy parallels these Akan concepts by bringing critical thinking, authenticity, and high standards into teacher–student–family relationships so that together they can create knowledge that brings benefit to the members of the classroom and community. This pedagogy is distinct from standardized testing and transmission pedagogy that are based on the retrieval of "right" answers. Instead, teachers guide instruction through their more developed knowledge base, with the assumption that everyone in the classroom has knowledge worth knowing, and that putting this knowledge together produces authentic demonstrations of high quality that bring something worthwhile to the community. By including the ideas, standards, expectations of families, and their understanding of community needs in creating curriculum and assessing what students produce, Culturally Authentic Assessment Pedagogy permeates the boundaries between classrooms and communities.

As an African-informed pedagogy, Culturally Authentic Assessment also encourages students to perform their learning—to connect the rhythms (life forces) that exist in movement, music, dance, drumming, words, and imagery (Akbar, 1984; Boykin, 1983; Jones, 1979; Welsh Asante, 1985). During performance—which "is considered as normal as speaking"—aesthetic and literary expressions are combined and intertwined with the histories and spiritual, social, and political practices and events in each African community (Stone, 2000, p. 7). Susan Goodwin (Goodwin & Swartz, 2008), refers to performance as an instructional approach that "connects teachers with learners in what becomes a three-way communication with the community audience…. Performance allows students to experience themselves as learners and teachers when they share and open themselves to community critique and affirmation" (p. 13). In the context of Culturally Authentic Assessment pedagogy, student demonstrations and performances are opportunities for interpersonal and reciprocal interactions that involve movement, flow, and improvisation between individuals and the group and between the material and spiritual worlds, which in African worldview are viewed as inseparable (Anyanwu, 1981b; Senghor, 1964). These performance interactions are common experiences among African cultures at home and in the Diaspora. As explained by Kariamu Welsh Asante (1985):

In the African sense, the work [song, dance, spoken word, drumming] itself must have life and be worthy of the praises and approbations of an audience. The African aesthetic in the oral element provokes collectiveness in terms of spirit and individuality in terms of artistry. Pride and self-satisfaction come from the harmony achieved with the ancestors, nature, family and village.

(p. 79)

Following this understanding, the pedagogy of Culturally Authentic Assessment is emancipatory in that it encourages the performance of knowledge—a way to give knowledge life through interaction with an audience. In an essay on African artistic and aesthetic experience, K. C. Anyanwu (1981b) describes the enduring epistemic features of the African cultural platform that supports the pedagogy of Culturally Authentic Assessment:

Life in an oral culture demands a high sense of imagination, intuition, memory, sense of hearing, observation and the ability to use language effectively. Here lies the significance of storytelling as a form of art. Language is used to create or recreate events so vividly that it produces the desired effects among the audience-participants. One must listen attentively to grasp the flow or rhythm of events and the individual must flow with them.

(p. 281)

For students whose ancestral cultures are oral and communal, performance that uses imagination and language effectively resides in their group memory (heritage knowledge). For other students, the community-enhancing possibilities of performance can be learned through access to this cultural knowledge. In either case, the emancipatory pedagogy of Culturally Authentic Assessment gives all students an opportunity to experience community through the integration of critical thought, words, imagination, and movement.

Culturally Informed Principle #6: A Collective Humanity

The actions of residents in the Black towns of the Midwest indicate their self-determination and understanding of freedom and justice as human entitlements—as inherent rights of all people in any time and place—rather than legal rights that depend upon who is in power in a particular time and place (Franklin, 1992; Harding, 1990). Their actions in this historical period certainly have precedents in the Black freedom struggle as far back as the earliest presence of African peoples in the Americas and in the resistance to Arab and European conquest and enslavement on the African Continent (Asante, 2007b; Hall, 1992; Hart, 1985/2002; Hilliard, 1995; Piersen, 1993). As a grassroots mass movement, emigrants from the

South circumvented a hierarchy of human worth to support each other and the vision of freedom and justice for everyone. In the early stages of building Black towns in the Midwest, Black and White farmers worked together and Black town leaders established a working relationship with White county and state officials. However, this cooperation turned to hostility once Black towns—as well as Black communities in Midwest towns and cities, such as Greenwood in Tulsa, Oklahoma—became successful (Brophy, 2002). When Black leaders sought political influence outside of their towns, White legislatures changed boundaries so that voters in Black towns would have less influence in county and state elections; and after that, legislatures denied Black people the vote in state elections, and finally passed Jim Crow laws to separate Black and White people on trains, in schools, and other public and privately owned places (Crockett, 1979; Katz, 1996; Painter, 1976/1986; Taylor, 1998). White banks denied credit to Black farmers (O'Dell, 2011); and acts of mob violence against Black people increasingly occurred outside the refuge of Black towns (Crockett, 1979; Loewen, 2005). The violence and hostilities of White people demonstrated their commitment to a hierarchy of human worth—the opposite of viewing all groups of people as equally belonging to the human collective.

Communal Responsibility—an Emancipatory Pedagogy

Communal Responsibility is the pedagogical application of the principle of a Collective Humanity. Ms. Hart uses this pedagogy to ensure an environment of reciprocity and shared responsibility—a coming together that corresponds to the principle of a Collective Humanity in the "re-membered" content she uses. This is how she describes it:

> It makes sense to me now that my pedagogy needs to match the content I'm using. So, if the content is inclusive and representational—with no hierarchy of human worth—then my pedagogy needs to communicate to students that everyone in our classroom is valued for what they contribute. This pedagogy is called Communal Responsibility. As the pedagogical part of Teaching *for* Freedom, Ms. Singleton and I have been working on six emancipatory pedagogies and Communal Responsibility is the sixth one. I use it to encourage students to see our class as a whole, not only as a group of individuals. So, we do a lot of partnering and group work and we make decisions by consensus, which means that students have many opportunities to consider each other, negotiate, and come to agreements through collaboration. This is such a different approach than what I thought I would be doing when I entered teaching. I don't foster competition; I try to create learning as a mutually beneficial and communal experience—one in which everyone considers the good of the group. As I've come to see it, that's how each individual benefits the most.

Notice that the community-oriented features of Communal Responsibility are also part of the other five emancipatory pedagogies. Eldering positions students in right relationship to their teacher, who understands knowledge as a collective and communal experience in which everyone has something to contribute; Locating Students at the center of teaching and learning acknowledges their cultural communities and normative cultural characteristics as reasonable and right contexts for learning; Multiple Ways of Knowing acknowledges cultural communities as the source of epistemic diversity; Question-Driven Pedagogy is a relational experience that builds on and scaffolds what students know to increase learning for the group; and Culturally Authentic Assessment pedagogy stimulates critical inquiry in the completion and evaluation of projects and performances designed to bring benefit to both the classroom and the community. Communal Responsibility brings together the community-oriented features of these five emancipatory pedagogies to guide students through collaborative experiences that teach unity and communal caring. As an embodiment of emancipatory vision and practice, Harriet Tubman is a forerunner of Teaching *for* Freedom. She knew that for anyone to be free, everyone had to be free—that freedom is a mutual experience of working together for the good of the community. Likewise, the praxis of Teaching *for* Freedom combines and uses emancipatory pedagogies in overlapping ways to bring about unity among teachers, students, and families as a shared responsibility for communal well-being and belonging.

An African Cultural Platform for Communal Responsibility

African worldview, philosophies, proverbs, cosmologies, and language concepts acknowledge community to be what Nigerian philosopher Polycarp Ikuenobe (2006) calls a "normative conceptual scheme" in African cultures (p. 53). He echoes a common theme among numerous African philosophers, such as K. C. Anyanwu (1981b), Kwame Gyekye (1987, 1998), Ademola Kazeem Fayemi (2009), Kimbwandende Kia Bunseki Fu-Kiau (2001), and Yusef Waghid (2014) when he states that "the community is at the center of every activity, practice, belief, and value" (p. 53). As an emancipatory pedagogy, Communal Responsibility—which teaches mutual consideration, working together for the good of the community, and being responsible for each other—is a cultural practice grounded in this view of community.

Language is one way to identify elements of the cultural platform that supports this pedagogy. Hassimi Oumarou Maïga (2010) explains how the lexicon of any language—what words exist *and* do not exist in a language—reveals the meaning of concepts, values, and the presence or absence of specific sociocultural practices. In *Songhoy-Senni* language (of Mali, West Africa), there are no words for "retirement," since elders do not retire, but are seen as essential to the well-being and functioning of their families and communities. Thus, for example, elders are counselors and guides in charge of rites of passage ceremonies for the young.

Likewise, there is no word in *Songhoy-Senni* for "orphanages," since there are none; the family is the institution that cares for children. The absence of these words from the *Songhoy-Senni* language—and therefore from Songhoy concepts and institutions—is a way to know about the African communal values and practices related to elders and children in traditional Songhoy and other African societies (Boakye-Boaten, 2010; Ikuenobe, 2006).

African proverbs and their wide-ranging functions in daily living also sit on the cultural platform that supports Communal Responsibility. As explained by Congolese scholar Kimbwandende Kia Bunseki Fu-Kiau (2001), African proverbs are a philosophical language; they communicate large and important ideas within a community:

> Proverbs, in African context, are laws, reflections, theories, customs, social norms and values, principles, and unwritten constitutions. They are used to justify what should be said or what has been said. Proverbs play a very important ethical role in storytelling, legends, etc. Very often parents as well as griots [*n'samuni*], and storytellers end their tales by very fitting proverbs.
>
> (p. 94)

Between 1964 and 1973, Fu-Kiau directed the collection of over 1500 proverbs that draw upon oral literature to reflect the cosmology of the Bântu-Kôngo (Central Africa). Many of these proverbs define and describe community (*kânda*), and in so doing are a cultural foundation for the pedagogy of Communal Responsibility. For example:

> *Mu kânda, babo longa ye longwa.*
> Within the community everybody has the right to teach and to be taught. Education is a matter of reciprocity. True knowledge is acquired through sharing.
>
> (pp. 99–100)

> *Kânda diansânsa, kânda isânsa.*
> The community took care of me; I will take care of that community. Community life is a process of receiving and transmitting/passing on. [tâmbula ye tambikisa] Teach a child completely and thoroughly about what you are as a community and your teaching will go on completely and thoroughly. Life and living is a seedling process.
>
> (p. 104)

> *Dièla dia kânda m'bikudi.*
> The wisdom of the community prophesizes. The community sees farther than an individual can. Anyone who learns to see through the community's eyes (wisdom) is a very bright person.
>
> (p. 106)

These longstanding proverbs of the Bântu-Kôngo foreshadow the unity, complementary and caring relationships, and right action that Communal Responsibility seeks to produce pedagogically. By teaching that true knowledge comes from group belonging and reciprocity; that being cared for by the community is received and passed on in the actions of community members; and that excellence and insight are accomplished by communal efforts, these Bântu-Kôngo proverbs provide guidance for the pedagogy of Communal Responsibility. With this cultural positioning of the community at the center of every activity and decision, the pedagogy of Communal Responsibility is well connected to "re-membered" content—written with the principle of a Collective Humanity—that reflects unity and the oneness of all humanity.

Concluding Thoughts

In this chapter, we have demonstrated how the praxis of Teaching *for* Freedom uses Afrocentric concepts and culturally informed principles to connect six emancipatory pedagogies with "re-membered" (democratized) content in the social studies. We have also shown how emancipatory pedagogies are supported by cultural platforms that carry African worldview, cosmologies, philosophies, and related cultural concepts and practices drawn from oral and written African literature. These cultural platforms, which demonstrate the reality of the cultural unity of African peoples (Diop, 1959/1990), are absent in standard school knowledge, not only for African Diasporan groups, but for other historically marginalized groups as well. In fact, cultural platforms are absent for all groups when the knowledge they convey is distorted by inaccurate scholarship and the obstruction of critical thinking. Knowing about the cultural platforms that support emancipatory pedagogies imbues these instructional practices with epistemic authority—with centuries of African knowledge, expertise, and wisdom about freedom—about how to bring goodness, harmony, and balance into the world; how to produce intellectual and cultural excellence; how to keep the past and the present connected; and how to facilitate community well-being and belonging.

We have shown how emancipatory pedagogies and "re-membered" content are outcomes of cultural practices, which means that both heritage knowledge and cultural knowledge figure prominently in their use. Members of all cultural groups have heritage knowledge, which is a repository of group memory related to their ancestry and other "re-membered" or recuperated knowledge about their heritage; and members of all cultural groups can gain cultural knowledge, which is knowledge of the histories and cultural legacies of other groups. When teachers and students draw upon their cultural memory or heritable legacy, and learn knowledge about their own People, they are connected to what they are learning. Instruction becomes an experience of belonging that acknowledges their cultural and individual identities. Likewise, when teachers and students gain and use cultural knowledge, they become part of preserving the cultural capital and continuity that school knowledge has historically ignored or obstructed, which is also an experience of belonging—in this case to a learning community engaged in ethically informed practices. As we saw demonstrated in this chapter, when students are encouraged to use heritage knowledge and cultural knowledge to collaboratively explore a topic—and when families are a substantive part of this process—students *and* their families truly know that the classroom is a place where they belong. In this way, Teaching *for* Freedom is an emancipatory praxis with an educational emphasis on community well-being and shared responsibility. Structuring learning opportunities through "remembered" content and emancipatory pedagogies demonstrates how accessing the knowledge carried on diverse cultural platforms is essential in efforts to produce academic and cultural excellence.

References

Akbar, N. (1984). Africentric social sciences for human liberation. *Journal of Black Studies, 14*(4), 395–414.

Allen, B. A., & Boykin, W. A. (1991). The influence of contextual factors on Afro-American and Euro-American children's performance: Effects of movement opportunity and music. *International Journal of Psychology, 26*(3), 373–387.

Allen, B. A., & Boykin, W. A. (1992). African-American children and the educational process: Alleviating cultural discontinuity through prescriptive pedagogy. *School Psychology Review, 21*(4), 586–596.

Allen, B. A., & Butler, L. (1996). The effects of music and movement opportunity on the analogical reasoning performance of African American and White school children: A preliminary study. *Journal of Black Psychology, 22*(3), 316–328.

Anyanwu, K. C. (1981a). The African world-view and theory knowledge. In E. A. Ruch & K. C. Anyanwu (Authors), *African philosophy: An introduction to the main philosophical trends in contemporary Africa* (pp. 77–99). Rome: Catholic Book Agency.

Anyanwu, K. C. (1981b). Artistic and aesthetic experience. In E. A. Ruch & K. C. Anyanwu (Authors), *African philosophy: An introduction to the main philosophical trends in contemporary Africa* (pp. 270–282). Rome: Catholic Book Agency.

Arthur, G. F. K. (2001). *Cloth as metaphor: (Re)reading the Adinkra cloth symbols of the Akan of Ghana*. Accra, Ghana: Cefiks Publications.

Asante, M. K. (1980/1988). *Afrocentricity*. Trenton, NJ: Africa World Press.

Asante, M. K. (1987/1998). *The Afrocentric idea*. Philadelphia, PA: Temple University Press.

Asante, M. K. (1991/1992). Afrocentric curriculum. *Educational Leadership, 49*(4), 28–31.

Asante, M. K. (2003). The Afrocentric idea. In A. Mazama (Ed.), *The Afrocentric paradigm* (pp. 37–53). Trenton, NJ: Africa World Press.

Asante, M. K. (2007a). *An Afrocentric manifesto*. Malden, MA: Polity Press.

Asante, M. K. (2007b). *The history of Africa: The quest for eternal harmony*. New York, NY: Routledge.

Bennett, L. Jr. (1982). *Before the Mayflower: A history of Black America*. Chicago, IL: Johnson Publishing Company.

Boakye-Boaten, A. (2010). Changes in the concept of childhood: Implications on children in Ghana. *The Journal of International Social Research, 3*(10), 104–115.

Boykin, A. W. (1983). The academic performance of Afro-American children. In J. Spence (Ed.), *Achievement and achievement motives* (pp. 321–371). San Francisco, CA: W. Freeman.

Boykin, A. W. (1986). The triple quandary and the schooling of Afro-American children. In U. Neisser (Ed.), *The school achievement of minority children* (pp. 57–92). Hillsdale, NJ: Lawrence Erlbaum.

Boykin, A. W. (1994). Afrocultural expression and its implications for schooling. In E. R. Hollins, J. E. King, & W. C. Hayman (Eds.), *Teaching diverse populations: Formulating a knowledge base* (pp. 243–273). Albany, NY: State University of New York Press.

Boykin, A. W. (2001). The challenge of cultural socialization in the schooling of African American elementary school children: Exposing the hidden curriculum. In W. H. Watkins, J. H. Lewis, & V. Chou (Eds.), *Race and education: The role of history and society in educating African American students* (pp. 190–199). Needham Heights, MA: Allyn and Bacon.

Boykin, A. W., & Bailey, C. T. (2000). *The role of cultural factors in school relevant cognitive functioning: Description of home environmental factors, cultural orientation, and learning preferences*, Report No. 43. Washington, DC: Center for Research on the Education of Students Placed at Risk (CRESPAR), supported by the Office of Educational Research and Improvement (OERI), U.S. Department of Education.

Boykin, A. W., & Cunningham, R. T. (2001). The effects of movement expressiveness in story content and learning context on the analogical reasoning performance of African American children. *The Journal of Negro Education, 70*(1/2), 72–83.

Boykin, A. W., Lilja, A. J., & Tyler, K. M. (2004). The influence of communal versus individual learning context on the academic performance in social studies of grade 4–5 African Americans. *Learning Environments Journal, 7*, 227–244.

Boykin, A. W., Albury, A., Tyler, K. M., Hurley, E. A., Bailey, C. T., & Miller, O. A. (2005). Culture-based perceptions of academic achievement among low-income elementary students. *Cultural Diversity and Ethnic Minority Psychology, 11*(4), 339–350.

Brophy, A. L. (2002). *Reconstructing the dreamland: The Tulsa riot of 1921: Race, reparations, and reconciliation*. New York, NY: Oxford University Press.

Campbell, L. (2014). Austin Steward: Home-style teaching, planning, and assessment. In J. E. King & E. E. Swartz (Authors), *"Re-membering" history in student and teacher learning: An Afrocentric culturally informed praxis* (pp. 105–120). New York, NY: Routledge.

Clarke, J. H. (1977). The University of Sankore at Timbuctoo: A neglected achievement in Black intellectual history. *Journal of Western Black Studies, 1*(2), 142–147.

Clarke, J. H. (1994). *Christopher Columbus and the Afrikan holocaust: Slavery and the rise of European capitalism*. Brooklyn, NY: A & B Publishers Group.

Crockett, N. L. (1979). *The Black towns*. Lawrence, KA: The Regents Press of Kansas.

Dill, E. M., & Boykin, W. A. (2000). The comparative influence of individual peer tutoring and communal learning contexts on the text recall of African American children. *Journal of Black Psychology, 26*(1), 65–78.

Diop, C. A. (1959/1990). *The cultural unity of Black Africa*. Chicago, IL: Third World Press.

Dixon, V. J. (1971). African-oriented and Euro-American-oriented world views: Research methodologies and economics. *The Review of Black Political Economy, 7*(2), 119–156.

Du Bois, W. E. B. (1947). *The world and Africa: An inquiry into the part which Africa has played in world history*. New York, NY: Viking Press.

Du Bois, W. E. B., & Padmore, G. (Eds.) (1962). *History of the Pan-African Congress.* London: Hammersmith Bookshop.

Fayemi, A. K. (2009). Human personality and the Yoruba worldview: An ethico-sociological interpretation. *The Journal of Pan African Studies, 2*(9), 166–176.

Franklin, V. P. (1992). *Black self-determination: A cultural history of African American resistance.* Chicago, IL: Lawrence Hill Books.

Fu-Kiau, K. K. B. (2001). *African cosmology of the Bântu-Kôngo, tying the spiritual knot: Principles of life and living.* New York, NY: Athelia Henrietta Press.

Gatto, J. T. (2001). *A different kind of teacher: Solving the crisis of American schooling.* Berkeley, CA: Berkeley Hills Books.

Goodwin, S. (1996). Teaching students of color. *Raising Standards: Journal of the Rochester Teachers Association, 4*(1), 23–35.

Goodwin, S. (2004). Emancipatory pedagogy. In S. Goodwin & E. E. Swartz (Eds.), *Teaching children of color: Seven constructs of effective teaching in urban schools* (pp. 37–48). Rochester, NY: RTA Press.

Goodwin, S., & King, J. E. (2006). *Criterion standards for contextualized teaching and learning about people of African descent.* Rochester, NY: RTA Press.

Goodwin, S., & Swartz, E. E. (2008). *Culturally responsive practice: Lesson planning and construction.* Rochester, NY: RTA Press.

Gordon, B. M. (1994). African American cultural knowledge and liberatory education: Dilemmas, problems, and potentials in a post-modern American society. In M. J. Shujaa (Ed.), *Too much schooling, too little education: A paradox of Black life in white societies* (pp. 57–78). Trenton, NJ: Africa World Press.

Gyekye, K. (1987). *An essay on African philosophical thought: The Akan conceptual scheme.* Cambridge, MA: Cambridge University Press.

Gyekye, K. (1997). *Tradition and modernity: Philosophical reflections on the African experience.* New York, NY: Oxford University Press.

Gyekye, K. (1998). Person and community in African thought. In P. H. Coetzee & A. P. J. Roux (Eds.), *The African philosophy reader* (pp. 317–336). New York, NY: Routledge.

Hall, G. M. (1992). *Africans in colonial Louisiana: The development of Afro-Creole culture in the eighteenth century.* Baton Rouge, LA: Louisiana State University Press.

Hamilton, K. M. (1991). *Black towns and profit: Promotion and development in the Trans-Appalachian West, 1877–1915.* Chicago, IL: University of Illinois Press.

Harding, V. (1981). *There is a river: The Black struggle for freedom in America.* New York, NY: Harcourt Brace Jovanovich.

Harding, V. (1990). *Hope and history.* New York, NY: Orbis Books.

Hart, R. (1985/2002). *Slaves who abolished slavery: Blacks in rebellion.* Kingston, Jamaica: University of the West Indies Press.

Hilliard, A. G. III (1986). Pedagogy in ancient Kemet. In M. Karenga & J. H. Carruthers (Eds.), *Kemet and the African worldview: Research, rescue, and restoration* (pp. 130–148). Los Angeles, CA: University of Sankore Press.

Hilliard, A. G., III (1995). *The Maroon within us: Selected essays on African American community socialization.* Baltimore, MD: Black Classic Press.

Ikuenobe, P. (2006). *Philosophical perspectives on communalism and morality in African traditions.* Lanham, MD: Lexington Books.

Jones, J. M. (1979). Conceptual and strategic issues in the relationship of Black psychology to American social science. In A. W. Boykin, A. J. Franklin, & J. F. Yates (Eds.), *Research directions of Black psychologists* (pp. 390–432). New York, NY: Russell Sage Foundation.

Karenga, M. (1980). *Kawaida theory.* Los Angeles, CA: Kawaida Publications.

Karenga, M. (1996). The Nguzo Saba (the Seven Principles). In M. K. Asante & A. S. Abarry (Eds.), *African intellectual heritage: A book of sources* (pp. 543–554). Philadelphia, PA: Temple University.

Karenga, M. (1999). *Odù Ifá: The ethical teachings.* Los Angeles, CA: University of Sankore Press.

Karenga, M. (2006a). Philosophy in the African tradition of resistance: Issues of human freedom and human flourishing. In L. R. Gordon & J. A. Gordon (Eds.), *Not only the master's tools: African American studies in theory and practice* (pp. 243–271). Boulder, CO: Paradigm Publishers.

Karenga, M. (2006b). *Maat, the moral ideal of ancient Egypt: A study in classical African ethics.* New York, NY: Routledge.

Katz, W. L. (1996). *The Black west: A documentary and pictorial history of the African American role in the westward expansion of the United States.* New York, NY: Touchstone/Simon & Schuster.

King, J. E. (1991). Dysconscious racism: Ideology, identity, and the miseducation of teachers. *Journal of Negro Education, 60*(2), 133–146.

King, J. E. (1994). The purpose of schooling for African American children: Including cultural knowledge. In E. R. Hollins, J. E. King, & W. C. Hayman (Eds.), *Teaching diverse populations: Formulating a knowledge base* (pp. 25–56). Albany, NY: State University of New York Press.

King, J. E. (2006). "If justice is our objective": Diaspora literacy, heritage knowledge and the praxis of critical studyin' for human freedom. *Yearbook of the National Society for the Study of Education, 105*(2), 337–360.

King, J. E., & Akua, C. (2012). Dysconscious Racism and Teacher Education. In J. A. Banks (Ed.), *Encyclopedia of diversity in education* (pp. 724–727). Thousand Oaks, CA: Sage Publications.

King, J. E., Goss, A. C., & McArthur, S. A. (2014). Recovering history and the "parent piece" for cultural well-being and belonging. In J. E. King and E. E. Swartz (Authors), *"Re-membering" history in student and teacher learning: An Afrocentric culturally informed praxis* (pp. 155–188). New York, NY: Routledge.

King, J. E., Swartz, E. E., with Campbell, L., Lemons-Smith, S., & López, E. (2014). *"Re-membering" history in student and teacher learning: An Afrocentric culturally informed praxis.* New York, NY: Routledge.

Kwame, S. (1995). *Readings in African philosophy: An Akan collection.* New York, NY: University Press of America.

Loewen, J. W. (2005). *Sundown towns: A hidden dimension of American racism.* New York, NY: New Press.

Maïga, H. O. (2010). *Balancing written history with oral tradition: The legacy of the Songhoy people.* New York, NY: Routledge.

Mazama, A. (2003). The Afrocentric paradigm, an introduction. In A. Mazama (Ed.), *The Afrocentric paradigm* (pp. 3–34). Trenton, NJ: Africa World Press.

Mbiti, J. S. (1990). *African religions and philosophy* (2nd ed.). Portsmouth, NH: Heinemann Educational Books.

McTighe, J., Seif, E., & Wiggins, G. (2004). You can teach for meaning. *Educational Leadership, 62*(1), 26–31.

Nkulu-N'Sengha, M. (2005). African epistemology. In M. K. Asante & A. Mazama (Eds.), *Encyclopedia of Black studies* (pp. 39–44). Thousand Oaks, CA: Sage Publications.

Nobles, W. W. (1972). African philosophy: Foundations for Black psychology. In R. L. Jones (Ed.), *Black Psychology* (pp. 18–32). New York, NY: Harper and Row.

Nobles, W. W. (1976). Extended self: Rethinking the so-called Negro self-concept. The *Journal of Black Psychology, 2*(2), 15–24.

Nobles, W. W. (1991). African philosophy: Foundations for Black psychology. In R. Jones (Ed.), *Black psychology* (3rd ed., pp. 47–63). Berkeley, CA: Cobb and Henry.

Nyang, S. S. (1980). Reflections on traditional African cosmology. *New Directions: The Howard University Magazine, 7*, 28–32.

Oakes, J., Rogers, J., & Lipton, M. (2006). *Learning power: Organizing for education and justice.* New York, NY: Teachers College Press.

O'Dell, L. (2011). *All-Black towns.* Retrieved from http://plainshumanities.unl.edu/encyclopedia/doc/egp.afam.006.

Painter, N. I. (1976/1986). *Exodusters: Black migration to Kansas after Reconstruction.* New York, NY: W. W. Norton & Company.

Piersen, W. D. (1993). *Black legacy: America's hidden heritage.* Amherst, MA: University of Massachusetts Press.

Senghor, L. S. (1964). *On African socialism* (Mercer Cook, Trans.). New York, NY: Frederick A. Praeger. (Original work published 1961.)

Shakes, G. (2004). Student experience. In S. Goodwin & E. E. Swartz (Eds.), *Teaching children of color: Seven constructs of effective teaching in urban schools* (pp. 97–105). Rochester, NY: RTA Press.

Shujaa, M. J. (1994). Education and schooling: You can have one without the other. In M. J. Shujaa (Ed.), *Too much schooling, too little education: A paradox of Black life in white societies* (pp. 13–36). Trenton, NJ: Africa World Press.

Sindima, H. (1995). *Africa's agenda: The legacy of liberalism and colonialism in the crisis of African values.* Westport, CT: Greenwood.

Smith, F. (2004). Classroom environment. In S. Goodwin & E. E. Swartz (Eds.), *Teaching children of color: Seven constructs of effective teaching in urban schools* (pp. 83–90). Rochester, NY: RTA Press.

Smitherman, G. (1977/1986). *Talkin and testifyin: The language of Black America.* Detroit, MI: Wayne State University Press.

Smitherman, G. (1994). *Black talk.* Boston, MA: Houghton Mifflin Company.

Spring, J. (2011). *The American school: A global context from the Puritans to the Obama era* (8th ed.). Boston, MA: McGraw-Hill.

Stiggins, R. J. (June 2002). Assessment crisis: The absence of assessment for learning. *Phi Delta Kappan, 83*, 758–765.

Stone, R. M. (2000). African music in a constellation of arts. In Ruth M. Stone (Ed.), *The Garland handbook of African Music* (2nd ed., pp. 7–12). New York, NY: Routledge.

Swartz, E. E. (2012). Distinguishing themes of cultural responsiveness: A study of document-based learning. *The Journal of Social Studies Research, 36*(2), 179–211.

Swartz, E. E. (2013). *Black community building: The African tradition of collective work and responsibility.* Rochester, NY: Omnicentric Press.

Taylor, Q. (1998). *In search of the racial frontier: African Americans in the American West, 1528–1990.* New York, NY: W. W. Norton & Company.

Tedla, E. (1995). *Sankofa: African thought and education.* New York, NY: Peter Lang.

Tedla, E. (1998). On the path to personhood: Teacher as elder, family, community builder. *Raising Standards: Journal of the Rochester Teachers Association, 6*(1), 31–38.

Tolson, A. L. (1974). *The Black Oklahomans: A history, 1541–1972.* New Orleans, LA: Edwards Printing Company.

Turner, L. D. (1949). *Africanisms in the Gullah dialect.* Chicago, IL: University of Chicago Press.

Waghid, Y. (2014). *African philosophy of education reconsidered: On being human.* New York, NY: Routledge.

Welsh Asante, K. (1985). The commonalities in African dance: An aesthetic foundation. In M. K. Asante & K. Welsh Asante (Eds.), *African culture: The rhythms of unity* (pp. 71–82). Westport, CT: Greenwood Press.

Willis, B. (1998). *Adinkra dictionary: A visual primer on the language of Adinkra.* Washington, DC: Pyramid Complex.

Woodson, C. G. (1922/1966). *The Negro in our history* (11th ed.). Washington, DC: The Associated Publishers.

Yosso, T. (2005). Whose culture has capital? A critical theory discussion of community cultural wealth. *Race, Ethnicity, and Education, 8*(1), 69–91.

3

HARRIET TUBMAN

"Re-membering" Cultural Continuities

That your Petitioners apprehend we have in common with all other men a natural right to our freedoms without Being depriv'd of them by our fellow men as we are a freeborn People and have never forfeited this Blessing by any compact or agreement whatever.

To his Excellency Thomas Gage Esq. Captain General and Governor in Chief in and over this Province [Massachusetts-Bay], May 25, 1774 in Aptheker, *A Documentary History of the Negro People in the United States: From Colonial Times Through the Civil War*, 1951/1969, p. 8

The praxis Teaching *for* Freedom offers us a way to access and build upon African heritage knowledge and cultural knowledge. The need for this praxis in student and teacher learning is evident in the omnipresence of eurocratic presentations of knowledge that omit and misrepresent the histories and cultural productions of perennially marginalized cultures and groups, and in so doing, disrupt the cultural continuities necessary for intergenerational community well-being. While we are reluctant to spend much time in this volume on what is damaging about eurocratic presentations of knowledge—preferring instead to provide examples of "re-membered" content—we ask Ms. Harriet Tubman's permission to discuss the ways in which she, and the grand narrative of slavery in which she is located, continues to be presented in standard social studies knowledge. While there are particularities and nuances in the too-numerous examples of omissions and distortions in standard school knowledge—many that we describe in our earlier volume (King & Swartz, 2014)—this one in-depth example should suffice here. We conclude this chapter by showing how the cultural continuities that Harriet Tubman's life and work represent can be "re-membered."

Ms. Tubman has been included in most school curricula and instructional materials for over four decades, yet the way in which she is represented still exemplifies the need to recuperate a more accurate account that keeps her connected to her African heritage. For this reason, she is an excellent example for the praxis of Teaching *for* Freedom. How can Tubman be taught so that she remains at the center of her story as an African woman who embodies the African understanding that for anyone to be free, everyone has to be free—that freedom is a shared responsibility and inherent right that she and others had never given up? In other words, how can Tubman's story be told in a way that maintains African Diasporan cultural continuity? Almost a century after Carter G. Woodson's (1919) assessment of the omissions and distortions of African and African American history in school curriculum, Tubman and other women and men of African ancestry continue to be deployed to represent the ubiquitous grand narratives that continue to shape school knowledge. As distorted explanations of national development, grand narratives—about macro-historical topics such as exploration, colonization, slavery, freedom and democracy, manifest destiny, and industrialization—are planted in the minds of children in their earliest school days and repeated throughout 12 or more years of schooling (Epstein, 2009; King & Swartz, 2014). These explanatory narratives are particularly pronounced in the social studies, but also shape knowledge related to literature, science, mathematics, media, and school celebrations of national holidays such as Thanksgiving and Columbus Day. Grand narratives include assumptions about the right of dominance, difference as deficit, cultural legitimacy, the origin of concepts and entire disciplines, progress and technology, and the inevitability of oppression that together play an epistemic role in maintaining eurocratic dominance and its hierarchy of human worth. To look at how young children are introduced to Harriet Tubman in school knowledge, we first need to examine the grand narrative of slavery into which she is inserted. This agreed-upon narrative conveys a set of ideas that are taught with varying degrees of detail at different grade levels.

The Grand Narrative of Slavery and its Assumptions

We are able to identify the contours of U.S. grand narratives in the social studies through a review of textbooks from the 19th century to the present (Bailey, 1956, 1971; Boyd et al., 2011a–e; Fiske, 1894; Gavian & Hamm, 1945; Klein, 1983; Hale, 1835; Morison & Commager, 1942; Bennett et al., 2013). While we acknowledge that textbooks are only one aspect of school curricula, corporate publishers have assured the predominance of these products in most classrooms through marketplace strategies that capitalize on current technologies. From no pictures to drawings to photographs; from black and white to color; from no graphics to colorful graphic layouts; and from hard copy to e-books to digital apps and other interactive materials, textbooks are redesigned to be attractive to teachers and students in each decade (Kessler, 2011; Pearson, 2013). Yet, with all their attempts at shifting shape, the grand narrative themes conveyed in these corporate materials remain consistent. The content that teaches these themes is called a master script, since it legitimizes the accounts of powerful groups (e.g., White, upper class, male, abled) as the knowledge worth knowing (Swartz, 1992, 2007a). The voices of others are either omitted or misrepresented as a way of *mastering* or bringing them under control so that they can be marginally included without challenging the hegemony of standard school knowledge (King & Swartz, 2014). This type of marginalizing inclusion occurs in master scripts when "others" are so significant to an account that it strains credibility to omit them. In cyclical fashion, these master scripts teach and perpetuate the grand narrative themes that have shaped them.

For example, the grand narrative of slavery explains—from an authoritative Euro-American stance—the origins, characteristics, development, and outcomes of this institution. As you read this grand narrative in Vignette 3.1, it may sound familiar, since it includes ideas and assumptions that have been consistently conveyed to most of us through state standards, master scripts, local curricula, textbooks, and other materials since we were very young children. Following Vignette 3.1, we will point out and discuss the numerous contradictions and inaccurate portrayals of historic events that exist within this grand narrative.

VIGNETTE 3.1

Grand Narrative of Slavery

Slavery refers to a lack of freedom and has existed all over the world for thousands of years. Arabs, Africans, and Europeans all participated in slavery in Africa. In the 1500s, African slaves were used to provide the large numbers of laborers needed to develop colonies in the Americas. When the United States became a country, it continued to use slave labor as a means of economic growth. Blacks were owned as property by someone else and forced to work hard, mostly on farms and plantations. While some slaves were treated badly, others were treated well. Over the years, slavery continued to grow, especially in Southern states. Northerners and Southerners debated about slavery and legal compromises were made about the political representation of slaves as well as where slavery could exist. Some slaves tried to rebel against slavery by running away, and they were helped by people called abolitionists who wanted to end slavery. Disagreements about slavery was one of the reasons for the Civil War, and before the end of that war, President Abraham Lincoln—who was opposed to slavery—wrote the Emancipation Proclamation.

By using Afrocentric theoretical concepts such as Centrality/Location, Self-Determination, and Subjects with Agency (see Chapter 1, Table 1.1 for descriptions of these concepts), we can identify numerous errors and distortions in the above grand narrative and the assumptions it fosters. Foremost, the very people who were enslaved are decentered; they are the objects of the narrative, not the subjects, even though they *are* the topic. And the self-determination and agency of free and enslaved people of African descent are nowhere to be found—hidden by the white supremacist assumption of the right to dominate. This assumption replicates the original objectifying nature of enslavement in current accounts that describe it.

Applying culturally informed principles, such as Representation, Indigenous Voice, and Accurate Scholarship (see Chapter 1, Table 1.2 for descriptions of these principles), to further examine the grand narrative of slavery uncovers additional omissions and distortions. For example, when the European slave trade began, there were no "Africans." Rather, the Indigenous Peoples of Africa (e.g., Akan, Songhoy, Wolof, Kôngo, etc.) as well as the Peoples of Europe (e.g., British, Dutch, Portuguese, Spanish, etc.), identified themselves not in pan-continental terms but with their respective Nation/nation states. (See King & Swartz, 2014, p. 53 for a detailed explanation of the use and capping of "Nations" and "Peoples.") Likewise, this grand narrative of slavery includes no representation or indigenous voice of the men, women, and children of various Nations who are referred to as "slaves," rather than as people who were kidnapped and *en*slaved. Labeling people "slaves" conceptually severs them from their families, communities, and heritage—as well as from the human family—while cloaking their enslavers and their worldview; and once in the Americas, the terms "blacks" and "slaves" are used interchangeably. Over time the various peoples of Europe, who waged interminable wars to dominate, control, and exploit the Americas, Africa, and other areas in the world, have come to be known collectively as "Europeans." We now use this commonplace conceptualization of "Europeans" and "Africans" even though it elides these important historical developments. Further, the claim that "Arabs, Africans, and Europeans all participated in slavery in Africa" not only collapses time, context, and meaning but it also assumes that the term "slavery" denotes common cultural practices across more than 1500 years. While Arabs began enslaving the European, Turkic, and East and North African people as early as the sixth century, our focus here is on what Kwasi Konadu (2010) describes as the "international enslavement enterprise" (p. 6)—commonly called the Atlantic slave trade, but more accurately called the European slave trade or *Maafa*. To the detriment of the Peoples and civilizations in Africa and the Americas, this "enterprise" resulted in a massive transfer of wealth from Africa to Europe, bringing system-wide economic benefit *only* to Europeans and their colonial descendants as seen in European and American scientific and industrial revolutions and global supremacy in commerce to this day (Davidson, 1972; Mills, 1997; Rodney,

1982; C. Williams, 1974; E. Williams, 1944/1966). Land theft and genocidal depredations suffered by the Indigenous peoples of the Americas also resulted in earlier untold wealth transfers from the Americas to Europe and the subsequent massive kidnapping, deportation, and enslavement of Africa's people (Sublette, 2008).

Reframing the Grand Narrative of Slavery and its Assumptions

The topic of "slavery" has unquestioningly generated extensive debate among generations of academics within varying schools of thought. Even with a range of ideological stances and shifting demographic and historical evidence, the topic of "slavery" remains tantamount in the popular imagination as an explanation of Black people's presumed deficits (King, 1991). Our interest here is not to engage in this academic debate, but to provide teachers with information that can expand either their heritage knowledge or their cultural knowledge and will to question and decipher agreed-upon historical narratives that function as ideology. We aim in this way to offer an antidote for the dysconsciousness that permeates our ranks as educators. Developed by Joyce E. King in 1991, the concept of dysconsciousness

> refers to an uncritical habit of mind (including perceptions, attitudes, assumptions, and beliefs) that justifies inequity and exploitation by accepting the existing order of things as a given. This cognitively limited mode of thinking shapes one's identity and distorts one's consciousness—that is, one's awareness and sense of agency. Dysconscious racism is an uncritical habit of mind that lacks any ethical judgment regarding or critique of systemic racial inequity. By unquestioningly accepting the status quo, this mind-set, which is identified as an outcome of miseducation, prevents teachers, for example, from questioning the existing racial order and leaves no room for them to imagine practical possibilities for social change or their role as change agents.
>
> (King & Akua, 2012, p. 724)

The unrelenting presence of grand narratives and master scripts to which we have all been exposed—through school knowledge, media, sociopolitical institutions, and corporate marketing—create an uncritical mind-set and obstruct teachers from questioning the existing order of knowledge. The absence of this critical capacity—long a concern of scholars in the Black intellectual tradition—is achieved by shutting out the perspective advantage of alterity, that is, the knowledge, experiences, and insights of those misrepresented or disregarded in dominant venues (King, 2004; Wynter, 1997, 2000, 2006). When knowledge from such marginalized or liminal locations is made

visible and centered, it critically challenges phenomena that remain unques-
tioned in the knowledge base of dominant groups (King, 2006). Thus, our
response to such dysconsciousness responds to the epistemic eurocratic authority that maintains it—an authority that continuously supports the dismissal and
denigration of "other" knowledge. The following reframing of the grand narrative of slavery includes content that teachers can use to critically assess their
own knowledge and their instructional materials and to supplement or select
other materials that more accurately represent this topic.

At the beginning of Portuguese exploration of the west coast of Africa in the
mid-15th century, varying forms of domestic servitude existed in Europe and
Africa (Rodney, 1966). Domestic servants could typically gain freedom and
eventually integrate into the society where they lived. While domestic servitude
was maintained in Africa, it was discarded in Europe, which turned to chattel
slavery of African people to propel their emerging merchant capitalist system—a
system that expanded exponentially with the 16th and 17th century development of colonial ventures in the Americas (Davidson, 1961). During these two
centuries, the records of the first European enslavers in Africa, the Portuguese,
make no reference to West African chattel slavery and include no mention of
enslaved people in that region's trade activities (Rodney, 1966). Along the
western coast of Africa, interest in trading with Europeans initially involved
local commodity exports (e.g., gold, ivory, copper, hides, cloth, indigo, salt) in
exchange for European goods (Dike, 1956; Miller, 1988; Rodney, 1966, 1982).
However, after more than two centuries of European disruption of African
social, economic, and political structures in search of people to enslave for
profit, including the British-financed defeat of the Songhoy Empire in 1591,
followed by European-induced wars among African Nations that were justified
by the Catholic Church as "Just Wars", a European-driven system of chattel
slavery took root.

It is important to note that African resistance to the voracious European slave
trading in the states of Matamba, Kôngo, Benin, and Dahomey—to name only
a few—is well documented (Rodney, 1982; Williams, 1974). Yet, with few
exceptions—Nzinga, Queen of Matamba being one—this resistance was overcome by the well-armed troops of European intruders who then required local
leaders to deliver quotas of enslaved people or themselves be enslaved (Davidson, 1961; Williams, 1974). Europe's steady provocation of internal conflicts
and purposeful devaluing of local currencies for economic control led to extensive social upheaval, dependency, and breakdown within African Nations.
These conditions made it possible for Europeans, who were competing among
themselves, to advance a system of race-based chattel slavery in the African societies they targeted, and over centuries, to disrupt their practices of justice and
shared responsibility for community welfare. However, as discussed in Chapter
2, the worldview, philosophies, and cultural concepts that were the foundation
for these traditional practices among the Yoruba, Akan, Songhoy, Kôngo, and

other African Nations were not lost; they constitute the cultural continuities that were retained and brought to the Americas by those who were enslaved (Konadu, 2010; Gomez, 1998; Gyekye, 1997; Maïga, 2010; Nkulu-N'Sengha, 2005; Piersen, 1993).

Europeans and Africans had very different conceptions of "slavery" (Davidson, 1961; King, 1992, 2006; Rodney, 1966). This is evident when considering the institution of chattel slavery that Europeans developed. The following example shows how knowledge of African language concepts can shed light on the meaning of these culturally distinct conceptions. In *Songhoy-senni*, the language of the Songhoy people of West Africa, the word *barnya* refers to "someone who doesn't even have a mother" (King, 2006, p. 352). Fleeing from danger, captured in war, or cast out of your community as punishment for wrongdoing (there was no word for "prisons" in pre-colonial Africa because there were none) meant that as *barnya* you no longer had the protection of your lineage or your mother's people. You would be taken in by another community, but your lineage disruption often positioned you in an indigenous system of domestic servitude that bore no resemblance to chattel slavery in the Americas, with its dehumanizing bondage in perpetuity (Davidson, 1961; King, 2006). As a domestic servant, you might become part of a system of trade, with your exchange signifying the wealth of your new "owner" who sought to buy your loyalty more than your labor (Davidson, 1961).

As exemplified in the Niger-Delta, domestic servitude was typically a socially mobile system in which freedom and elevation in social status was gained through hard work and ingenuity that brought benefit to the head of your household who valued and rewarded your achievements (Dike, 1956). However, the grand narrative of slavery and the K-12 master scripts that convey it collapse these different cultural conceptions and practices by referring to them with the same term—"slavery." Stating that slavery existed all over the world, without examining local language meanings, indigenous historical accounts, substantive differences in different eras, and the range of practices from domestic servitude to chattel slavery erroneously suggests that slavery is universal in definition and description and therefore an inevitable phenomenon (King, 2005; Maïga, 2010). When referring to the European slave trade, the encapsulating use of the term "slavery" in K-12 instructional materials serves to erase its particularities and obstruct the accountability of its perpetrators and beneficiaries; and it infers that both Africa and Euro-America are responsible for the holocaust experienced by the former that brought benefits and worldwide dominance to the latter.

The grand narrative of slavery also ignores scholarship that could result in greater accuracy and a more complete account, and as a result blocks the critical thinking and moral agency of teachers (King, 1991). For example, proclaiming the "need for large numbers of laborers" as the reason for slavery ignores scholarship about the knowledge and skills of specific African Nations that were sought and exploited by Europeans and their descendants through the system of slavery. African people came to the Americas with knowledge and skills in such fields as agriculture, architecture, astronomy, metallurgy, husbandry, fishing, gold mining, the military, business and trade, sculpture, culinary arts, weaving and textile production, and medicine (Holloway, 1990; Littlefield, 1981; Phillips, 1990; Wahlman, 2001). This can be seen in the growing of products unfamiliar to Europeans, such as rice, tobacco, and indigo; in the construction and adornment of Southern plantations by African craftsmen; and in primary source accounts that verify African influences on the nation's agricultural, industrial, and aesthetic development (Carney, 2001; Hall, 2005; Maïga, 2010; Piersen, 1993; Sublette, 2008; Walker, 2001). If students and teachers have no access to accounts of African intellectuality and accomplishments, it is likely that dominant cultural assumptions about difference as deficit will lead to the false conclusions that still predominate in the school textbooks and the popular imagination. These false conclusions—which obstruct any critical examination of the *Maafa*—include the belief that Africans provided only unskilled labor, that the existence of domestic servitude in Africa justified the institution of chattel slavery in the Americas, and that the low socioeconomic positioning of African people, then and now, is a "reasonable" outcome of these factors.

Likewise, failing to name White people as the enslavers and describing slavery as something that just "grew" assumes its inevitability and cloaks those responsible for the well-documented horrors of enslavement and post-emancipation systems of oppression—as if they operated without perpetrators and beneficiaries. In addition, as Europeans became "white" and the dehumanization of African people became normative, the grand narrative of slavery perpetuated a cultural model built on the ideology of white racial superiority (Fields & Fields, 2014; Painter, 2011; Wynter, 1984). Within this normative belief structure of race, racist scholarship has shaped the current grand narrative of slavery that "silently" positions African people as non-cultural beings in order to justify enslavement as normative (Mills, 1997; Wynter, 2000).

Once enslaved, the grand narrative of slavery provides no reference to how people retained African practices as well as how they created new cultural forms and continuities that have sustained them in the Americas (Bennett, 1975; King & Goodwin, 2006; Walker, 2001). The meager references to rebelling and "running away" in no way characterize the ongoing resistance and successful liberation efforts by individuals and groups who wrote and spoke about never having given up their natural right to be free (Aptheker, 1951/1969; Bennett, 1975; Hart, 1985/2002; Price, 1979; Thompson, 1987; Williams, 2010). Assumptions about agency—who has it and who does not—erase the substantive role of Africans who resisted slavery on the continent and during the middle passage and the resistance of enslaved Africans in the Caribbean. Also erased are the Black men and women in the abolition movement in the United States, inferring that, with few exceptions, abolitionists were White. And the truth about Lincoln's disinterest in ending slavery is omitted (Bennett, 2000; Quarles, 1969; Still, 2007). His Emancipation Proclamation was not a position against slavery, and in fact freed no one that Lincoln had the power to free. The Proclamation was both a war measure issued to further weaken the Confederacy (Welles, 1862/1960) and a gradual plan of emancipation that would keep as many African people enslaved as possible until they could be deported, which was Lincoln's favored plan that he was unable to effect (Bennett, 2000).

The culturally informed principle of a collective humanity—that we are all one humanity and that no human groups are more worthy than any others—is absent in the grand narrative of slavery as seen in references to enslaved people being treated well and slavery being something about which to debate and compromise. Whether we are beaten less often, wear better clothes, or eat better food than people on the next plantation does not change that we are all enslaved (S. Goodwin, *personal communication*, October 17, 2008). Neither being held against our will in perpetuity or being worked to death (Bland, 2001), or systematic sexual coercion to deliberately "breed" crops of humans to be sold as "slaves," qualifies as "good treatment" (Bridgewater, 2014; Smithers, 2013). And "Northerners" and "Southerners" (coded geographic designations that refer to White people in the grand narrative of slavery) debating and compromising over our existence—as if freedom is not a human entitlement—makes it clear that assumptions about difference as deficit obstruct the idea of equitable human worth in this grand narrative.

Grand Narratives, Master Scripts, and Time

The grand narrative of slavery in Vignette 3.1 has changed very little over time. It and other grand narratives endure because they are protected and perpetuated by master scripts that change somewhat to accommodate the sensibilities of each era. For example, textbooks used at the end of the 19th and first half of the 20th century contained justifications and support for the system of slavery that depended on the absence of African voices about the experiences of enslavement, the acceptance of White domination as given, racial slurs, slanderous stereotypes, false assumptions of docility, and justifications of dehumanization (Bailey, 1956; Fiske, 1894; Johnston, 1904; Gavian & Hamm, 1945; Harlow, 1947; Morison & Commager, 1942). The grand narrative of slavery in Vignette 3.1 fits as well with these much earlier textbooks as it does with current textbooks that have dropped the racial slurs and slanderous stereotypes, since old and new texts justify the system of slavery through omissions, distortions, and the absence or misuse of indigenous voice (Appleby, Brinkley, Broussard, McPherson, & Ritchie, 2014; Bennett et al., 2013; Boyd et al., 2011a; Viola et al., 2008; Zimmerman, 2004). A notable exception to this textbook rule is Carter G. Woodson's (1945) *The Story of the Negro Retold*, originally published in 1935. This high-school textbook not only locates people of African ancestry as the subjects of its accounts, it fully reveals their agency and self-determination in the pursuit of freedom. Reading this textbook, written 80 years ago, makes it quite clear that it was not lack of scholarship that resulted in consistently omitted and distorted content in the standard school texts of this era that persist in our day. In fact, current textbooks continue to present African enslavement in a matter-of-fact and objectifying manner—as just the way it was back then (Mbatha, 2012; Swartz, 2012a). The master scripts in these texts still cloak the perpetrators of slavery, omit the ideology of racial superiority, and silence any discussion of the inhumanity of chattel slavery.

A few current textbooks say that the conditions of slavery in the Americas were cruel or harsh, but they do not describe the institution as unethical or inhumane, which can actually be found in much older textbooks. For example, in Salma Hale's 1835 high-school textbook, he wrote that slavery was "a traffic abhorrent to humanity, disgraceful to civilization, and fixing the foulest stain upon the character of the age and people" (p. 22). Nothing close to this ethical assessment can be found in the master scripts of current textbooks, which instead use sound-bites from personal accounts and speeches of once-enslaved African people, such as Frederick Douglass. For example, a current high-school textbook by Appleby et al. (2014) includes a quote from a speech made by Frederick Douglass in Rochester, New York on July 5, 1852:

> What, to the American slave, is your 4th of July? I answer: a day that reveals to him, more than all other days in the year, the gross injustice and cruelty to which he is the constant victim. To him your celebration is a sham; your boasted liberty, an unholy license; your national greatness, swelling vanity; your sounds of rejoicing are empty and heartless; . . . a thin veil to cover up crimes which would disgrace a nation of savages.
>
> (p. 178)

Douglass, not the textbook, concludes that slavery is unjust, disgraceful, and criminal. While brief and infrequent quotes by people of African ancestry insert ethical moments into master scripts, these insertions are not supported by the content that surrounds them. These "moments" create an illusion that textbooks are now multicultural and inclusive, but the lack of text support for these brief insertions fails to challenge the prevailing grand narrative of slavery and the master scripts that teach it (King & Swartz, 2014). In fact, these moments of realness lend credibility to textbook accounts by suggesting that the exclusion of marginalized or omitted voices in the past has now been corrected. Thus, even when those voices challenge the practices of their era—as in the above quote of Frederick Douglass—their anomalistic presence in no way alters the master script. As for inclusions that are more than sound-bite quotes, as is the case with the corporate delivery of figures such as Harriet Tubman, the content in no way challenges or critiques the grand narrative or master scripts that convey it.

The Corporate Delivery of Harriet Tubman

While Harriet Tubman is included as an agent of the Underground Railroad in Carter G. Woodson's (1945) high-school textbook, *The Story of the Negro Retold*, she doesn't appear in most standard school curricula and instructional materials until the late 1960s (e.g., Bailey, 1971; Fenton, 1970; Klein, 1983; Morison, Commager, & Leuchtenburg, 1969; Wineburg & Monte-Sano, 2008). Her inclusions range from one in-text sentence to a picture and caption to a paragraph to a vignette. Yet, in whatever form, the content is consistent across corporate publishers in that it fits within the grand narrative of slavery. It is noteworthy that one of the earlier textbooks to include Harriet Tubman, *The Americans: A history of the United States* (Fenton, 1970), used a story form that provided much more information about her than later and current texts. While parts of this account take some liberties with scholarship on Tubman, and the account still fits within the grand narrative of slavery (e.g., enslavement is not contested and its perpetrators are not named), it provides indigenous voice and representation that connect Tubman to her family, community, and ancestral heritage. This is another example that suggests caution about assuming that content related to historically omitted and marginalized groups increases or improves in a linear fashion from earlier decades to the present.

Our review of elementary, middle, and high-school social studies textbook accounts of Harriet Tubman over the past decade shows that inclusions varied in length, but the content was remarkably similar across publishers (Appleby et al., 2014; Banks et al., 2005a–d; Bennett et al., 2013; Berson, Howard, & Salinas, 2012a & b; Boyd et al., 2011a–d; Cayton, Israels Perry, Reed, & Winkler, 2007; Garcia, Ogle, Risinger, & Stevos, 2005). Thus, it is possible to claim that examining any one of these textbooks is representative of the current corporate delivery of knowledge about Harriet Tubman. So, let's look at a recent elementary social studies series by Scott Foresman in which Tubman is included in vignettes, text, pictures, and sound-bite quotes in their first-, second-, third-, and fifth-grade textbooks (Boyd et al., 2011a–d). As a heuristic for critiquing corporate versions of knowledge about Tubman, and as a prelude to "re-membering" knowledge about her, we selected for review one of Scott Foresman's lengthier accounts—a two-page vignette in their first-grade textbook *All Together* (Boyd et al., 2011b).

At the top of this two-page vignette is a red, white, and blue banner of stars and stripes with the title "Citizen Heroes" (Boyd et al., 2011b, pp. 68–69). Citizen Heroes is a feature of this elementary textbook series that highlights individuals at different grade levels who each represent one of the characteristics of good citizenship, which are defined in the series as caring, respect, responsibility, fairness, honesty, and courage. Need it be said that Harriet Tubman—considered a fugitive slave by the laws of the United States—was not a citizen of this country in the 1840s and 1850s. Using language and flag imagery to signify otherwise disingenuously appropriates Tubman into the dominant national and patriotic narrative of "democracy and freedom for all," which did not apply to Tubman. In fact, by passing the Fugitive Slave Act of 1850, the U.S. government made Tubman and other self-liberated African women and men no longer safe from capture and enslavement, even in the North. Thus, "our country" would have supported her re-enslavement if she had been caught.

The first paragraph in the vignette reads: "Some customs and ways of life have changed from long ago. Harriet Tubman lived in *our country* when some African Americans were not free. She wanted fair treatment for everyone" (p. 68; emphasis added). Apparently the "customs and ways of life that changed from long ago" refers to enslavement, which isn't mentioned prior to this vignette—or actually anywhere in this first-grade textbook. How are six-year-olds to understand why "some [it was actually millions] African Americans were not free"? What did they do to be not free? This introduction of Harriet Tubman gives students no information about enslavement, about Tubman's ancestry, and whether she was one of the African Americans who was "not free." What they are told is: "She wanted fair treatment for everyone." To state that Tubman wanted "fair treatment," but not to say from whom and for whom, invisibilizes the power and presence of the ideology of whiteness that in practice obstructed freedom for enslaved African Americans. In the same paragraph, the text invites students to identify with "*our country*"—a country that enslaved and denied Harriet Tubman and millions of other African Americans human dignity and the rights of citizenship. The misrepresentation of Tubman's work as a desire for fairness (from White people who go unnamed) is used to infer that there was/is one country experienced the same by all—a country that valued fairness. Actually, Harriet Tubman was not interested in seeking any kind of treatment from White people. Quite the contrary, she was seeking liberation for Black people, which she understood as everyone's inherent right. Not only does the misinformation in this paragraph make critical thinking next to impossible, the absence of indigenous African voice portrays a cruel and oppressive system as benign.

"Fair treatment" remains a theme in the second paragraph, with Harriet Tubman working hard to achieve it by helping "African Americans move to new places where they could be free. The people she helped followed a special path in the woods. The path was called the Underground Railroad" (p. 68). Tubman sounds more like a travel agent than a conductor of the Underground Railroad, and the "special path in the woods" sounds like a nature hike rather than a route to freedom fraught with hardships and dangers.

The third paragraph states that "Harriet Tubman was a very brave woman" (p. 69), remembered for believing in fairness and freedom for African Americans. Yes, she was a brave woman, but her bravery is presented in a way that disconnects her from her community. The absence of any information about her own liberation from enslavement and her repeated and perilous trips into the South to liberate others ignores scholarship that could provide a more

accurate, more complete, and indigenously voiced account that would acknowledge her bravery and connect it to its source. Harriet Tubman personifies an
African worldview in what Maulana Karenga (2006) calls her pursuit of a "collective practice of self-determination in community" (p. 247)—a communal orientation of practicing freedom as a shared responsibility. Explaining this source of
her bravery maintains continuity between Harriet Tubman and the African community that taught her the meaning of freedom. In summary, the absence of indigenous voice and the appropriation of Tubman into the dominant and patriotic
national narrative objectify and deculturalize her; the focus on fair treatment rather
than liberation obstructs accurate scholarship regarding enslavement and racial
ideology. Moreover, cloaking the White perpetrators of slavery sanitizes the institutionalized system of enslavement, representing it rather benignly as "unfair treatment" that, according to the text, seems inevitable and benefiting no one. In these
ways, this vignette is a master script that disrupts African Diasporan cultural continuities and protects and teaches the grand narrative of slavery.

A "Re-membered" Account of Harriet Tubman

So far in this chapter we have used Afrocentric theory and culturally informed
principles to examine one grand narrative and the master scripts that sustain it.
We also use this theory and these principles to create "re-membered" accounts
of the past in such forms as one-to two-page rewrites of textbook content
(Swartz, 2005, 2006, 2011) and stand-alone texts on specific topics (Swartz,
2007b, 2008, 2010, 2012b, 2013). In this section our "re-membered" account
of Harriet Tubman (Swartz, 2011) is a two-page re-write of the Scott Foresman
first-grade vignette discussed in the previous section. Our "re-membered"
vignette (see Vignette 3.2 below) follows a format similar to the Scott Foresman
vignette. The "re-membered" content is of course different. We decided to
only include a copy of our re-written, "re-membered" vignette about Tubman
in this chapter, not a copy of the Scott Foresman first-grade vignette. We
believe that including the latter would likely qualify for "fair use" under current
copyright law, since 1) it is being used for scholarly/educational purposes; (2)
the portion used (only two pages out of a 272-page text) is not substantial; and
(3) it is unlikely that including the vignette in this chapter will affect the textbook's marketability (since it was published in 2011 and pre-adoption samples
of the 2015 edition are currently being advertised) (Pearson, 2015; TEA, 2015;
U.S. Government Printing Office, 2014). However, given the unlikelihood of
receiving Scott Foresman's permission to include and critique a portion of their
textbook in this volume, we decided to avoid possible legal questions by only
describing and quoting small portions of the textbook vignette in the above
section. Interested readers can request a copy of the Scott Foresman vignette for
study in professional development contexts by sending an e-mail to omnicen-
tricpress@gmail.com or by buying the 2011 first-grade text *All Together* from

Scott Foresman at http://pearsonschool.com/index.cfm?locator=PSZwAe. Vignette 3.2 below is our "re-membered" text vignette about Harriet Tubman, along with a discussion of its content. This vignette is also written for first grade, but can be used in other elementary grades; it can also be used as an exercise in critical analysis at upper grade levels. To inquire about obtaining an 8.5 x 11 inch color copy of this vignette that can then be copied for classroom use, contact omnicentricpress@gmail.com.

Our Harriet Tubman uses the same general layout of the Scott Foresman textbook vignette, but that is where the similarities end. As an African woman, Harriet Tubman and her people are located at the center of the "re-membered" student text in Vignette 3.2. This is first seen in the words and imagery of the title. Rather than being inaccurately referred to as a "Citizen Hero," Tubman is called a "Heroine of Right Action." This tells young children that her actions were just and right, which is why she is someone to learn from and admire. And rather than the stars and stripes, the banner at the top of the page includes Kente cloth made by people of the Asante Nation. Some Tubman biographers either omit any discussion of her African ancestry (Lowry, 2007) or are tentative about identifying her Asante lineage (Clinton, 2004). When interviewed by journalist Frank C. Drake in 1907 (as cited in Larson, 2004), Tubman stated that she was told by women in her community about her Asante heritage. Ghana, a current African nation that is the homeland of the Asante People, has agreed. In 2000, Ghanaian officials visiting New York City enstooled (a tradition that recognizes the contributions of a community member) Harriet Tubman as Queen Mother of Ghana; and in 2005 Ghanaian officials received her great-grandnieces in the Ghanaian city of Aburi for a week of activities honoring their great-grandaunt (USA Today, 2005). Thus, the Kente cloth is a visual reference to the first sentence in the vignette that connects Tubman to Africa: "Harriet Tubman came from a long line of African men and women." Freedom is then defined in the context of an African worldview as a shared responsibility that applies to everyone (Karenga, 2006). By framing the first paragraph with three Afrocentric concepts—Centrality/Location, Collective Responsibility, and Reclamation of Cultural Heritage—the presentation of Harriet Tubman is "re-membered" by drawing upon an African knowledge base that is omitted in standard accounts.

Accurate Scholarship, Indigenous Voice, and Critical Thinking are culturally informed principles used to describe the enslavement of African people in the second paragraph (Aptheker, 1951/1969; Bennett, 1975; Franklin & Moss, 1994). The content in this paragraph obviates the grand narrative assumptions of slavery as a benign and inevitable system. Rather than assuming the white right of dominance, it names slavery's perpetrators, calls their actions wrong, and states how they benefit from stealing the knowledge, skills, and labor of African people, all of which allow teachers to guide students in exploring the unethical dimensions of the system of slavery. This becomes a critical thinking opportunity, one that is

VIGNETTE 3.2

HEROINE OF RIGHT ACTION

Harriet Tubman

Harriet Tubman came from a long line of African men and women. They knew that everyone had to be free in order to have justice in the world. This means that freedom is a shared responsibility.

Before and during Harriet Tubman's lifetime, the freedom of millions of African people was taken away. Their knowledge skills, and labor were stolen by White people to make money. This is called slavery. Slavery is not a right action. It is cruel and wrong.

Harriet Tubman was enslaved. But, she and all other enslaved Black people never gave up their right to be free. So, like many others, she found a way to take back her freedom.

Harriet Tubman was born in Dorchester County, Maryland.

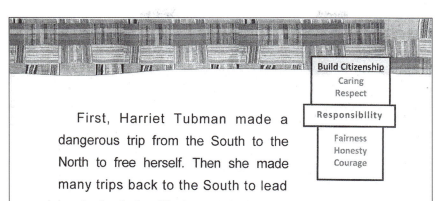

Build Citizenship
Caring
Respect
Responsibility
Fairness
Honesty
Courage

First, Harriet Tubman made a dangerous trip from the South to the North to free herself. Then she made many trips back to the South to lead hundreds of other Black people to freedom. She used the help of Black and White people. They worked together to hide and feed the people she was guiding to freedom. The plans they made and the hiding places they used were called the Underground Railroad.

Most travelers on the Underground Railroad walked all the way to freedom. Others were able to ride part of the way. Some were hidden in secret spaces in wagons.

Courtesy, Mendenhall Plantation, Historic Jamestown Society

Harriet Tubman was a caring member of her community. Her courage came from knowing that in order for any one person to really be free, everyone had to be free.

silenced when standard school knowledge presents enslaved labor as an inevitable driver of economic growth—as if that compels its justification and removes it from ethical review in the present.

The third paragraph presents Harriet Tubman as an enslaved member of a community that had never given up its right to freedom (Aptheker, 1951/1969; Bennett, 1975; Hart, 1985/2002). Students learn that she and others in her community found ways to liberate themselves (Bennett, 1975; Franklin, 1992; Price, 1979; Quarles, 1969; Thompson, 1987; Williams, 2010). This section uses Indigenous Voice, Representation, and Accurate Scholarship to write student content that is framed by the Afrocentric concepts of Subjects with Agency and Self-Determination. There is no voiceless request for fair treatment from a cloaked, unseen oppressor. Instead, there is a voice-full account of a person's and a People's taking back what was always theirs—a markedly different portrayal of enslavement and freedom that emerges from locating African people at the center of their own story.

In the fourth paragraph, students learn of Tubman's Underground Railroad work and her collaborations with White and Black people, which demonstrate the Afrocentric concepts of Collective Responsibility, Agency, and Self-Determination and the culturally informed principle of a Collective Humanity—all of which counter the ideology and practice of white racial supremacy. Black people and some White people saw themselves as equally part of the human collective and together they acted to resist this ideology as practiced in the system of slavery (Aptheker, 1993; Bennett, 1968; Quarles, 1969; Still, 2007). White resistance is presented in the context of the African struggle for human freedom—not leading it, but more accurately assisting it. Harriet Tubman exemplifies this: as she engineered her journeys to freedom, she sought and acquired the assistance of Black and White abolitionists. By placing African people at the center, an African knowledge base and experiences are "re-membered"—and are also combined, in this case, with the knowledge base and experiences of White people. Tubman is no longer a marginalized object of discussion in a White narrative of slavery, but the subject of a reconnected, culturally informed narrative about her and her people.

Another Afrocentric concept, the Reclamation of Cultural Heritage, frames the final paragraph. It describes the communal source of Harriet Tubman's courage and caring. She embodies the African understanding that freedom is a communal concept and experience, and that for anyone to be free, everyone has to be free. Human freedom is a shared responsibility, which demonstrates what *is* African about Harriet Tubman's actions. Thus, in this rewritten vignette, Harriet Tubman represents the citizenship characteristic of Responsibility (as a community), rather than Fairness (as an individual). This vignette demonstrates how cultural continuities can be "re-membered" when extant knowledge—in this case about Tubman—is shaped by African knowledge and worldview. Yes, Harriet Tubman was a brave and exceptional woman; not everyone could or can be a Harriet Tubman. But her exceptionality, as seen in her understandings, courage, and caring, was shaped by the African community to which she belonged.

Conclusion

While it is necessary to engage in critical analysis of standard school knowledge, it is equally necessary to acknowledge that such critique is endlessly reactive. Standard instructional materials, which are responsive to state interests in maintaining dominant national narratives, are produced by a well-funded corporate delivery system that is impervious to criticism, especially of the grand narratives it perpetuates (Buras, 2008; Spring, 2010; King & Swartz, 2014). Rather than continuously reacting to "official knowledge" (Apple, 1999) that has become entrenched in social, political, and economic institutions, not the least of which are schools, the Teaching *for* Freedom praxis we suggest and demonstrate here produces instructional materials for students that "re-member" cultural continuities. In describing his efforts against the fugitive slave law as a way of destroying slavery, Frederick Douglass (1881/1983) wrote that

> it was like an attempt to bail out the ocean with a teaspoon, but the thought that there was *one* less slave, and one more freeman—having myself been a slave, and a fugitive slave—brought to my heart unspeakable joy.
>
> (p. 272)

In drawing upon this metaphor, we recognize that the examples of "re-membered" cultural continuities that we produce fill only a teaspoon in comparison to the ocean of omnipresent corporate-state productions of standard knowledge. Under such circumstances, and guided by the Black intellectual tradition, we are still "outthinking and outflanking" hegemony (Du Bois, 1932, p. 71) if only 100 teachers and several thousand students are given access to instructional materials that "re-member" the multiple and shared knowledge bases and experiences that shaped our collective past. By framing student materials with Afrocentric theory, and writing them using culturally informed principles, there will be fewer children and adults mentally enslaved to limited sets of knowledge that obstruct human freedom by continuously replaying and reifying the past in the way it is told in the present. Rather, there will be more children and adults whose understanding of the past and present is informed by access to the cultural continuities that make it possible to disrupt grand narratives and master scripts while concurrently providing a fuller rendering of our collective history.

References

Apple, M. (1999). *Official knowledge: Democratic education in a conservative age* (2nd ed.). New York, NY: Routledge.

Appleby, J., Brinkley, A., Broussard, A. S., McPherson, J. M., & Ritchie, D. A. (2014). *United States history & geography*. New York, NY: McGraw Hill Education.

Aptheker, H. (1951/1969). *A documentary history of the Negro people in the United States: From colonial times through the Civil War* (Vol. I). New York, NY: The Citadel Press.

Aptheker, H. (1993). *Anti-racism in U.S. history: The first two hundred years*. Westport, CT: Praeger.

Bailey, T. A. (1956). *The American pageant: A history of the republic*. Boston, MA: D. C. Heath and Company.

Bailey, T. A. (1971). *The American pageant: A history of the republic*. Lexington, MA: D. C. Heath.

Banks, J. A., Boehm, R. G., Colleary, K. P., Contreras, G., Goodwin, A. L., McFarland, M. A., & Parker, W. C. (2005a). *We live together* New York, NY: Macmillan/McGraw-Hill.

Banks, J. A., Boehm, R. G., Colleary, K. P., Contreras, G., Goodwin, A. L., McFarland, M. A., & Parker, W. C. (2005b). *Our communities*. New York, NY: Macmillan/McGraw-Hill.

Banks, J. A., Boehm, R. G., Colleary, K. P., Contreras, G., Goodwin, A. L., McFarland, M. A., & Parker, W. C. (2005c). *Our country's regions*. New York, NY: Macmillan/McGraw-Hill.

Banks, J. A., Boehm, R. G., Colleary, K. P., Contreras, G., Goodwin, A. L., McFarland, M. A., & Parker, W. C. (2005d). *Our nation*. New York, NY: Macmillan/McGraw-Hill.

Bennett, L., Jr. (1968). *Pioneers in protest*. Chicago, IL: Johnson Publishing Company.

Bennett, L., Jr. (1975). *The shaping of Black America*. Chicago, IL: Johnson Publishing Company.

Bennett, L., Jr. (2000). *Forced into glory: Abraham Lincoln's White dream*. Chicago, IL: Johnson Publishing Company.

Bennett, L., Cummins, J., Kracht, J. B., Tatum, A., Colonial Williamsburg Foundation, & White, W. E. (2013). *My world social studies, the growth of our country*. Boston, MA: Pearson Education.

Berson, M. J., Howard, T. C., & Salinas, C. (2012a). *Our communities*. Boston, MA: Houghton Mifflin Harcourt.

Berson, M. J., Howard, T. C., & Salinas, C. (2012b). *The United States: Making a new nation*. Boston, MA: Houghton Mifflin Harcourt.

Bland, S. L. (2001). *African American slave narratives: An anthology* (Vol. 1). Westport, CT: Greenwood Publishers.

Boyd, C. D., Gay, G., Geiger, R., Kracht, J. B., Ooka Pang, V., Risinger, C. F., & Sanchez, S. M. (2011a). *The United States*. Boston, MA: Pearson.

Boyd, C. D., Gay, G., Geiger, R., Kracht, J. B., Ooka Pang, V., Risinger, C. F., & Sanchez, S. M. (2011b). *All together*. Boston, MA: Pearson.

Boyd, C. D., Gay, G., Geiger, R., Kracht, J. B., Ooka Pang, V., Risinger, C. F., & Sanchez, S. M. (2011c). *People and places*. Boston, MA: Pearson.

Boyd, C. D., Gay, G., Geiger, R., Kracht, J. B., Ooka Pang, V., Risinger, C. F., & Sanchez, S. M. (2011d). *Communities*. Boston, MA: Pearson.

Boyd, C. D., Gay, G., Geiger, R., Kracht, J. B., Ooka Pang, V., Risinger, C. F., & Sanchez, S. M. (2011e). *Regions*. Boston, MA: Pearson.

Bridgewater, P. D. (2014). *Breeding a nation: Reproductive slavery, the Thirteenth Amendment, and the pursuit of freedom.* Cambridge, MA: South End Press.

Buras, Kristen L. (2008). *Rightist multiculturalism: Core lessons on neoconservative school reform.* New York, NY: Routledge.

Carney, J. A. (2001). *Black rice: The African origins of rice cultivation in the Americas.* Cambridge, MA: Harvard University Press.

Cayton, A., Israels Perry, E., Reed, L., & Winkler, A. M. (2007). *America: Pathways to the present.* Boston, MA: Pearson Education/Prentice Hall.

Clinton, C. (2004). *Harriet Tubman: The road to freedom.* New York, NY: Little, Brown.

Davidson, B. (1961). *Black mother: The years of the African slave trade.* Boston, MA: Little, Brown and Company.

Davidson, B. (1972). *In the eye of the storm: Angola's people.* Garden City, NY: Doubleday & Company.

Dike, K. O. (1956). *Trade and politics in the Niger Delta, 1830–1885: An introduction to the economic and political history of Nigeria.* London: Oxford at the Clarendon Press.

Douglass, F. (1881/1983). *The life and times of Frederick Douglass.* Secaucus, NJ: Citadel Press.

Du Bois, W. E. B. (1932). Education. *The Journal of Negro Education, 1*(1), 60–74.

Epstein, T. (2009). *Interpreting national history: Race, identity, and pedagogy in classrooms and communities.* New York, NY: Routledge.

Fenton, E. (Ed.) (1970). *The Americans: A history of the United States.* New York, NY: American Heritage Publishing Company.

Fields, K., & Fields, B. J. (2014). *Racecraft: The soul of inequality in American life.* New York, NY: Verso.

Fiske, J. (1894). *A history of the United States for schools.* Boston, MA: Houghton, Mifflin and Company.

Franklin, V. P. (1992). *Black self-determination: A cultural history of African American resistance.* Chicago, IL: Lawrence Hill Books.

Franklin, J. H., & Moss, A. A., Jr. (1994). *From slavery to freedom: A history of African Americans* (7th ed.). New York, NY: McGraw-Hill.

Garcia, J., Ogle, D. M., Risinger, C. F., & Stevos, J. (2005). *Creating America: A history of the United States.* Evanston, IL: McDougal Littell.

Gavian, R. W., & Hamm, W. A. (1945). *The American story: A history of the United States of America.* Boston, MA: D. C. Heath and Company.

Gomez, Michael A. (1998). *Exchanging our country marks: The transformation of African identities in the colonial and antebellum South.* Chapel Hill, NC: University of North Carolina Press.

Gyekye, K. (1997). *Tradition and modernity: Philosophical reflections on the African experience.* New York, NY: Oxford University Press.

Hale, S. (1835). *History of the United States, from their first settlement as colonies, to the close of the war with Great Britain in 1815 to which are added questions, adapted to the use of schools.* New York, NY: N. & J. White.

Hall, G. M. (2005). *Slavery and African ethnicities in the Americas: Restoring the links.* Chapel Hill, NC: University of North Carolina Press.

Harlow, R. V. (1947). *Story of America.* New York, NY: Henry Holt and Company.

Hart, R. (1985/2002). *Slaves who abolished slavery: Blacks in rebellion.* Kingston, Jamaica: University of the West Indies Press.

Holloway, J. E. (Ed.) (1990). *Africanisms in American culture.* Bloomington, IN: Indiana University Press.

Johnston, A. (1904). *High-school history of the United States, with maps, plans, and illustrations.* New York, NY: Henry Holt and Company.

Karenga, M. (2006). Philosophy in the African tradition of resistance: Issues of human freedom and human flourishing. In L. R. Gordon & J. A. Gordon (Eds.), *Not only the master's tools: African American studies in theory and practice* (pp. 243–271). Boulder, CO: Paradigm Publishers.

Kessler, S. (2011). *Publishers launch first digital-only textbook for K-12*. Retrieved from http://mashable.com/2011/06/27/iste-textbooks-k-12/.

King, J. E. (1991). Dysconscious racism: Ideology, identity, and the miseducation of teachers. *Journal of Negro Education, 60*(2), 133–146.

King, J. E. (1992). Diaspora literacy and consciousness in the struggle against miseducation in the Black community. *Journal of Negro Education, 61*(3), 317–340.

King, J. E. (2004). Culture-centered knowledge: Black studies, curriculum transformation, and social action. In J. A. Banks & C. A. McGee Banks (Eds.), *Handbook of research on multicultural education* (2nd ed., pp. 349–378). San Francisco, CA: Jossey-Bass.

King, J. E. (2005, February 3). *Heritage knowledge for human freedom: Student-centered learning*. Paper presented at a meeting of the Parent/Teacher and Community Education Forum, Rochester Teacher Center, Rochester, New York.

King, J. E. (2006). "If justice is our objective": Diaspora literacy, heritage knowledge and the praxis of critical studyin' for human freedom. *Yearbook of the National Society for the Study of Education, 105*(2), 337–360.

King, J. E., & Akua, C. (2012). Dysconscious racism and teacher education. In J. A. Banks (Ed.), *Encyclopedia of diversity in education* (pp. 724–727). Thousand Oaks, CA: Sage Publications.

King, J. E., & Goodwin, S. (2006). *Criterion standards for contextualized teaching and learning about people of African descent*. Rochester, NY: Authors.

King, J. E., Swartz, E. E., with Campbell, L., Lemons-Smith, S., & López, E. (2014). *"Re-membering" history in student and teacher learning: An Afrocentric culturally informed praxis*. New York, NY: Routledge.

Klein, S. (1983). *Our country's history*. Austin, TX: Steck-Vaughn.

Konadu, K. (2010). *The Akan diaspora in the Americas*. New York, NY: Oxford University Press.

Larson, K. C. (2004). *Bound for the promised land: Harriet Tubman, portrait of an American hero*. New York, NY: Ballantine.

Littlefield, D. C. (1981). *Rice and slaves: Ethnicity and the slave trade in colonial South Carolina*. Baton Rouge, LA: Louisiana State University Press.

Lowry, B. (2007). *Harriet Tubman: Imaging a life*. New York, NY: Doubleday.

Maïga, H. O. (2010). *Balancing written history with oral tradition: The legacy of the Songhoy people*. New York, NY: Routledge.

Mbatha, W. (2012). "My family's not from Africa—we come from North Carolina!": Teaching slavery in context. *Rethinking Schools, 27*(1), 37–41.

Miller, J. C. (1988). *Way of death: Merchant capitalism and the Angolan slave trade, 1730–1830*. Madison, WI: University of Wisconsin Press.

Mills, C. W. (1997). *The racial contract*. Ithaca, NY: Cornell University Press.

Morison, S. E., & Commager, H. S. (1942). *The growth of the American republic* (Vol. 1, 3rd ed.). New York, NY: Oxford University Press.

Morison, S. E., Commager, H. S., & Leuchtenburg, W. E. (1969). *The growth of the American republic* (Vol. 1, 6th ed.). New York, NY: Oxford University Press.

Nkulu-N'Sengha, M. (2005). African epistemology. In M. K. Asante & A. Mazama (Eds.), *Encyclopedia of Black studies* (pp. 39–44). Thousand Oaks, CA: Sage Publications.

Painter, N. I. (2011). *The history of white people*. New York, NY. W. W. Norton Publishers.

Pearson (2013). *Learning social studies? Pearson's got an app for that!* Retrieved from www. pearsoned.com/learning-social-studies-pearson%E2%80%99s-got-an-app-for-that/#. Un1UVCeIbYQ.

Pearson (2015). *Pearson 2015 Elementary social studies: Grades pre-K-6.* Retrieved from www.pearsonschool.com/index.cfm?locator=PS2oOe&acornRdt=1&DCSext.w_ psvaniturl=http%3A%2F%2Fwww.pearsonschool.com%2Fk12catalogs.

Phillips, J. E. (1990). The African heritage of White Americans. In Joseph E. Holloway (Ed.), *Africanisms in American culture* (pp. 225–239). Bloomington, IN: Indiana University Press.

Piersen, W. D. (1993). *Black legacy: America's hidden heritage.* Amherst, MA: University of Massachusetts Press.

Price, R. (Ed.) (1979). *Maroon societies: Rebel slave communities in the Americas* (2nd ed.). Baltimore, MD: The Johns Hopkins University Press.

Quarles, B. (1969). *Black abolitionists.* New York, NY: Oxford University Press.

Rodney, W. (1966). African slavery and other forms of social oppression on the Upper Guinea Coast in the context of the Atlantic slave trade. *The Journal of African History,* 7(3), 431–443.

Rodney, W. (1982). *How Europe underdeveloped Africa.* Washington, DC: Howard University Press.

Smithers, G. D. (2013). *Slave breeding: Sex, violence, and memory in African American history.* Gainesville, FL: University Press of Florida.

Spring, J. (2010). *The politics of American education.* New York, NY: Routledge.

Still, W. (2007). *The Underground Railroad: Authentic narratives and first-hand accounts* (edited and with an introduction by I. F. Finseth). Mineola, NY: Dover Publications. (Original work published 1872.)

Sublette, N. (2008). *The world that made New Orleans: From Spanish silver to Congo Square.* Chicago, IL: Chicago Review Press.

Swartz, E. E. (1992). Emancipatory narratives: Rewriting the master script in the school curriculum. *The Journal of Negro Education,* 61, 341–355.

Swartz, E. E. (2005). *Rewrite: The coming conquest.* Rochester, NY: Omnicentric Press.

Swartz, E. E. (2006). *Rewrite: Acting for freedom.* Rochester, NY: Omnicentric Press.

Swartz, E. E. (2007a). Stepping outside the master script: Re-connecting the history of American education. *The Journal of Negro Education,* 76(2), 173–186.

Swartz, E. E. (2007b). *Reconstruction: Moving toward democracy.* Rochester, NY: Omnicentric Press.

Swartz, E. E. (2008). *Journeys to freedom: Self-determination, abolition, and the Underground Railroad.* Rochester, NY: RTA Press.

Swartz, E. E. (2010). *Early African presence in the Americas.* Rochester, NY: African and African American Studies Department of the Rochester City School District and the Rochester Teachers Center.

Swartz, E. E. (2011). *Rewrite: Heroine of right action: Harriet Tubman.* Rochester, NY: Omnicentric Press.

Swartz, E. E. (2012a). Removing the master script: Benjamin Banneker "Re-membered." *Journal of Black Studies,* 44(1), 31–49.

Swartz, E. E. (2012b). *Remembering our ancestors.* Rochester, NY: Rochester City School District.

Swartz, E. E. (2013). *Freedom and democracy: A story remembered.* Rochester, NY: Omnicentric Press.

TEA (Texas Educational Agency) (2015). *Proclamation 2015 pre-adoption samples, social studies, K-8.* Retrieved from http://tea.texas.gov/Curriculum_and_Instructional_

Programs/Instructional_Materials/Review_and_Adoption_Process/Proclamation_2015_ Pre-adoption_Samples,_Social_Studies,_K-8/.

Thompson, V. B. (1987). *The making of the African diaspora in the Americas 1441–1900.* New York, NY: Longman.

U.S. Government Printing Office (2014). *Sec. 107—Limitations on exclusive rights: Fair use.* Retrieved from www.gpo.gov/fdsys/pkg/USCODE-2010-title17/pdf/ USCODE-2010-title17-chap1-sec107.pdf.

USA Today (2005). *African city to honor America's Harriet Tubman.* Retrieved from www. usatoday.com/travel/destinations/2005-08-11-ghana-tubman_x.htm.

Viola, H. J., Witham Bednarz, S., Cortes, C. E., Jennings, C., Schug, M. C., White, Charles S. (2008). *Houghton Mifflin Social Studies: United States history early years.* Boston, MA: Houghton Mifflin Harcourt.

Wahlman, M. S. (2001). *Signs and symbols: African images in African American quilts.* Atlanta, GA: Tinwood Books.

Walker, S. S. (Ed.) (2001). *African roots/American cultures: Africa in the creation of the Americas.* Lanham, MD: Rowman & Littlefield Publishers.

Welles, G. (1862/1960). *Diary of Gideon Welles, Vol. 1* (edited by H. K. Beale). New York, NY: W. W. Norton & Company.

Williams, C. (1974). *Destruction of Black civilization: Great issues of a race from 4500 B.C. to 2000 A.D.* Chicago, IL: Third World Press.

Williams, E. (1944/1966). *Capitalism and slavery.* New York, NY: Capricorn Books.

Williams, E. (2010). The slaves and slavery. In L. Dubois & J. S. Scott (Eds.), *Origins of the Black Atlantic* (pp. 323–333). New York, NY: Routledge.

Wineburg, S., & Monte-Sano, C. (2008). *"Famous Americans": The changing pantheon of American heroes.* Retrieved from www.journalofamericanhistory.org/textbooks/2008/ wineburg.html.

Woodson, C. G. (1919). Negro life and history as presented in the schools. *The Journal of Negro History, IV,* 273–280.

Woodson, C. G. (1945). *The story of the Negro retold* (3rd ed.). Washington, DC: The Associated Publishers. (Original work published 1935.)

Wynter, S. (1984). The ceremony must be found: After humanism. *Boundary 2, 12–13*(3), 19–70.

Wynter, S. (1997). Alterity. In C. Grant & G. Ladson-Billings (Eds.), *Dictionary of multicultural education* (pp. 13–14). New York, NY: Oryx.

Wynter, S. (2000). The re-enchantment of humanism: An interview with Sylvia Wynter by David Scott. *Small Axe, 8,* 119–207.

Wynter, S. (2006). On how we mistook the map for the territory, and re-imprisoned ourselves in our unbearable wrongness of being, of Désêtre: Black studies toward the human project. In L. R. Gordon & J. A. Gordon (Eds.), *Not only the master's tools: African American studies in theory and practice* (pp. 107–169). Boulder, CO: Paradigm Publishers.

Zimmerman, J. (2004). Brown-ing the American textbook: History, psychology, and the origins of modern multiculturalism. *History of Education Quarterly, 44*(1), 46–69.

4

"RE-MEMBERING" THE JEANES TEACHERS

To be a teacher in the Jim Crow South demanded a faith in the future and a belief that education could make a difference in the lives of individual students and their communities.

> Joanne Abel, *Persistence and Sacrifice*, 2009, p. 120

Some African American leaders still held out hope that at least northern whites could be turned back from the rising venality of white Americans.

> Douglas Blackmon, *Slavery By Another Name*, 2008, p. 270

...[w]hite southerners and politicians were suspicious of any education for blacks that involved reading, writing, and arithmetic that would lead to black demands for political equality.

> Phyllis McClure, *Jeanes Teachers*, 2009, p. 19

To dialogue deeply with African cultures means, more than anything else, using them as a *resource* rather than as a mere *reference*. It means communicating critically and becoming conversant with continental and diasporan African thought- and practice-traditions that point to new passions and new possibilities.

> Reiland Rabaka, *Against Epistemic Apartheid*, 2010, pp. 276–277

This chapter illustrates another example of the praxis of Teaching *for* Freedom. It uses Afrocentric theoretical concepts and African worldview elements (see Chapter 1) that "re-member" African American rural school supervisors in the South, who were called "Jeanes Teachers," named after Anna T. Jeanes, the wealthy Northern Quaker philanthropist whose funds partially paid their salaries. This chapter situates the thought and pedagogical practices, community building work, and teacher training activities of these exceptionally able Black teachers within the historical reality of how "negro" education has been used to maintain white supremacy (Fairclough, 2007; Watkins, 2001). Although the Southern white power structure employed Jeanes teachers ostensibly to "improve" woefully inadequate and often dilapidated "rural negro schools," many devised ways to resist the deprivations and depredations of white-controlled Jim Crow education in their communities (Abel, 2009; Fairclough, 2000). This chapter asks: How was this possible? What ways of being and knowing, values, virtues, and principles are consistently found in their work? And how does an African worldview guide us to "read" the African Diasporan cultural continuity of these Jeanes teachers as an example of the praxis of Teaching for Freedom?

Northern White industrial philanthropists and education agents, who catered to the ideology of Southern White planter regime's more overt racism and the "social consensus" that excluded Black political participation through institutionalized structures of white racial domination, are implicated in the betrayal of Black aspirations for freedom and advancement through education (Anderson, 1988). For while education was the fervent hope of the masses of the four million formerly enslaved African Americans, abject impoverishment, the denial of education altogether, and the systematically intentional provision of substandard education were involved in the re-imposition of white supremacy upon Black people in the post-Reconstruction Jim Crow South (Fultz, 1995). There are well-documented accounts of the epic efforts of Black communities to build, fund, and operate their own schools during and following the Civil War (Du Bois & Dill, 1911). Following the war, however, state, religious, and philanthropic involvement in education for African people was ideologically driven by White interests in social, political, and economic control, not in fostering freedom and self-reliance (Butchart, 1988). Thus, Black women teachers were paid less than half of what White male teachers earned; schools did not exist in many rural communities—for Blacks or Whites; and both funding and educational quality were unequal in every other respect—which violated the "separate but equal" provision of the 1896 Plessy *v* Ferguson Supreme Court decision, the legal framework that normalized segregation and made it mandatory as Reconstruction was overturned (Anderson, 1988).

While some Southern Whites believed a "racially separate pedagogy" that offered a modicum of education for farm and domestic work—"manual arts"—would prevent Black people from migrating to the cities and reconcile them to their subordinated status, McClure (2009) observes that wealthy Northern industrialists and philanthropists, such as John D. Rockefeller, Julius Rosenwald, and John Slater, among others, "had their own reasons" for endorsing and financing this type of education for rural Blacks in the South. McClure's (2009) observation is worth quoting on this point:

> The cotton crop and mills and the railroads in which they had their own investments were central to the economy of the South. A trained black

southern worker would deter any attempts to unionize labor. With the reformist intensions and a missionary spirit, Northerners threw their support behind the Tuskegee Institute and the Hampton Institute as the leading promoters of the type of black education that would help drag the region out of poverty.

(p. 19)

Situating the Jeanes teachers within this historical, political, economic, and cultural dialectic of domination/resistance is required to pinpoint and then reconnect the collusion and corrosive power of White Northern philanthropists, Southern elites and a rampantly racist media to opposing dynamics among the Black intellectual leadership and Black scholarly activism of this period that challenged the racial orthodoxy of white supremacy and Black people's so-called degeneracy (Butchart, 1988; Du Bois, 1935/1972; Woodson, 1922). Black intellectuals and educators, including Booker T. Washington, challenged the ideology of white supremacy by:

contradicting the pervasive message of black degeneracy and criminality. The Negro as degenerative beast and rapist became an image so destructive that it had to be altered for the race to make progress. A more positive reputation for black Americans was needed to defuse some of the explosive feelings that had built up against blacks since Reconstruction, especially during the 1890s.

(Norrell, 2005, p. 47)

Carter G. Woodson, W. E. B. Du Bois, Ida B. Wells, Anna Julia Cooper, Booker T. Washington, and the Jeanes teachers were part of this dynamic (Lemert & Bahn, 1998; Davidson, 2009; Du Bois, 1897).

Within this complex nexus of powerful white political intransigence, lethal ideological subjugation, and social terror, the work of the Jeanes teachers—also called "Jeanes supervisors," "Jeanes agents," or "Jeanes supervising industrial teachers"—involved both apparent accommodation and tenacious covert resistance. Locating the Jeanes teachers as normative Subjects with Agency at the center of the Jim Crow regime "re-members" and reclaims their contributions to the Black freedom struggle as heritage knowledge, and is intended to illuminate other Afrocentric theoretical concepts and African worldview elements (see Chapter 1) that are recognizable in the pioneering work of these women, their knowledge of Black cultural strengths, and their way of being in the world. For example, African Collective Consciousness, Collective Responsibility, and Self-Determination can also be seen in their actions. As Chirhart (2013) reports: "Many Jeanes teachers were accomplishing more than educational improvements for African Americans." In Georgia:

> Those who were members of the National Association for the Advancement of Colored People and the Georgia Teachers and Education Association (GTEA) also informed African American communities about the work, promoted by both organizations, for equal schools and voting rights. By communicating African American goals at the state and national level to local communities, many Supervisors served as leaders of the early civil rights movement during the 1950s.
>
> (Chirhart, 2013, n.p.)

While this conscious definition and demonstration of concern for cultural and communal well-being on the part of the Jeanes teachers is part of Black cultural heritage, this legacy has been nearly obliterated from history as well as from our memory.

Fortunately, there is growing interest in the Jeanes teachers (Fairclough, 2007; Harris & Taylor, 1999; Jones, 1937; Littlefield, 1999; McClure, 2009; Pincham, 2005; Smith, 1997; Williams, 1981). Moreover, Afrocentric theory reveals a more complete context for analyzing and interpreting the freedom implications of their thought and their pedagogical practices. Yet, the expressions of African worldview in the thought and practice of the Jeanes teachers epitomize persistent contradictions within the Black freedom struggle, particularly with regard to white patronage, control, and influence, and the need to appease Whites versus maintaining racial dignity and loyalty (Fairclough, 2000). In numerous articles and books, several theses, oral histories, and other web resources, the story of the Jeanes teachers typically begins with the altruism of Northern philanthropists. The concerns of these Northern White elites about the "problems of Negro education" in the South led them to establish several funds, including a generous gift of Quaker Anna T. Jeanes, who, in consultation with Booker T. Washington, scion of "industrial" (that is, vocational or manual) education for the formerly enslaved, established a $1 million endowment to improve education in rural Negro schools in the South. This fund paid a portion of the salaries of Black supervisors—Jeanes teachers—most of whom were women assigned to supervise and support typically under-prepared and under-paid Black teachers in country schools in impoverished counties where the local education authorities elected to use them. The first Jeanes supervisor, Mrs. Virginia Estelle Randolph, was appointed in Virginia, then others, following the model "Henrico Plan" that she developed, were hired in 16 southern states from 1908 through 1968 (Pincham, 2005). The predominate educational philosophy envisioned and intended for rural Black schools was not academic preparation for higher education but the "industrial" Hampton-Tuskegee model developed by Samuel C. Armstrong and promoted by his "prized pupil" Booker T. Washington (Anderson, 1988, p. 32). Before examining the "school of thought" (McClure, 2009, p. 96) and pedagogical practices of the Jeanes teachers and the ways they navigated this contradictory ideological and political terrain, it is important to connect them to the broader sociopolitical, economic, cultural, and ideological context that defined the white supremacy racism regime that circumscribed or denied Black education altogether. Thus, "re-membering" the Jeanes teachers entails critically examining this broader context from an African worldview perspective in order to consciously recover and reclaim what was both African and emancipatory about their thought and their pedagogical practice.

The Great Fear: "To Prevent the 'Africanization' of the South"

In his 1895 Atlanta Exposition Address, when Booker T. Washington advised Black people to "cast down [their] buckets where they were" in "agriculture, mechanics, commerce, domestic service," he articulated the educational philosophy that would inspire Northern philanthropists, assuage white fears, and define white expectations for Black education for a generation, including the rural schools and the work of the Jeanes teachers (Williams, 2006, p. 188). However, this training program for manual labor and domestic work not for real industrial jobs that were closed to African Americans in the South was controversial from the beginning among the masses of Black people as well as for leading Black intellectuals like W. E. B. Du Bois and Carter G. Woodson, who viewed Booker T. Washington's educational philosophy as an accommodationist obstacle to Black progress (Anderson, 1988; Fairclough, 2000). Scholars also argue, however, that Washington's championing of "black self-reliance and thus, Black people's *capacity* for progress contradicted white supremacist ideology" (Frederickson, 1995, p. 35, emphasis added). Norrell (2005) explains that Washington's "Atlanta Compromise" speech merely articulated what was already the reality of Black political disenfranchisement.

> In the Atlanta speech Washington began a sustained challenge to the ugly images then current in white intellectual and cultural presentations of beastly, immoral African Americans. The speech represented Washington's attempt to counter the presumption on the part of the white South, and much of the rest of the nation, that in freedom African Americans had declined in character and morality.
>
> (p. 46)

Thus, Washington believed that Reconstruction, a time when Black people had been voted into political office, was a failed and futile experiment and the "industrial model of education was the only way to accommodate Whites" (Riley, 2002, p. 4).

The racial climate in the United States in 1908 when the first Jeanes teacher was appointed was defined by what Du Bois described as White people's "Great Fear" (Riley, 2002, p. 3) that was manifested in a period of rising white racism, disenfranchisement, the terror and trauma of lynching, the deadly economic exploitation of Black people which continued slavery through peonage, and the system of convict leasing or "slavery by another name" (Blackmon, 2008). The media popularized the myth of Black people's inherent criminality and violent immorality in the popular 1915 film "The Birth of a Nation." White researchers also promulgated the belief in the imminent extinction of the Black population as a result of such deviant degenerative racial traits (Muhammad, 2010). This "mentality," or arsenal of white power, contrasts with the "race knowledge" and Black scholarly activism in the fight against white supremacy, which included a growing interest in and recognition of "the achievements of blacks in ancient Africa" (Williams, 2006, p. 134)—another reference to an Afrocentric concept called the "Anteriority of Classical African Civilizations" (see Chapter 1). Williams argues that through Booker T. Washington's association with the sociologist Monroe N. Work, who had in turn been influenced by W. E. B. Du Bois and Franz Boas, Washington was gradually influenced by this viewpoint. However, as far as prevalent white sentiment that Northern philanthropists and Southern education administrators were both so keen to respect, little had changed since President Andrew Johnson's 1867 annual message to Congress, when he stated that African Americans who had "less capacity for government than any other race of people," would "relapse into barbarism" if left to their own devices (EIJ, 2015, p. 7). Also worth noting is the role of U.S. philanthropy in the adoption of Tuskegee-style "industrial education," including the use of traveling Jeanes teachers, in rural British colonial and missionary schools in Africa (Kenya, South Africa, Rhodesia, Uganda, Zambia) and British Honduras (Berman, 1971; Franklin, 2011; McClure, 2009; Watkins, 2001).

"Thinking Black": Self-Determination and Freedom as an Inherent Right

Carter G. Woodson's fight against white supremacy ideology is evident in a revealing historical inter-connection between the Afrocentric theoretical concept of Collective Consciousness, the value of service to others, namely racial uplift, and Self-Determination, another Afrocentric theoretical concept demonstrated by both Woodson and the Jeanes teachers. Like the Jeanes teachers, Woodson had received considerable Northern industrial philanthropic funding to establish and support the Association for the Study of Negro Life and History and to maintain the publication of the *Journal of Negro History*—which were seminal to his campaign for "Negro history" to uplift the consciousness of both the Black masses and the Black educated class. In spite of his ongoing critical need for Rockefeller support at the time, he nevertheless resisted all pressure from his White benefactors to "affiliate" his research program and publications with a "Negro College" that was receiving Rockefeller funding—adamantly choosing instead to maintain his scholarly autonomy. The common denominator was Jackson Davis, whose career represented the pattern of white control of Black education reflecting both Northern interests and Southern domination over Black lives and opportunities for education. Davis was Virginia Randolph's White "boss" when he served as State Superintendent of Schools and secured Jeanes funding to appoint her as the first Jeanes teacher in Virginia. Davis "admired the initiative she took in improving her school and organizing the parents and teachers for community betterment" (McClure, 2009, p. 29). She also advocated "industrial training" in her first report:

> The destiny of our race depends, largely, upon the training children receive in the schoolroom.... The great majority of the children in the country schools will never reach high school; therefore we must meet the demands of the schools in the Rural Districts by introducing [industrial] training in every school room.
>
> (p. 31)

Davis promoted Mrs. Randolph's teaching approach as a model throughout the South. By the time of his appointment as Director at the General Education Board (a precursor of the Rockefeller Foundation) in 1915, the same year Woodson established the Association, Davis, a proselytizer of the Hampton-Tuskegee philosophy of manual training for Black people, was considered possibly the nation's "leading white authority on black education" (McClure, 2009, p. 28).

Woodson was at the center of the ideological clash about Black education and was the target of a sustained campaign to curtail his work. As part of the pressure Davis and the other foundation officers exerted on Woodson, an "independent" assessment of the publications produced by the Association for the Study of Negro Life and History was undertaken—reviewed by some of the same White historians Woodson's scholarship criticized. Even though this surreptitious review deemed the Association's publications "useful," Rockefeller funding was withdrawn when Woodson refused their demands to surrender his independence. According to the historian Darlene Clark Hine (1986), Woodson asserted: "for a black university to assume a publishing responsibility for the *Journal* would amount to a 'disestablishment of the Association'" (p. 419).

It was Davis who delivered the news to Woodson that *all* the Rockefeller trusts had agreed that further funding would not be forthcoming unless Woodson heeded their directive. Previously, however, Woodson had declared that in the final analysis the work of researching and writing Negro history "must be done by Negroes ... who have the advantage of being able to think black" (Hine, 1986, p. 409). Moreover, while Woodson maintained that Whites did "not appreciate the feeling, thought, and aspirations of the Negro and therefore cannot think black" (Goggin, 1993, p. 131), by the 1930s Woodson also "argued that black educational institutions were 'mis-educating' black students, failing to teach them about their racial and cultural heritage, but also how to make a living" (p. 155). Thus, he refused any efforts of White people to control or guide his research and at the same time his position was that no Black college was up to the task of supporting the Negro History Movement (Woodson, 1933/1990). Hine states what "Davis reported to his colleagues":

> I made it clear to Dr. Woodson that the Board had invested large sums of money in these institutions and that it seemed to the officers that the opportunity and responsibility of the Board was in helping them to become centers of study and research rather than to build up independent agencies without institutional connections.
>
> (Hine, 1986, p. 420)

After 1933, no foundations made any contributions to the Association and Woodson "would not endorse or participate in any projects financed by whites that he could not control" (Goggin, 1993, p. 111).

Subsequently, Woodson relied almost totally upon the Black community for financial support—through paid Association memberships, $1 subscriptions purchased primarily by Black teachers, and book sales—to continue his scholarly and organizing endeavors on behalf of Black people. During the hard times of the Depression, through economizing, greater efficiencies, outreach efforts, and creativity, at great personal sacrifice he not only maintained the production schedule of the scholarly *Journal of Negro History*, Woodson also began several new research projects and published the mass-appeal *Negro History Bulletin* as well. He broadened his base of support among the Black masses and organizations, such as the mail carriers union (in his home state of Virginia); he offered correspondence courses through the Association's Home Study Department and teacher training institutes for educators that likely included Jeanes teachers; and he established chapters of the Association through which he engaged a "mass audience in the collection and dissemination of source materials for the study of black history" (Goggin, 1993, p. 118). Woodson also trained and paid salesmen to sell black history books in a door-to-door campaign across the Deep South and cities, including Chicago and Philadelphia (Greene, 1996).

"Reading" African Diasporan Cultural Continuities in Emancipatory Pedagogy Born in Struggle

Woodson's emphasis on the importance of being able to "think black" in the interest of Black people's advancement—that is to say, for freedom as an inherent right—demonstrates agency and self-determination using black history research and teaching as emancipatory tools for black liberation and to combat white supremacy. As discussed in Chapter 1, the Afrocentric concept of Subjects with Agency describes African people who "have the will and capacity to act in and on the world—not only as individuals, but as members of their cultural group." Likewise, the Jeanes teachers also relied on the Black community to support their work and, like Woodson, were committed to education and freedom for the Black masses. Other examples of this community-minded "black thinking" on the part of the Jeanes teachers will be evident in the examples of their emancipatory pedagogical practices—a praxis of Teaching *for* Freedom that also exemplifies African Diasporan cultural continuities and Afrocentric theoretical concepts, such as Collective Consciousness, Collective Responsibility, Subjects with Agency, and Reclamation of Cultural Heritage.

Collective Consciousness: Community-Minded Service to Others

Historical records of Jeanes teachers reveal Collective Consciousness in their intergenerational knowing/thinking and "educational and communal values" (Anderson, 1988, p. 173) on behalf of Black people's freedom and well-being. This Collective Consciousness was part of the heritage knowledge bequeathed to them from formerly enslaved parents and the ideology of "racial uplift" and memories of freedom that defined post-Reconstruction Black communities. Whether their families were relatively privileged or impoverished, Jeanes teachers Virginia Randolph, Sarah Delany, and Carrie Thomas Jordan, for example, were rooted and grounded in an ethos of community-mindedness and a strong sense of belonging in familial, community, and professional networks that displayed African ways of being, knowing, and values that shaped and made their extraordinarily dedicated professional work as Jeanes teachers possible.

Virginia Randolph, born in 1874 in Henrico, County Virginia, was the second of four children "of a widowed mother born in slavery" (McClure, 2009, p. 29). She became a legendary Jeanes teacher in her own lifetime. While Superintendent Davis appointed her as the first Jeanes teacher because he admired her effective relations with the parents and community and her initiative in improving the school where she worked in neighboring Goochland County (with so very little material resources), Mrs. Randolph "realized that she could use the industrial courses [imposed by Northern benefactors and local Southern education officials] to improve the lives of her students and their parents, and as a supplement to and not a replacement of the traditional curriculum, while pleasing Superintendent Davis" (Abel, 2009, p. 32). McClure gives a detailed account of Mrs. Randolph's methods and the challenges she encountered working with teachers in 20 Henrico County schools in order to:

> instruct them on how to impart skills that would improve the lives and physical surroundings of poor children. The curriculum incorporated training in personal hygiene, making schoolrooms clean and attractive, and learning how to plant and harvest gardens. She was a prodigious

fund-raiser; she collected pennies from parents, solicited contributions from sympathetic whites, and pled with the Jeanes Fund for extra money. All cash and donations went to planting trees and gardens, painting class-rooms, hanging curtains, and opening summer programs. Randolph organized exhibits of quilts and other items made by students.... With money raised from black families and cajoled out of the county school board, Randolph worked to provide more years of schooling than the small primary schools offered.

(McClure, 2009, pp. 31–32)

In 1921, Virginia Randolph purchased three acres of land next to the four-teacher Rosenwald training school that had been built and named after her. This land was used for a girls' dormitory that eventually opened in 1924. She turned the deed over to the County as required by the Jeanes Fund. Boarding allowed students who lived too far away to continue their education beyond primary school.

Sarah "Sadie" Delany, one of the celebrated "Delany Sisters," was born in 1889 (Delany & Delany, 1993). She grew up with nine brothers and sisters on the campus of Saint Augustine College where her father, Henry Delany, was Vice-principal. Although he was born into slavery and he and his family were freed "with nothing," they did have certain advantages: they were still together; he could read; and he learned carpentry skills from his father. Her mother, whose White father and Black mother could never marry, had been a house servant and also could read. Henry Delany studied theology on scholarship at Saint Augustine's, the school the Methodist Episcopal church had established for freed men and women. Her mother, Nanny Logan Delany, also a graduate, taught home economics and domestic science and served as the college "Matron." Henry Delany was eventually ordained as a deacon, then a priest, Archdeacon, and in 1918 rose through the hierarchy to become the first African American Bishop elected in the (segregated) Episcopal Church in North Caro-lina. Bishop Delany was active in the promotion of church-based education for Black people; he helped organize church-affiliated schools throughout the state of North Carolina; and he was also "one of the few education advocates who worked to bring educational opportunities to black prisoners in local jails" (Rupert, n.d.).

Sadie recalls that, on the day she graduated from "St. Aug" in 1910, her father said: "Daughter, you are college material. You owe it to your nation, your race, and yourself to go.... And if you don't, shame on you! I have no money.... You must make your own way" (Delany & Delany, 1993, p. 79). Her father also advised her not to accept any scholarship money, warning that she would be beholden to the people who gave her the money. This advice is an example of the attitude of self-determination among the formerly enslaved, which they passed on to the next generation. So to save money and pay her own college expenses, she applied and was appointed to a position as a Jeanes supervisor setting up "domestic science" programs; she also assumed administrative duties and was responsible for rural schools all over Wake County, North Carolina—with no additional pay or recognition. Such additional duties were routinely assigned to Jeanes teachers (Tillman, 2004). Though she was accustomed to the amenities of city living in Raleigh, her relatively more privileged background was not a barrier in her work, as she made trips to visit schools and boarded with local rural families living in the most impoverished circumstances. Miss Delany described the conditions she found in the rural schools:

> Oftentimes, "school" was held at a church and the children would kneel on the floor and use the pews as desks. There were usually no facilities to teach domestic science, so I would borrow someone's kitchen and once I got a class started I would hire a teacher to take up where I left off.
>
> (Delany & Delany, 1993, pp. 113–114)

Mrs. Carrie Thomas Jordan, who was appointed as the third Jeanes supervisor in Durham, North Carolina from 1923–1926, was the daughter of Reverend Lawrence Thomas, a founder of Morris Brown College and a pastor of Big Bethel AME, the oldest Black church in Atlanta. A graduate of Morris Brown College in 1889, she had been a teacher and a principal who was guided by a racial uplift educational philosophy. Mrs. Jordan is credited with raising money to build 12 Rosenwald schools and she implemented various educational innovations, including an enriched curriculum based on the State Course of Study Guide that was intended for White students. This curriculum, which included the subjects of spelling, geography, and nature study, was intended "to prepare Black children for a world that neither they nor their community could envision" (The Artishia and Frederick Jordan Scholarship Fund, n.d.). In her report to the Division of Negro Education, Mrs. Jordan indicated:

> An effort was made to develop in each child a spelling conscience—the ability to know when a word is spelled correctly or incorrectly; to teach the use of the dictionary and the need for looking up words when uncertain of the spelling or meaning of a word. Games and spelling devices were used to motivate the drill and put life and interest into the spelling class.
>
> (Abel, 2009, p. 75)

Mrs. Carrie T. Jordon documented the ways she helped teachers to improve classroom instruction, thereby hoping to improve student interest and attendance:

> In order to increase the Black students' knowledge of geography, Carrie solicited funds from the Black community and the Black Teachers'

Association to purchase maps, globes, and travel magazines which gave her students "an incentive for doing school tasks which they had not had heretofore."

(The Artishia and Frederick Jordan Scholarship Fund, n.p.)

She modeled place-based science teaching innovations and project-based geography lessons using the local environment. She developed other long-lasting innovations: commencement programs and rallies to showcase Black students' academic accomplishments that drew hundreds of parents (Abel, 2009). Engaging students in learning and demonstrating their knowledge of science as related to the context in which they lived foreshadowed the emancipatory pedagogies we discuss in Chapters 1 and 2, such as Locating Students, Multiple Ways of Knowing, and Communal Responsibility.

The Collective Consciousness of these Jeanes teachers, which can be seen in their community building, was linked to teacher development and improving instruction through organizing: Parent Teacher Associations, Homemaker's Clubs, teachers' Reading Circles, Parent Unions, Health Clubs, Home Improvement Associations, Corn Clubs, Pig Clubs, fundraising, teaching in summer institutes for teachers, and encouraging teachers to complete professional certification. All these activities are indicative of the epistemology of relational knowing and the ancestral continuity their lives represented. As Abel (2009) notes, to do their work, "each Jeanes teacher had to put her teachers, students, and communities first, pushing the white authorities as far as she could" (p. 32).

Collective Responsibility: Justice and Interdependence

Linking the Rosenwald Rural Negro School Fund—financed by Sears Roebuck magnate Julius Rosenwald—and the "industrial education" Jeanes teachers were responsible for promoting and overseeing was the brainchild of Booker T. Washington. As Anderson (1988) points out, however, the aim was never to produce qualified skilled workers for the industrializing South. Rather, the plan was to further entrench the Hampton-Tuskegee educational approach to prepare teachers who would instill in the Southern Black population the attitude of acquiescence to the prevailing racial hegemony in the guise of self-reliance—"convincing them to accept their subordination as a normal and inevitable fact of life ... while leaving the door of hope and opportunity ajar" (Leloudis, 1996, p. 182). John Hope Franklin offered a clear analysis of the situation:

> The collusion was complete as Northern financiers and industrialists reaped enormous benefits from economic developments in the South. And, if these Northerners sinned as accessories in stimulating share cropping, peonage,

and convict labor, they did penance by offering pittances to educate the former slaves in ways that would not be offensive to Southern mores and predispositions.

(Cecelski & Tyson, 1998, p. x)

Thus, classes in cooking, sewing, and manual training were typically found only in Black schools supervised by Jeanes teachers. Such "industrial training" was viewed as a supplement to the curriculum for White schools but as the "ideal linchpin of black schooling" (Thuesen, 2013, p. 51). Thuesen makes this point:

> Industrial lessons taught students to prepare food and clothing for their families. In cash-strapped tenant and sharecropping families Jeanes teachers schooled children in cooking, sewing, gardening, basketry, shuck mat making, cobbling, housekeeping, pine straw work, rug making, embroidery, and flower arrangement. In encouraging these skills, many Jeanes teachers organize Home-Makers' Clubs, where children worked to grow corn, can [preserve] produce, raise chickens and pigs, and make pickles and jellies.
>
> (p. 52)

While the "Rosenwald Fund required its schools to include facilities for such activities," however, many Jeanes teachers were not content with limited aspirations for Black children (Thuesen, 2013, p. 51). These Jeanes teachers, who shared other Black educators' concerns about the limitations of this approach, found ways to resist this racialized curricular inequality that "curried the favor of local whites" by promising "more efficient domestic and agricultural laborers" (Thuesen, 2013, p. 51). Jeanes teachers also took the lead in grassroots fund-raising to build schools, supplement teachers' salaries, purchase supplies and equipment, extend the school term, etc. In harmonious, reciprocal, and interdependent relationship with impoverished tenant farmers and sharecropping families who contributed at least a third of the funds needed to build a Rosenwald school, Jeanes teachers and the rural population took advantage of cracks in the system to collectively seek more justice.

One Jeanes teacher and her husband, a Black pastor and teacher in Fayette County, Tennessee, helped to build 20 Rosenwald Schools throughout the county. What this meant in reality was that Black citizens—ex-slave subsistence tenant and share-cropping farmers and their children working in the cotton fields, with contributions from more well-to-do others in their communities—collectively helped to build these schools. They contributed their labor and donated building materials and land, mortgaged their property and, as an example, raised as much as $2,200 of the $3,500 needed for one school. Anderson (1988) reports that, in this instance, "the Rosenwald fund donated $500 and the county public school authorities appropriated $800" (p. 166). By 1928, one in five schools for Black students across the South was a Rosenwald school. When the program ended in 1932:

> this fund had helped to build more than 4,977 new school facilities, 217 teachers' homes, and 163 shop buildings ... at a total cost of $28.5 million. Of that $28.5 million, the Fund donated $4.3 million and local African-American communities had raised $4.7 million. These schools served 663,615 students in fifteen southern states.
>
> (National Registry of Historic Places, 2008, p. 11)

In addition to providing more up-to-date facilities to offer more rural students improved "industrial education," Rosenwald schools became sites for various community activities, including theatrical productions, pageants, graduation ceremonies, Juneteenth celebrations, agricultural exhibitions, extension demonstrations, church services, and even political activism. For example, Jeanes supervisor Mrs. Carrie T. Jordan "turned the Rosenwald Schools of Durham [North Carolina] into organizing tools and community centers" (Abel, 2009, p. 118). Not only did she elevate academic instruction, as noted above:

> She would bring members of various churches, land owners, sharecroppers, tenant farmers, workers in the factories and mills of East or West Durham together to work for the common goal of improving their children's schools.... The schools became centers of community life, where Moonlight schools [evening schools for adults], Home Makers' Clubs, Betterment Leagues, P.T.A.'s, and other community meetings took place.
>
> (Abel, 2009, pp. 119)

Also, according to Abel (2009), some Jeanes teachers "organized cooperatives to buy land so tenant farmers and sharecroppers could become landowners" (p. 33). In addition, besides emphasizing cleanliness and self-sufficiency, which might be the most obvious "next needed thing"—as expressed in their motto—Jeanes teachers also "transformed their students into entrepreneurs" (Gilmore, 1996, p. 161). In North Carolina in 1915:

> their Home-Makers Clubs, Corn Clubs, Pigs Clubs involved over 4,000 boys and girls and 2,000 adults in 32 counties. The clubs were intended to teach farming, of course, but they also enabled poor rural African Americans to make money on their produce. The students raised more than $6,000 selling fruits and vegetables that year.
>
> (Gilmore, 1996, pp. 162–163)

During the Depression in the 1930s, growing and preserving home-grown foodstuffs made vital contributions to family survival. Engaging in these practices through shared or Collective Responsibility for communal well-being and belonging was "emancipatory in that their collaborative enactment increase[ed] justice and right action for African people and the whole of humanity" (see Table 1.1 in Chapter 1). The evidence for this claim is more visible when examples of Jeanes teachers' educational activism are analyzed and interpreted through the lens of African worldview elements, such as ways their Faith, Creativity, and community mindedness informed their ethical consciousness and participation in the Black struggle for Justice (see Figure 1.1 in Chapter 1) under conditions of overt racial repression, which is discussed next.

Subjects with Agency: Teacher Activism, Struggles for Equity

Demonstrating agency *and* self-determination within a white supremacy regime—"to advance within a system designed by white people to stop them from advancing" (Fairclough, 2007, p. 262)—called forth diligent stratagems. The nature of the struggle was transparently clear:

> it was an unpalatable fact that instead of narrowing, the inequalities between black schools and white schools widened in the 1920s and 1930s. Black schools improved but white schools improved more. Every educational innovation had to be first started in the white schools; a decade or two then went by before whites considered extending it to black schools.
>
> (Fairclough, 2007, pp. 262–263)

Thus, there is more than irony in the fact that the intended schooling for Black children living in the most impoverished circumstances—where Black citizens were doubly taxed by being required to raise their own funds to build badly needed schools—was not designed for their betterment but to make them better fitted for permanent exploitation. Worse still, it was also documented that Black people paid more in taxes than the state (of North Carolina) spent on Black education, and Black people's taxes were routinely used to educate White children (Gilmore, 1996, p. 159). Whites were encouraged to support this "right kind of education" for Black people because: "Each year Durham will be supplied with better trained cooks, servants, and housekeepers" (Abel, 2009, p. 69).

In *Gender and Jim Crow*, Glenda E. Gilmore (1996) observes how Jeanes teachers attempted to upend and exploit this ideological hegemony using it to the advantage of the Black community:

> While paying lip service to the ideal of producing servants for white people, black women quietly turned the philosophy into a self-help endeavor and the public schools into institutions resembling social settlement houses. Cooking courses became not only vocational classes but nutrition courses where students could eat hot meals. Sewing classes ...

had the advantage of clothing poor pupils so they could attend school more regularly.

(Gilmore, 1996, pp. 160–161)

Indeed, in a chapter entitled "Diplomatic Women," Gilmore argues that the Rosenwald Negro Rural School Fund gave Black teachers in the state of North Carolina "what they needed to incorporate social work into the public school system" (p. 161).

In North Carolina, where Jeanes teachers helped to build the largest number of Rosenwald schools in any state (412), Whites supported the program because they claimed it "yielded a more docile and less restless black population" (Abel, 2009, p. 35). Paradoxically, "the Rosenwald Fund rewarded Black self-help"—a kind of agency, with "white paternalism but discouraged notions of black entitlement" (Abel, 2009, p. 35). In fact, White officials assured the White community that "the colored people do not expect as much money shall be spent on their school as is spent on the white school" (p. 35). Less visible are examples of Jeanes teachers' tactful but vigorous "push-back" as demonstrated, for example, when Mrs. Marie McIver was appointed State Supervisor of Negro Elementary Schools in North Carolina. In 1937, she provided her White supervisor with her assessment of a primary reader that was being developed specifically for Black children. Mrs. McIver's critique of the text, entitled *Tobe*, which depicted Black tenant farming families in blatant "blackface" stereotypes, found its way into the final published version. Not only had she strongly objected to the representation that "tends to make *farm tenancy* ideal," she also noted: "I would like to call attention to the expression on the face of the father on page thirty-eight 'Daddy's Got a Watermelon'" (Abel, 2009, p. 33).

In her account of this example, Abel observes: "While showing respect for her boss, Mrs. McIver was also true to herself and the community she served" (p. 35). This tightrope was arguably much more manageable for Black women teachers than Black men (Fairclough, 2000). The overall stratagem was to use Northern philanthropy to compel local officials to allocate *some* funding for Black education within the limits of the Jim Crow legal framework and White control where none would otherwise have been made available because the power structure was engaged in maintaining manifestly separate and *un*equal conditions. As community activists, Jeanes teachers, community leaders, pastors, and other Black professionals joined with the grassroots Black community to extract at least some benefits from the system. They did this while transgressing the narrow confines of the type of education provided by the Jeanes program and the Rosenwald Negro Rural Schools Fund. Abel (2009) describes what the Jeanes teachers knew that enabled them to breach these parameters in the rural schools of Durham, North Carolina:

When teaching subjects that whites considered industrial education, the Jeanes teachers knew that they were improving the lives of their students and their communities. Canning clubs would again become very important sources of food during the Great Depression. The Jeanes teachers knew that this sort of vocational education was not going to lead to jobs in the industrializing South, but they played along with the white Northern funders and state education officials who still believed it was the best sort of education for African Americans. For Durham's Jeanes teachers, vocational education was not emphasized.

(Abel, 2009, pp. 117–118)

The Jeanes teachers also held the rural teachers they supervised to high standards, while encouraging them to attain more education—which was another way to undermine the edifice of black inferiority upon which the system of Jim Crow mis-education was constructed. By the 1930s, "industrial education gradually gave way to a more academic emphasis by Jeanes Supervisors" (Noland, n.d.). That their agency and various forms of resistance were impactful is evident, even though it was not in line with the official purpose of the Jeanes Fund. In 1931, President of the Jeanes Fund Henry Dillard advised Black teachers to "teach academics selectively and not to abandon plain, humble handiwork" because children "study words too much, and words cause thoughts and thoughts are what is troubling the world today" (Thuesen, 2013, p. 53). The examples in the following sub-section further illustrate "troubling thoughts" (for White people) as seen in the values and ethical principles that Jeanes teachers reclaimed from Black cultural heritage, which sustained them in the struggle for right action through an emancipatory praxis of Teaching *for* Freedom that brought benefit to oppressed Black people on behalf of justice in the world.

Reclamation of Cultural Heritage: In Their Own Words

An oral history and an autobiography of two college-educated Jeanes teachers who supervised rural segregated schools in North and South Carolina in the 1940s and 1950s present compelling examples—in their own words—of Black cultural heritage and the African worldview elements they consciously reclaimed and embodied to aid them in their work. Among these elements are their faith in God, which allowed them to transcend feelings of hate and anger, and their close identification with the Black community, including the poor, which can be understood philosophically in terms of the African ontology of *Odù*, "gathering together in harmony," and the epistemology of *Ubuntu*, or "I am because we are and because we are, therefore I am" (Mbiti, 1990; Nobles, 1973). Related elements involve affirming their humanity and ethical consciousness.

As these Jeanes teachers described the anguish and anger they felt when attempting to respond to grossly unjust educational conditions the teachers and students experienced in the schools they supervised, their recollections demonstrate these four examples of reclaiming Black cultural heritage: (1) they consciously called upon their faith and prayed to God to help them maintain their own humanity and (2) they relied upon close relations and organizing networks within the Black community—securing the active engagement of even the most impoverished parents and community members and partnering with other Black professionals and community leaders. Thus, being college-educated was not a barrier that set them apart from poor parents and they used their social standing to gain access to arenas of power and influence, which they used for the benefit of the community. Further, as their testimony reveals, (3) consciously re-affirming their own humanity in dehumanizing situations also enabled them to seek out and garner assistance from sympathetic White people. In addition, (4) demonstrating ethical consciousness, consistent with the ideals of *Maat*, for example, enabled them to embody the African American cultural legacy of justice as a standard that fosters community well-being. Each of these Black cultural heritage and African worldview elements helped these Jeanes teachers to persevere.

Mrs. Lucy Saunders Herring was born into a family of 12 children in 1900 in Union, South Carolina, where she had limited education opportunities. Eventually, earning a master's degree at the University of Chicago, Mrs. Herring's career as a teacher, principal, education consultant, reading specialist, and award-winning Jeanes supervisor in Harnett County, North Carolina spanned 52 years (Krause, 2005). She started teaching in Ashville in a one-room schoolhouse at age 16. She died in 1995. Dr. Lela Haynes Session was also born in South Carolina, in the town of Moncks Corner, in 1921; she died in 2013. Dr. Session was appointed as a Jeanes teacher in Berkeley County, South Carolina from 1952–1959. Her outstanding career of leadership in education, her church, and civic activities were recognized with a tribute that U.S. Representative James E. Clyburn entered into the *Congressional Record* on July 25, 1995 (p. E1508). Mrs. Lucy Herring's experience recorded in an oral history interview (Herring, 1977/2001) is presented first, followed by excerpts from Mrs. Lela Haynes Session's autobiography (Session, 2012).

Lucy Saunders Herring

Whenever there was an old bus replaced, it went to the black kids, and the white kids got the new [one]. And the same thing was true of equipment; [we got] desks after ... the white kids would have them and cut them up. Well, our people got them; so, we were accustomed to this kind of second-hand thing.... It was painful in Harnett County to see white kids riding to consolidated schools on nice yellow buses, and black kids walking to school long distances, and most of them going to cotton fields when they should have been in school because they were tenant farmers and they had no choice. The landlord had charge, and if they stayed on the farms, they had to work. So many of these kids would ride to the fields, cotton fields and tobacco fields on wagons, and the white kids were going to school in nice yellow buses. But that's the thing you tolerated and worked to improve, and asked God to help you, you know, to make it, to make conditions better.

. . .

You didn't feel good over it, but you couldn't afford to lose your mind over it, you know what I mean? So, quite often you prayed over it to keep from losing your temper and from climbing the wall, and that's the way we maintained our sanity by not letting ourselves become too emotionally disturbed. We could just pray over that. That has been the salvation of the black man: to pray over a thing, and just work and wait!

. . .

I describe all of this, you see. About the struggle that the black people have had to get an education. It has been a very rugged path, but there is something about the black person that is of this kind of endurance; maybe it's a part that our forebears passed on to us, this matter of bearing the burden, of being patient and working on, but still hoping and never giving up, never despairing of the fact that you will eventually reach your goal.... But it's a struggle that I guess you just become—you're not totally immune to it, but you become reconciled to the fact that God is not dead and things will eventually change, and it's that kind of hope, you see, that's helped us to go on.

(Herring, July 26, 1977 [2001])

Lela Haynes Session

Some barns were converted into schools ... with unpleasant odors from the animals at times. Some of the schools were rooms in churches and individual homes. The majority of the buildings had no water supply ... outside toilets were used.

(Session, 2012, p. 69)

My work as a Jeanes teacher/social worker included finding clothing for the children and medical supplies...

(p. 72)

Some of the teachers had thirty students from grades elementary to high school in one room.

(p. 74)

Starting their day off with devotion, prayer, scripture, and the pledge of allegiance to the flag were great therapeutic techniques to cope with the situation and hope it will change.

(p. 74)

Dr. Lela H. Session also co-signed loans with the local bank for fathers who were employed cutting trees in the lumber industry but, during rainy weather, they could not work. Her financial intervention, trusting the families to pay these debts, made it possible for children to continue to come to school. Also, Dr. Session acknowledged that she did not experience these conditions in her own personal life—she attended private school and she admitted she "never knew the real picture of education in South Carolina" (p. 69). In the passage below, she shared how confronting these conditions affected her and what she had to overcome to be effective.

> The first and most important hurdle I had to overcome was my personal anger, disbelief, hurt, and feelings of prejudice mounting within me. These strong feelings of prejudice inside of me frighten me. I did not want to hate. But the conditions that the students and teachers had to cope with made me furious at the governor, senators, congressmen and school officials in Berkeley County [and] the President of the United States and everyone who was associated with funding and making decisions about education. I was irate that black people were not voting in mass crowd[s] and had a little voice in government. I made up my mind I had to get involved on a larger scale by getting involved in the politics of education.... Flashbacks of [my] mother's words and sacrifices danced in my head concerning education. I just gave thanks to a kind and loving Savior who still had me in the palm of His hand.... I prayed and asked Him to help me not to have hate in my heart and not to let the conditions of my people cloud my judgments to classify all white as enemies.... I ask my Father in heaven to help me not to blame people as a race but be aware of the state of mind of an individual. My prayer was to use my strength and wisdom to find solutions and not a moment complaining. These are times you are glad for your favorite scriptures or bible stories to rely upon for comfort. I know that once my emotional health was in control and I had a healthy perspective of myself, there was nothing stopping me from successfully helping mankind.
>
> (pp. 69–70)

Mrs. Lucy Herring likewise emphasized the power of faith and prayer to bolster her effectiveness in the struggle and her ability to persevere:

> You've got to have faith; you've got to have a vision. You have to have patience; you have to be tolerant. And my one prayer has been that I would never hate anybody or anything because that is the thing that will tear you apart. When you start hating, that's the time you start destroying your effectiveness.
>
> (Herring, July 26, 1977 [2001])

Odù/Ubuntu/*Ethical Consciousness*

The way Mrs. Lucy Herring responded to ethical challenges that she encountered with both her White supervisor and members of the "Negro school committee" that she had to work with further demonstrates her commitment to bringing goodness and well-being to the communities where she labored. Upholding a standard of excellence in spite of possible risks to her own position, she described how she responded when the Superintendent indicated that he wanted her to terminate and replace teachers who did not hold a state certificate. Instead she used her Black professional network to develop an in-service training program that included extension courses and summer school opportunities with instructors coming from a nearby HBCU. Mrs. Herring stated what she told the Superintendent:

> I'm not concerned with trying to replace people so much as I am to lift people and to improve the teachers. Some of them, although they don't have degrees, they are doing a good job, and I know it.... Some of these teachers probably, although they have not gone beyond the ninth grade, have good backgrounds in the basic skills, and with assistance they could develop into very, very good teachers.
>
> (Herring, August 2, 1977 [2001])

Her explanation seemed to convince the Superintendent and she explained the results of her approach:

> So the point is ... we got some teachers to go back to school, the young ones who had just finished the high school which was the ninth grade, and the standards were not very high. We got them to go back to school; some went to Fayetteville College, and they did work that was really below the high school level. Many went back and went through in-service training.
>
> (Herring, August 2, 1977 [2001])

Mrs. Herring also recognized a systemic inequity related to teacher certification that particularly disadvantaged Black teachers with respect to the problem of "substandard" and temporary certification:

> In Fayetteville, which is in Cumberland County, a much more prosperous county than Harnett, the superintendent there reportedly hired mostly black substandard teachers in order to avoid paying big salaries, but the white teachers were paid a different salary. And they would take white teachers with State certificates, but they took very few black teachers with State certificates because they didn't want to pay them that salary.
>
> (Herring, August 2, 1977 [2001])

Mrs. Herring's commitment to many of the African worldview elements evident in the *Odù Ifá* can be seen in her ways of being and knowing, values, principles, and virtues that are part of the Diasporan African legacy (see Chapter 1). Survival of the Group, Harmony, community-mindedness, Justice, and Faith (see Figure 1.1 in Chapter 1) are evident in her response to the ethical implications of a challenge to this worldview: A school committeeman offered her $50 to place a person that he wanted hired into a teaching position (Herring, August 2, 1977 [2001]). It was the responsibility of three-man Trustees or "Negro Advisory Committees" to recommend teachers to be hired by the County Superintendent. (See "The Jeanes Teachers: The Women Who Ran the Schools," http://durhamcountylibrary.org/exhibits/jeanes/teachers.php, Note 12.) The *Maatian* Virtue of Propriety in Mrs. Herring's response demonstrated her worldview; it was tactful but uncompromising:

> "I'm sorry sir. I don't operate like that! No, you can't pay me anything! You couldn't pay me a $1,000! (I knew she wasn't qualified). The superintendent has told me to get qualified teachers—to recommend qualified teachers. I have recommended a qualified teacher for that place.... I would never take any kind of money for any kind of service! That would be dishonest!"
>
> (Herring, August 2, 1977 [2001])

Dr. Session also emphasized the importance of the community for her teachers' effectiveness and a lack of such ethical consciousness on behalf of *Ubuntu* ("I am because we are") would have undermined this important cultural legacy: "The teachers were well respected in the communities. Most lived in the community where they taught and had an invested interest in the community beyond the school activities. They had specific roles in the church as Sunday school teachers" (Session, 2012, p. 74).

In sum, these testimonies regarding Reclamation of Cultural Heritage illustrate Fairclough's observation about the importance of faith but also the need for organization, which these Jeanes teachers masterfully and wisely demonstrated: "The faith of women teachers sustained black schools and strengthened black communities at a time when white supremacy could not be directly challenged. But it would require organization, as well as faith, to bring about equality" (Fairclough, 2007, p. 263). The ongoing struggle of the Jeanes teachers is an integral part of the Black freedom struggle and was not only for equality of educational opportunity but for equality with cultural integrity that reflected elements of their African worldview.

The Legacy of Hope That's Helped Us To Go On

In this chapter, there are numerous examples of how Jeanes teachers "played along" with Northern industrial philanthropists and the local white supremacy power structure to take advantage of whatever opportunities could be extracted and used for the benefit of the Black community (Abel, 2009). In this sense, their "hope" represents an epistemic legacy—one that builds on knowing what is possible when people work together to develop community well-being and belonging. The Jeanes teachers' ontological communal focus on Survival of the Group, Collective Responsibility, and Interdependence should come as no surprise when the African Diasporan cultural legacy and the history of the Black freedom struggle are considered. Thus, this chapter also demonstrates the importance of using Continental and Diasporan thought- and practice-traditions as a *resource* in the explication of our experience (Rabaka, 2010). The "black thinking," or African worldview, in the emancipatory pedagogical approaches and activism of the Jeanes teachers has been underappreciated, while the cultural continuities these teachers embody are evident from the perspective of an Afrocentric theoretical analysis. This chapter identifies the ways of being, knowing, values, virtues, and principles that are consistently found in their work. The *Maatian* Virtues of Truth, Justice, Harmony, Balance, Order, Reciprocity, and Propriety are reflected in their community building and tenacious resistance bequeathed to the next generation as the battle against white supremacy and Jim Crow, which also included the scholarly activism of Carter G. Woodson and other "black thinking" intellectuals, evolved into the civil rights movement and took center stage out in the open. "Re-membering" the Jeanes teachers illuminates this legacy of "hope that's helped us to go on."

References

Abel, J. (2009). *Persistence and sacrifice: Durham County's African American community and Durham's Jeanes teachers build community schools, 1900–1930*. MA Thesis. Graduate School of Duke University. Durham, NC: Duke University.

Anderson, J. (1988). *The education of Blacks in the south: 1860–1935*. Chapel Hill, NC: University of North Carolina Press.

Berman, E. H. (1971). American influence on African education: The role of the Phelps-Stokes fund's education commissions. *The Comparative Education Review, 15*(2), 132–145.

Blackmon, D. A. (2008). *Slavery by another name: The re-enslavement of Black Americas from the Civil War to World War II*. New York, NY: Random House.

Butchart, R. E. (1988). Outthinking and outflanking the owners of the world. An historiography of the African American struggle for education. *History of Education Quarterly, 28*(3), 333–366.

Cecelski, D. S., & Tyson, T. B. (1998). *Democracy betrayed: The Wilmington race riot of 1898 and its legacy*. Chapel Hill, NC: University of North Carolina Press.

Chirhart, Ann S. (2013, August 6). Jeanes teachers. *New Georgia Encyclopedia*. Retrieved from www.georgiaencyclopedia.org/articles/education/jeanes-teachers.

Congressional Record (1995, July 25). Volume 141, Number 121, p. E1508.

Davidson, J. W. (2009). *"They say": Ida B. Wells and the reconstruction of race*. New York, NY: Oxford University Press.

Delany, S. L., & Delany, A. E. (1993). *Having our say: The Delany sisters' first 100 years.* New York, NY: Random House.

Du Bois, W. E. B. (1897). The conservation of races. *The American Negro Academy Occasional Papers, 2,* 1–15.

Du Bois, W. E. B. (1935/1972). *Black reconstruction in America.* New York, NY: Atheneum.

Du Bois, W. E. Burghardt, & Dill, Augustus Granville (1911). *The common school and the Negro American.* Atlanta, GA: The Atlanta University Press.

EIJ (Equal Justice Institute) (2015). *Lynchings in America. Summary Report.* Montgomery, AL: Author.

Fairclough, A. (2000). "Being in the field of education and also being a Negro ... seems ... tragic:" Black teachers in the Jim Crow South. *The Journal of American History, 87*(1), 65–91.

Fairclough, A. (2007). *A class of their own: Black teachers in the segregated south.* Cambridge, MA: Harvard University Press.

Franklin, V. P. (2011). Transnational education, collective cultural capital, and Opportunities Industrialization Centers International. *The Journal of African American History, 96*(1), 44–61.

Frederickson, G. M. (1995). *Black liberation: A comparative history of Black ideologies in the United States and South Africa.* New York, NY: Oxford University Press.

Fultz, M. (1995, Spring). Teacher training and African American education in the South, 1900–1940. *Journal of Negro Education, 64*(2), 196–210.

Gilmore, G. E. (1996). *Gender and Jim Crow: Women and the politics of white supremacy in North Carolina, 1896–1920.* Chapel Hill, NC: University of North Carolina Press.

Goggin, J. (1993). *Carter G. Woodson: A life in Black history.* Baton Rouge, LA: Louisiana State University Press.

Greene, L. J. (1996). *Selling Black history for Carter G. Woodson: A diary 1930–1933.* Columbia, MO: University of Missouri.

Harris, N. J., & Taylor, D. (1999). *African-American education in Dekalb County.* Charleston, SC: Arcadia Press.

Herring, L. S. (2001). *Lucy S. Herring oral history.* Heritage of Black Highlanders Collection. D.H. Ramsey Library. Special Collections. University of North Carolina. Retrieved from http://toto.lib.unca.edu/findingaids/oralhistory/SHRC/herring_lucy.html.

Hine, D. C. (1986, May). Carter G. Woodson, White philanthropy and Negro historiography. *The History Teacher, 19*(3), 405–425.

Jones, L. (1937). *The Jeanes teacher in the United States, 1908–1933.* Chapel Hill, NC: University of North Carolina Press.

Krause, B. J. (2005, April). "We did move mountains!" Lucy Saunders Herring, North Carolina Jeanes Supervisor and African American educator. *The North Carolina Historical Review, 80*(2), 188–212.

Leloudis, J. L. (1996). *Schooling for the new South: Pedagogy, self and, and society in North Carolina, 1880–1920.* Chapel Hill, NC: University of North Carolina Press.

Lemert, C., & Bahn, E. (1998). *The voice of Anna Julia Cooper: Including A Voice from the South and other important essays, papers, and letters.* Lanham, MD: Rowman and Littlefield Publishers.

Littlefield, V. W. (1999). "To do the next needed thing": Jeanes teachers in the southern United States 1908–1934. In K. Weiler & S. Middleton (Eds.), *Telling women's lives* (pp. 130–145). Philadelphia: Open University Press.

Mbiti, J.S. (1990). *African religions and philosophy* (2nd ed.). Portsmouth, NW: Heinemann Educational Books.

McClure, P. (2009). *Jeanes teachers: A view into Black education in the Jim Crow South.* Lexington, KY: Phyllis McClure.

Muhammad, K. G. (2010). *The condemnation of blackness: Race, crime, and the making of modern urban America.* Cambridge, MA: Harvard University Press.

National Registry of Historic Places (2008). *The Rosenwald School Building Program in South Carolina, 1917–1932.* Retrieved from www.nationalregister.sc.gov/MPS/MPS050.pdf.

Nobles, W. (1973). Psychological research and the Black self-concept: A critical review. *Journal of Social Issues, 29*(1), 11–31.

Noland, J. (n.d.). Jeanes supervisors. *The Encyclopedia of Alabama.* Retrieved from www.encyclopediaofalabama.org/article/h-2327.

Norrell, R. J. (2005). *The house I live in: Race in the American century.* New York, NY: Oxford University Press.

Pincham, L. B. (2005). A league of willing workers: The impact of northern philanthropy, Virginia Estelle Randolph and the Jeanes teachers in early twentieth-century Virginia. *Journal of Negro Education, 74*(2), 112–123.

Rabaka, R. (2010). *Against epistemic apartheid: W. E. B. Du Bois and the disciplinary decadence of sociology.* Lanham, MD: Rowman and Littlefield.

Riley, K. L. (2002). "A toilet in the middle of the court house square": The Summer Teaching Institute of 1915 and the influence of Booker T. Washington on Negro teacher education in Alabama. *Education and Culture, 28*(1), 2–9.

Rupert, A. (n.d.). Delany, Henry Beard, (1858–1928). *Blackpast.org.* Retrieved from www.blackpast.org/aah/delany-henry-beard-1858-1928.

Session, L. H. (2012). *Unconditional love.* Bloomington, IN: ArthorHouse.

Smith, A. B. (1997). *Forgotten foundations: The role of Jeanes teachers in Black education.* New York, NY: Vantage Press.

The Artishia and Frederick Jordan Scholarship Fund. (n.d.). *Carrie Thomas Jordan, 1870–1968.* Retrieved from www.jordanscholarship.org/about/history/carrie-thomas-jordan.

Thuesen, S. C. (2013). *Greater than equal: African American struggles for schools and citizenship in North Carolina, 1919–1965.* Chapel Hill, NC: University of North Carolina Press.

Tillman, L. C. (2004). (Un)Intended consequences? The impact of the Brown v. Board of Education Decision on the employment status of Black educators. *Education and Urban Society, 36*(3), 280–303.

Watkins, W. (2001). *White architects of Black education: Ideology and power in America, 1865–1954.* New York, NY: Teachers College Press.

Williams, M. (1981). The Jeanes story: A chapter in the history of American education, 1908–1968. *The Journal of Negro History, 66*(1), 149–151.

Williams, V. (2006). Monroe N. Work's contribution to Booker T. Washington's fight against white supremacy. In G. Cunnigen, R. M. Dennis, & M. G. Glascoe (Eds.), *The racial politics of Booker T. Washington* (pp. 133–148). Oxford, UK: Elsevier.

Woodson, C. G. (1922). *The Negro in our history.* Washington, DC: Associated Publishers.

Woodson, C. G. (1933/1990). *The mis-education of the Negro.* Trenton, NJ: Africa World Press.

5

"RE-MEMBERING" CULTURAL CONCEPTS

> By dialoguing with African culture, I mean constantly asking it questions and seeking from it answers to the fundamental concerns of humankind. Moreover, it is to continuously bring forth from this quest the best of what it means to be African and human in the fullest sense, speak this special cultural truth to the world, and use it to make a unique contribution to the forward flow of human history.
>
> Maulana Karenga, *Maat, the Moral Ideal in Ancient Egypt*, 2006a, p. 409

Worldview and cultural concepts are evident in what we do. While both are discussed in each preceding chapter, the idea of their presence in what we do and how we live our lives is exemplified in Chapters 3 and 4 through the lives of Harriet Tubman and the Jeanes teachers. These historical figures demonstrated numerous elements of African worldview (e.g., Collectivity, Interdependence, relational knowing, community mindedness, Reciprocity, Self-Determination) and embodied African cultural concepts such as *the inherent right of freedom, exhibiting self-determination that considers the needs of the collective*, and *demonstrating concern for human welfare through actions based on community mindedness and service to others* (Anyanwu, 1981a; Bennett, 1975; Gyeke, 1997; Karenga, 2006b; King & Swartz, 2014). The cultural concepts they embodied—which are consistently held patterns of thought and observable manifestations and expressions of their African worldview—brought change into a world that was out of order and out of balance through centuries of enslavement, denial of opportunities, and exploitation of one segment of the population by another. In this chapter, we explain and exemplify not only how the divergent worldviews and cultural concepts people hold have informed and shaped historical events, but how they have informed and shaped (and can shape) the ways in which we teach about those events. When practitioners of Teaching *for* Freedom invite students to gain knowledge through the lens of cultural concepts, all events and actions become more than mere historical occurrences; they are made meaningful by teaching that illuminates the worldviews and cultural concepts of the people involved and how they lived their lives. Since these concepts endure across time and place, teachers can guide students to use them in the present. Then, learning about Harriet Tubman, the Jeanes teachers, and other people and events becomes a way for teachers, students, and families to experience cultural continuity by using cultural concepts in their own communities, such as *sharing responsibility for communal well-being and belonging* and *pursuing freedom and justice as communal responsibilities*. As Mutombo Nkulu-N'Sengha (2005) states: "The ontological and cosmological dimensions of African knowledge imply also that knowledge is not a mere language game or a pure dialectical entertainment. Knowledge is active. Indeed, it is action!" (p. 43). The Afrocentric praxis of Teaching *for* Freedom incorporates this idea of knowledge as action by modeling how to engage teachers, students, and families with democratized content and emancipatory pedagogies that recognize culture as an interactive medium in which worldview and cultural concepts that have steadily informed and shaped people's actions in the past can be used to shape people's actions in the present.

Cultural Concepts: Disconnected or "Re-membered"

Compared to Teaching *for* Freedom, the fate of cultural concepts is different in mainstream schooling. There, cultural concepts—if they are acknowledged at all—are disconnected from content and pedagogy, and what and how we teach appears universal as if conceived outside of culture. For example, cultural concepts such as *competition as essential to making progress, achievement understood as excelling above others*, and *expecting and accepting a certain amount of student failure* are rarely acknowledged as the consistently held patterns of thought that shaped and maintain the school practices of assessing what is taught with high-stakes standardized testing and tracking students based on test results (Au, 2009; Hilliard, 1989, 1997; Kumashiro, 2008; Meier, 1994). Thus, these cultural concepts—which are observable manifestations and expressions of a European worldview in which Competition and Survival of the Fittest are predominant ways of being—are decoupled from the educational practices they have shaped (Akbar, 1984; Dixon, 1971; Nobles, 1976). Teachers transmit content, students compete for "right" answers, and it is accepted that some students will fail as if these practices are normal and inevitable. However, these practices are not normal or inevitable; they were shaped by cultural concepts that express a particular worldview. Developed and refined over time, their impact on mainstream schooling affects all of our children. Yet, these omnipresent cultural concepts and their links to educational practices are virtually invisible—like the air we breathe.

There are, of course, from within different worldview perspectives, other ways to view knowledge and knowing, which as we will show in this chapter have implications for what and how we teach. Cultural concepts such as *knowing as a communal experience in which everyone has something to contribute* and *inquiring (the acknowledgment of not knowing) as a source of true knowledge* are observable manifestations of an African worldview in which Collectivity, Cooperation, relational knowing, and symbolic imagery (use of proverbs, gestures, rhythms, metaphors, and affect) are predominant ways of being (Akbar, 1984; Dixon, 1971, 1976; Fu-Kiau, 2001; Nobles, 1976; Nkulu-N'Sengha, 2005). These cultural concepts—and the content and pedagogies they shape—are absent in mainstream schooling due to the devaluation of all things African (Asante, 2007). Thus, whether invisible due to being omnipresent or to being devalued, cultural concepts are disconnected from mainstream educational practices, which makes the meaning of these practices difficult to identify and changing them even more difficult.

When teachers use cultural concepts to "re-member" content and pedagogy—that is, when culture becomes a medium for interaction around what knowledge and teaching mean—the school experience can produce cultural continuity for all groups of students. Such cultural continuity does not currently exist. For example, teaching about African people in the Americas typically begins with enslavement. Yet, when students are taught about European people in the Americas, they learn, with increasing depth over the years, about the history and heritage that Europeans brought with them to the Americas. The history of European people does not begin with the late 15th century arrival of the Spaniards in the Caribbean or with the arrival of Portuguese, Dutch, British, French, or any other Europeans. While the worldview and cultural concepts underlying this narrative of European history and heritage are typically not acknowledged and are therefore invisible, and while this narrative is sanitized due to omissions and distortions, learning about Europeans in the Americas does involve some degree of continuity across time and place. However, in mainstream content, there is no similar experience of African Diasporan cultural continuity, which can only happen if students learn, with increasing depth over the years, about the history and heritage that African Peoples brought with them (see King & Swartz, 2014, p. 53, for a detailed explanation of the use and capping of "Nations" and "Peoples"). Their history also does not begin in the Americas, with the kidnapping and forced deportation of Kôngo, Akan, Igbo, Yoruba, Fon, Hausa people or people from other African Nations to the Americas—or even with the much earlier pre-Columbian African presence (Diop, 1967; Hall, 2005; Hayes, 2008; Van Sertima, 1976; Wiener, 1922). Nor does African people's history begin with the presence of free African people in Europe (Freeman, 2005; Horne 2014). The history of African people begins with humanity's origins and thousands of years of African heritage and cultural production. If this knowledge were included in the curriculum, learning about

Africans in the Americas would also involve some continuity across time and place. With the devaluation of all things African, however, access is blocked to the worldview and cultural concepts that foster African Diasporan cultural continuity, which therefore remains limited and in most classrooms non-existent. Yet, as we show in this chapter and Chapter 6, cultural concepts can be identified in the actions of African people and their descendants who brought concepts to the Americas such as *the inherent right of freedom, perceiving the interconnectedness of all life including the unseen world, the authentic authority of eldership*, and *knowing that cultural sovereignty is a common right of all Peoples*. When diverse cultural concepts are "re-membered" with content, that is, re-connected with the actions and events they shaped—and with the pedagogy used to teach about those actions and events—teachers and students can access meaning and experience cultural continuity that foster agency and action in *their* lives.

Dysconsciousness in the Anglosphere

In addition to blocking meaning and cultural continuity, obscuring the worldviews and cultural concepts that shape and maintain eurocratic school policies and practices produces a narrow cultural field that leads to dysconsciousness or uncritical habits of mind (King, 1991). From the colonial period to the present, European worldview and cultural concepts have shaped the content and pedagogical practices of public, private, and religious educational systems in the Anglosphere. This relationship between worldview, cultural concepts, content, and pedagogical practices, which we introduced above, is further developed in Figure 5.1 and the narrative that follows it.

Figure 5.1 presents some elements of European worldview, several cultural concepts, and mainstream content and pedagogical practices shaped and maintained by those worldview elements and cultural concepts. In this figure, European worldview includes Competition, Individualism (a way of being that raises the needs of individuals above the collective), excessive reliance on the scientific method as authoritative knowledge, a hierarchy of human worth, and only the strong survive. Over time, people holding these worldview elements developed and manifested cultural concepts such as *valorizing individual versus group identity, teaching as the transmission of agreed-upon information, achievement understood as excelling above others, expecting and accepting a certain amount of student failure, perceiving mistakes as negative and leading to loss*, and *distributing resources by status/rank* (Akbar, 1984; Baldwin & Hopkins, 1990; Boykin, 1986; Dixon, 1971; Kliewer & Fitzgerald, 2001). In turn, these cultural concepts shape and maintain content and pedagogical practices, such as sanitized eurocratic content, transmission pedagogy, standardized assessments, and a hierarchal system of tracking (Au, 2009; Meier, 1994; Swartz, 2007, 2012). These practices require individual students to compete with each other by taking in and successfully (more than others) giving back agreed-upon information and ideas that are transmitted to them by authorities (e.g.,

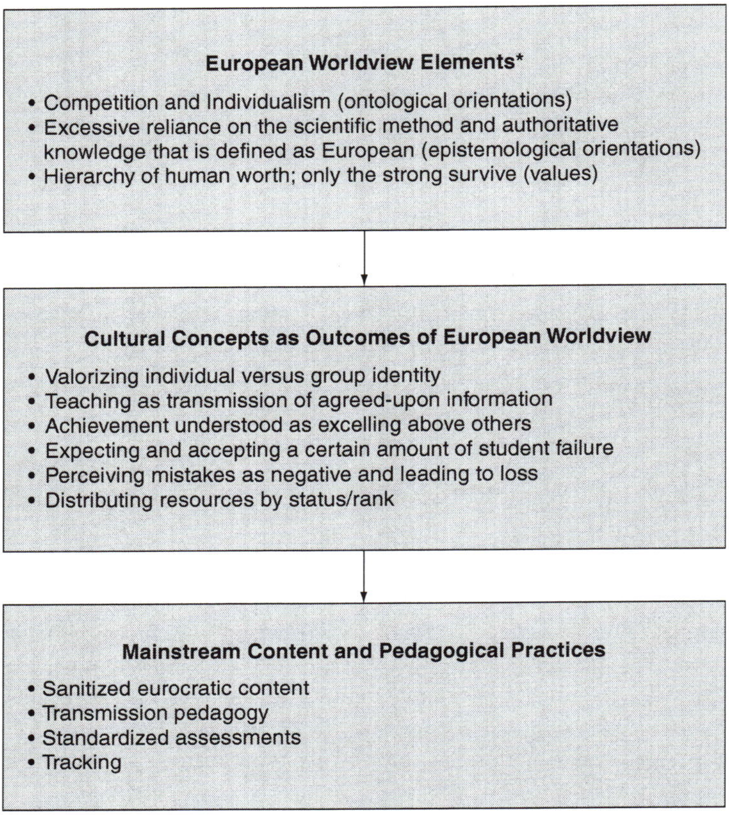

European Worldview Elements*

- Competition and Individualism (ontological orientations)
- Excessive reliance on the scientific method and authoritative knowledge that is defined as European (epistemological orientations)
- Hierarchy of human worth; only the strong survive (values)

Cultural Concepts as Outcomes of European Worldview

- Valorizing individual versus group identity
- Teaching as transmission of agreed-upon information
- Achievement understood as excelling above others
- Expecting and accepting a certain amount of student failure
- Perceiving mistakes as negative and leading to loss
- Distributing resources by status/rank

Mainstream Content and Pedagogical Practices

- Sanitized eurocratic content
- Transmission pedagogy
- Standardized assessments
- Tracking

FIGURE 5.1 European Worldview, Cultural Concepts, and School Practices.

Note
* Worldview is a cultural framework that endures across time and influences everything that people who share a cultural heritage produce.

teachers, texts, state standards). Each student's individual worth is then measured by statistically driven standardized assessments (constructed and justified through the scientific method) that are based on the ubiquitous bell curve, which concurrently "requires" and explains poor performance, guarantees failure, and claims to represent natural laws of distribution that do not exist (Fendler & Muzaffar, 2008; Oakes, Wells, Jones, & Datnow, 1997). These high stakes assessments sort students in a system of tracking, with the "best" students valued as worthy of receiving more educational benefits (e.g., higher expectations, advanced/enriched curricula, opportunities for critical thinking and active learning). Achievement outcomes on these assessments are claimed to be the result of individual effort, even though student scores are predicted by race and class (Au, 2009; Berliner & Biddle, 1995; Oakes, 1985). Standardized assessments and tracking—even though they distribute educational benefits unequally—are dysconsciously viewed as reasonable by many educators and the public, since they are based on culturally embedded assumptions that transmitting information is an effective way to learn, that a certain amount of student failure is to be expected (and therefore accepted), that achievement and progress require excelling above others, and that sorting and tracking students into a performance hierarchy mirrors the supposed "natural" bell curve of intelligence.

Within this worldview—and its related cultural concepts—let's look at an example of curricular content and how it is taught. In 1898, the U.S. annexed Hawaii, which occurred against the will of its people and its leaders who resisted in defense of their sovereignty (Liliuokalani, 1898; Schamel & Schamel, 1999). The actions of U.S. leaders were informed by their worldview that included Survival of the Fittest (ontological orientation), excessive reliance of authority (epistemology), and might makes right (value) as seen in the cultural concepts they embodied, such as *viewing cultural sovereignty as only the right of "advanced" cultures* (the fittest) and *gaining imperial possessions* (through the use of authority and might) *as descriptive and determinant of a country's worth* (Akbar, 1984; Nobles, 1976; P. J. Williams, 1991; W. A. Williams, 2007/1980).

Transmission pedagogy is typically used to teach content about the annexation of Hawaii (and other social studies topics) in preparation for standardized and other assessments that compare students with each other. These assessments are competitions that view progress as increasing the number of students who excel (above others). However, since standardized, norm referenced assessments (which are now attached to most subject areas and grade levels) are designed to produce a certain amount of failure (bell curve), there is a limit on the expected amount of excellence—and therefore a limit on teachers' expectations. In terms of content, notice that the sanitized agreed-upon state knowledge about the annexation of Hawaii—as seen in standardized state assessments—mirrors the same worldview and cultural concepts exhibited in the annexation itself. One New York State Regents exam referred to the annexation as imperialism, yet in no way contested it, thereby presenting U.S. imperialism as an acceptable way of interacting with other sovereign Nations (NYS Board of Regents, 2006). Another New York State Regents exam asked students to describe the historical circumstances that led the United States to expand by acquiring two territories (suggested territories are Ohio River valley, Louisiana Territory, Florida, Texas, Oregon Territory, California, Alaska, Hawaii, and Puerto Rico), and to "discuss the *positive **and/or** negative* effects of these acquisitions on the United States" (NYS Board of Regents, 2014, p. 11). Stating that 1) there is something positive about taking over other People's sovereign Nations; 2) referring to sovereign lands as territories—which implies empty land devoid of Nations, with their social, political, and economic structures; and 3) the absence of asking about the effects of these "acquisitions" on Hawaii or other "acquired" territories reproduce the value of might makes right and assumes that only "advanced" cultures like the United States (the fittest) have the right to cultural sovereignty. Imperial actions presented as a way of "expanding" territory, and state assessments and transmission pedagogy that echo a might makes right worldview are all rendered normative by reflecting the ubiquitous yet invisible European worldview and cultural concepts that shaped and maintain them.

Together, mainstream content and pedagogical practices have resulted in a school experience of programmed dysconsciousness or uncritical habits of mind (King, 1991). After 12 or more years of this programming, most students accept as normative and given such societal practices and outcomes as the pursuit of unlimited wealth, past and present economic exploitation, and vast inequalities in income and health care; U.S. imperialism and political, economic, and military intervention in other countries; environmental abuse and poisoned air, water, and food supplies; a linear view of progress that obscures or marginalizes knowledge and achievements preceding the rise of the Western world; the privatization of public spaces, including schools; and ongoing wars, surveillance, mass incarceration, and state violence in the name of national security (Alexander, 2012; Ayers, 2014; Bittman, 2012; Bullard & Wright, 2012; Chomsky, 2013a & b; Davis, 2014; Engelhardt, 2015; Hedges, 2014; King & Akua, 2012; Klein, 2014; Mills, 1997; Parry, 2014; Pierce, 2014; Ravitch, 2013; Waln, 2014).

Widening the Cultural Field

In response to the culturally skewed character of content and pedagogy—and the dysconsciousness they produce in U.S. schools and in the general society—we suggest drawing worldview elements and cultural concepts from beyond the Anglosphere. Let's look at two examples, one related to education and the other related to the environment. In the United States, educators have advocated the practice of cooperative learning and environmentalists have advocated an end to the irresponsible extraction of fossil fuels and other natural resources—the former to reap the benefits of communal learning and the latter to reduce harm to life on the planet (Johnson & Johnson, 1985; Klein, 2010, 2014; Slavin, 1983, 1987). However, the support needed to make such practices effective does not exist in the European worldview that predominates in the societies where these educators and activists labor. In fact, the success of cooperative learning and environmental well-being is compromised by this worldview, with its ontological orientations of Competition and Domination over Nature, epistemological orientation of excessive reliance on authority, and a value such as only the strong survive. Over time, people holding these worldview elements have manifested and expressed them through cultural concepts (e.g., *competition as essential to making progress; nature as hostile, alien, and needing to be controlled*) that in turn shape and maintain isolated learning and destructive environmental practices.

Traditional African and Indigenous worldview elements and cultural concepts would better support the above changes sought by educators and environmentalists (Cajete, 1994; Dixon, 1971; Hall, 1994; Karenga, 1999, 2006b; Simpson, 2011). These elements include 1) ontological orientations such as Collectivity (the well-being of the group supersedes the needs of individuals who benefit *because* the group benefits), Wholeness (all life viewed as one interconnected phenomenon), Interdependence (self is constructed in the context of reciprocal interactions with others), and Harmony (a natural rhythm and movement that exists among all living things); 2) epistemological orientations such as relational knowing (learning from reciprocal interactions), symbolic imagery, and intuition-reasoning (learning from heart-mind knowledge, which are together not separate); and 3) values such as community mindedness, equanimity, and right action (Abímbólá, 1976a; Anyanwu, 1981a & b; Boykin, 1986; Cajete, 1994; Dixon, 1971, 1976; Gyekye, 1987; Ikuenobe, 2006; Mohawk, 1993; Nkulu-N'Sengha, 2005; Nobles, 1976; Shenandoah, 1988; Simpson, 2011). It follows that people holding a worldview that includes Collectivity, Cooperation, relational knowing, and community mindedness express this worldview through a cultural concept such as *knowing as a communal experience in which everyone has something to contribute*; and that this worldview and cultural concept would support an educational practice such as cooperative learning. Likewise, it follows that people holding a worldview that includes Harmony, Wholeness, intuition-reasoning, and equanimity express this worldview through a cultural concept such as *perceiving the interconnectedness of all life including the unseen world*; and that this worldview and cultural concept would support a movement attempting to protect the planet. However, in our current situation—with traditional African and Indigenous knowledge marginalized in the academic literature, virtually absent in school knowledge, including teacher preparation, and well below the radar in the knowledge base of most people— the worldview and cultural concepts that *could* transform school and other societal practices remain inaccessible at best and hidden or distorted at worst.

Cultural Concepts

We have already referred to a number of African cultural concepts in this chapter. Table 5.1 below lists these and other African cultural concepts discussed throughout this volume. This list, while partial, offers a number of concepts drawn from consistently held patterns of traditional African thought—practiced over centuries—that are alternatives to the cultural concepts that have produced and maintain the programmed school experience of dysconsciousness described above. The African cultural concepts listed in Table 5.1—and referred to throughout this volume—are known through their practice, since they have been consistently enacted and refined across time and location by African people in ways that express their worldview. In this sense, cultural concepts represent

TABLE 5.1 African Cultural Concepts*

1	*sharing responsibility for communal well-being and belonging*
2	*perceiving the interconnectedness of all life including the unseen world*
3	*the inherent right of freedom*
4	*the inherent worth of all humans*
5	*being responsible to bring good into the world through actions that are ethical, just, generous, compassionate, and peaceable*
6	*pursuing freedom and justice as communal responsibilities*
7	*pursuing knowledge as inseparable from pursuing wisdom*
8	*love, dignity, and decency as shared by all*
9	*the authentic authority of eldership*
10	*knowing as a communal experience in which everyone has something to contribute*
11	*inquiring (the acknowledgment of not knowing) as a source of true knowledge*
12	*knowing that cultural sovereignty is a common right of all peoples*
13	*exhibiting self-determination that considers the needs of the collective*
14	*gaining knowledge for the purpose of bringing goodness, harmony, and balance into the world*
15	*demonstrating concern for human welfare through actions based on community mindedness and service to others*
16	*sharing freedom as a human entitlement*
17	*protecting childhood as a collective responsibility (each child is everyone's child) and*
18	*viewing nature as whole and complementary (not contradictory), including the material and social worlds*

Notes

* See Abímbólá, 1976a; Anyanwu, 1981a & b; Aptheker, 1951/1969; Asante, 2009; Bennett, 1975; Boakye-Boaten, 2010; Fu-Kiau, 2001; Gyeke, 1987; Ikuenobe, 2006; Karenga, 1999, 2005, 2006a & b; Nkulu-N'Sengha, 2005; Senghor, 1964; Tedla, 1995; and Waghid, 2014.

an African mode of existence that is communal and recognized by African Diasporan people throughout the world.

Worldview: Central Tendencies of Cultural Groups

If educators are going to widen the cultural field by using cultural concepts from beyond the Anglosphere—such as those in Table 5.1—we need to understand how these concepts are related to specific conceptions of the world called worldview. Examining culture through the worldview of its members, however, has raised concerns by some scholars that to do so reifies and essentializes culture by ignoring individual and intra-cultural differences (Allwood, 2011; Davidheiser, 2008; Hwang, 2011). These concerns rightly exist given the well-documented deployment of categorical schema by Europeans and their descendants who—over the last several centuries—have essentialized race and culture by developing entire branches of science and using other disciplines to institutionalize overgeneralizations and stereotypes like viewing colonized and subjugated groups as less evolved and pathological and their oppressors as more advanced and virtuous (Blaut, 1993; Gould, 1981; Mills, 1997; Rodney, 1982; Shields, 2004; Wilder, 2013). Thus, discussing European, African, Indigenous, Asian, or other worldviews may be discomforting to those who read the discussion as a rigid and totalizing representation of cultures and world regions. The scholars of worldview we cite throughout this volume identify diverse worldview characteristics as consistently observed in cultural concepts and practices over time, but make no claim that these characteristics are held in common or to the same degree by all members of any culture or society or that they are biologically based. Instead they suggest that cultures have observable central tendencies, and that knowledge of these tendencies is useful in understanding the ideas, productions, and practices of specific cultures and world regions. One example may suffice.

The idea and phrase "survival of the fittest" originated in a European context. Englishman Herbert Spencer (1864) coined the phrase to further describe the concept of natural selection, which was part of the evolutionary theory presented by Charles Darwin (1859) (also an Englishman). This phrase was used later by Darwin (1869) in his fifth edition of *On the Origin of Species*. Survival of the fittest soon became an economic and biological construct—as well as a social theory, as seen in Social Darwinism—that since then has influenced the work of European and European-identified scientists and philosophers (Mills, 1997; Williams, 2000). In diverse disciplines, "survival of the fittest" has been used to describe the actions of individual members of a group or species competing to survive, that is, competing at the levels of individual and group fitness (von Sydow, 2014). Thus, it was in British thought and practice that an idea like "survival of the fittest" had resonance and took root, not in Yoruba or Haudenosaunee or Bântu-Kôngo or Lakota thought and practice. In these and other traditional African and Indigenous societies one is more likely to find an idea like Survival of the Group, in which the group is seen as the source of everyone's strength, with individual well-being depending on group survival. For example, in various African cultures, this way of being or ontological orientation is a central tendency aptly described by John Mbiti (1990) in this way: "I am, because we are; and since we are, therefore I am" (p. 106). As part of worldview, Survival of the Group is expressed in African and Indigenous cosmological assumptions, philosophies, and observable practices of communalism that are still evident today (Anyanwu, 1981b; Gyekye, 1987, 1998; Grande, 2004; Fayemi, 2009; Fu-Kiau, 2001; Simpson, 2011; Waghid, 2014).

Bear in mind that to identify varying worldview elements and cultural concepts in Ewe and Songhoy cultures or the continent of Africa, in Nishnaabeg and Cherokee cultures or the Indigenous continent of the Americas, or to do the same in Britain, Germany, or the continent of Europe, is a heuristic framework for exploring the central tendencies of those cultures and world regions. Worldview is a dynamic concept and individuals and intra-cultural groups are not bound by it—only to live and work in ways determined by the predominant worldview tendencies in their culture (Gyekye, 1997). We suggest that eurocratic (and eurocratic-thinking) scholars who continue to levy the charge of essentialism in order to deny the validity of identifying a group's shared worldview and cultural concepts have dysconsciously accepted European worldview elements and cultural concepts as given. Thus, Individualism (a way of being), excessive reliance on authority (a way of knowing), only the strong survive (a value), and *competition as essential to making progress* (a cultural concept) are simply normative within this worldview—as long as these worldview elements and cultural concepts go unnamed. Once named and viewed in comparison to African and Indigenous worldview and cultural concepts, eurocratic scholars (as self-proclaimed referees) cry an essentialist foul. Thus, attempts to understand cultural differences as more than idiosyncratic are rejected by those who dysconsciously accept a European worldview and cultural concepts as normative, not only for themselves and their descendants, but for all others.

All Worldviews Are Not the Same

The central tendencies of African and European worldviews—and the cultural concepts that are observable manifestations and expressions of each worldview—can be examined side-by-side, with each providing examples that fit its cultural context. However, that is where their equivalence ends. That which is African predates that which is European by millennia, which means that the former—while denigrated for the past 500 years by the latter—has a much longer trajectory of evolving its cultural concepts and practices (Akbar, 1984). For example, the African concept of *perceiving the interconnectedness of all life including the unseen world* (#2 in Table 5.1) is found in a trove of African philosophies, cosmologies, and spiritual practices that are thousands of years old (Abímbólá, 1976a & b; Anyanwu, 1981a & b; Karenga, 1999, 2006a & b). Only since the early to mid-20th century has "modern" science, in the form of quantum physics, proposed and sought to verify that all living things are an integrated whole—that there is an "unbroken wholeness of the totality of the universe" (including its observers) that forms a web of life sustained by nature (Bohm, 1980, 1989, 1990; Bohm & Hiley, 1975, p. 103; Capra, 1996, 2007; S. Goodwin, personal communication, November, 12, 2005; Wolf, 1981/1989, 2011). Maulana Karenga (2006b) describes the African cultural context from which *perceiving the interconnectedness of all life including the unseen world, sharing freedom as a human entitlement*, and other cultural concepts have evolved:

> It is Africans who stood up at the dawn of human history and spoke the first human truth, searching intently for the meaning and motion of things. It is they, too, who in the quest to understand what it is to be human first defined humans as bearers of divinity and dignity. Moreover,

it is Africans who first insisted on the interrelatedness and oneness of being, the sacredness of life, and the integrity of the environment. It is Africans who first advocated freedom for the oppressed, justice for the wronged and injured, and cooperative harvesting and sharing of the world's good for everyone.

(p. 248)

Thus, it is Africans who first developed these cultural concepts and introduced their outcomes to the world, which were either taken in part by others such as the Greeks who studied philosophy as well as advanced science and mathematics in Kemet or "rediscovered" later—as in quantum physics—through different epistemologies (Bernal, 1987; Diop, 1967, 1985; Hilliard, 1995). In either case, examining available knowledge with integrity makes accurate scholarship possible, which is necessary to identify sources that have long been obscured or denied. Our point here is that being the known source of a concept and practicing and refining it longer than others suggests that all worldviews and what they produce are not the same, that is, are not equivalent in the depth of knowledge they offer and the guidance they can provide to transforming educational systems.

Using Other Worldviews and Cultural Concepts

While we are presenting the praxis of Teaching *for* Freedom as a model based on African worldview, cosmologies, philosophies, and cultural concepts, this does not preclude other worldviews and what they provide from being used in this praxis. Vietnamese culture offers an example related to its concept of self and the relationship of self to others and the natural environment. In the Vietnamese language, there are several words for the personal pronoun "I"—each referring to one's relationship with others based on factors such as age, gender, status, kinship, formality, feelings, and attitude (Nguyễn Vũ Hoàng, 2009). For example, *tôi* ("I") is used in polite speech to establish a relationship of willingness to be of service to another; *tao* ("I") is used when talking to a family member; *ta* ("I") is used when the speaker has higher status; and *mình* ("I") is used in an intimate relationship, such as between a husband and wife (Berrigan & Nhat Hanh, 1975; Nguyễn Vũ Hoàng, 2009). In other words, there is a relational cultural concept within the Vietnamese language—one that guides individuals to establish their specific connection to others during communication. This reflects a worldview in which people are understood as interdependent, and a related cultural concept of *self as defined in relation to others*.

Similarly, in the Buddhist tradition, Thich Nhat Hanh (2001, 2008), who is a Zen Master, Vietnamese spiritual leader, peace activist, and author explains that there is no separation between oneself and the social or natural environment. In this volume's Chapter 2, Leopold Senghor (1964) explains the same concept of identifying "with the Other" (p. 73)—whether person or object—an experience of commonness and connection. Both men's worldview is informed by the ontological orientation of Wholeness in which all life is viewed as one interconnected phenomenon. Their cosmological assumption is that the world is complementary, without dualities or fixed opposites that separate each of us from what and who we observe and experience. Thich Nhat Hanh (2008) claims that "[t]he environment is you" (p. 17), meaning that there is a reciprocal relationship in which you create the environment and it creates you. Breathing in and breathing out is the way he describes how you are continuously in both places—how you are the environment and the environment is you. His call for mindfulness and a "collective change of consciousness" (2008, p. 20) to avoid planetary destruction draws upon Vietnamese cultural concepts in Buddhism such as *unconditional love for all beings* (Nhat Hanh, 2001, p. 69) and *the connection and continuity between all that exists and has existed*. The way in which the Vietnamese language conceptualizes our individual selves in relation to others and the ways in which Buddhist practice views human relations with the social and natural worlds suggest that Vietnamese culture offers cultural concepts that—when "re-membered" with democratized content and emancipatory pedagogies—can also be used to transform mainstream school practices.

Learning Through Heritage Knowledge and Cultural Knowledge

The Afrocentric praxis of Teaching *for* Freedom is an inclusive model of democratic praxis with the capacity to bring knowledge and examples of African as well as other People's cultures into the school experience. The worldviews and cultural concepts of each culture exist in the heritage knowledge or group memory of its members (Clarke, 1994; King, 2006). Thus, all cultures have heritage knowledge that "holds" cultural legacies and patterns that can inform what is taught and how it is taught. Let's return to Harriet Tubman for a moment, and take a closer look at how teachers and students can gain knowledge about the African worldview and cultural concepts at the foundation of her emancipatory actions. Her worldview included Collectivity, Collective Responsibility (contributing to the well-being of the group), community mindedness, and Justice, which shaped the cultural concepts she embodied (e.g., *the inherent right of freedom, pursuing freedom and justice as communal responsibilities, demonstrating concern for human welfare through actions based on community mindedness and service to others*). Tubman's worldview and cultural concepts, which were part of her heritage knowledge or group memory, were experienced and practiced by her ancestors (Ikuenobe, 2006; Gyekye, 1997; Karenga, 1999, 2006b). Her African Diasporan cultural community had developed and practiced philosophies of communalism, values of right action and equanimity, and cultural concepts such as those above as well as *sharing freedom as a human entitlement*, and *perceiving the interconnectedness of all life including* (ancestors in) *the unseen world*, which Tubman called upon during her numerous journeys to freedom and her role as an army scout (Anyanwu, 1981a & b; Fu-Kiau, 2001; Karenga, 2006b; Nkulu-N'Sengha, 2005).

Teachers can have access to students' heritage knowledge that includes the worldview, philosophies, cosmologies, and cultural concepts within their culture(s). As teachers and students learn about or recover content about historical figures, events, cultural concepts, and accomplishments within their families and cultural communities, this content expands their heritage knowledge. When teachers and students learn about the worldviews, philosophies, cosmologies, cultural concepts, and content of cultures other than their own, the knowledge they gain is called cultural knowledge. Thus, when students of African ancestry learn about Harriet Tubman they are building on and expanding their heritage knowledge, while other students are gaining cultural knowledge. The knowledge that all students gain is not only about what Tubman did, but about her worldview and the cultural concepts that are a foundation for her actions. Figure 5.2 below shows how African cultural concepts that informed Harriet Tubman's actions come from specific worldview elements; and how these worldview elements and cultural concepts shape the development of emancipatory pedagogies. Along with "re-membered" content, these emancipatory pedagogies expand some students' heritage knowledge and assist other students in gaining cultural knowledge. In this way, all students have access to the same worldview elements, cultural concepts, content, and pedagogies. While Figure 5.2 references African Diasporan culture and Harriet Tubman, it is applicable to any cultural group and topic. The figure is accompanied by a narrative that describes how emancipatory pedagogies are outcomes of African worldview elements and cultural concepts.

Let's follow the thread in Figure 5.2 related to the practice of emancipatory pedagogies. In terms of African worldview, the ontological orientation of Interdependence, the epistemological orientation of relational knowing, the values of equanimity and right action, the *Maatian* Virtue of Reciprocity, and the *Nguzo Saba* Principle of Self-Determination work together to maintain cultural concepts that view (1) *demonstrating concern for human welfare through actions based on community mindedness and service to others*; (2) *knowing as a communal experience in which everyone has something to contribute*; and (3) *inquiring (the acknowledgment of not knowing) as a source of true knowledge*. Teachers can use these African cultural concepts to shape and support specific emancipatory pedagogies to teach all students any topic. For example, teachers use the pedagogies called Locating Students, Question-Driven Pedagogy, and Culturally Authentic Assessment when they view knowledge as communal, inquiry as a source of true knowledge, and assessment as a way to involve students and families in real-world demonstrations of concern and service to their communities. These teachers understand that curriculum is co-created and builds on what students know (individually and culturally) as they reciprocally interact to name and define their ideas based

African Worldview Elements
(bearing influence on Harriet Tubman and on emancipatory pedagogies)

Ontology—e.g., Collective Responsibility, Interdependence
Epistemology—e.g., intuition-reasoning, relational knowing
Values—e.g., equanimity, right action
Virtues (*Maat*)—e.g., Justice, Reciprocity
Principles (*Nguzo Saba*)—e.g., Self-Determination, Purpose

African Cultural Concepts
(manifested in Tubman's actions and/or in emancipatory pedagogies)

- the inherent right of freedom
- pursuing freedom and justice as communal responsibilities
- the interconnectedness of all life including the unseen world
- demonstrating concern for human welfare through actions based on community-mindedness and service to others
- knowing as a communal experience in which everyone has something to contribute
- inquiring (the acknowledgment of not knowing) as source of true knowledge

Emancipatory Pedagogies
(practices used to teach all students)

- **Locating students** (students' cultures "hold" information that can center them in learning)
- **Question-driven pedagogy** (asking students thought-provoking questions that build on what they know)
- **Culturally authentic assessment** (asking students to demonstrate/perform knowledge based on standards—including community-informed standards—developed with parents to assess student learning)

Building on and Expanding Heritage Knowledge

- Group memory of **worldview elements** (e.g., Collective Responsibility, Interdependence)
- Knowing and/or learning about a related African **cultural concept**: *the inherent right of freedom*
- Learning from **"re-membered"** content that—as an African woman—Tubman knew that Black people had never given up their right to be free. So, after emancipating herself, she returned many times to the South to guide hundreds of others to freedom.

Learning about other Cultures through Cultural Knowledge

- Learning about African **worldview elements** (e.g., Collective Responsibility, Interdependence)
- Learning about a related African **cultural concept**: *an inherent right of freedom*
- Learning from **"re-membered"** content that—as an African woman—Tubman knew that Black people had never given up their right to be free. So, after emancipating herself, she returned many times to the South to guide hundreds of others to freedom.

FIGURE 5.2 Learning Through Heritage Knowledge and Cultural Knowledge.

on critical questions. You saw how Ms. Hart—guided by her mentor Ms. Singleton—demonstrated these and other emancipatory pedagogies in Chapter 2. By using these pedagogies, practitioners of Teaching *for* Freedom build upon and expand the heritage knowledge of all students *at the same time as* giving students opportunities to be centered as they gain cultural knowledge about other cultures.

Conclusion

As discussed in this chapter, the central tendencies of European worldview represent a narrow cultural field that is unable to transform the dysconsciousness or uncritical habits of mind that predominate in mainstream schooling. We provide several examples that show what European and African worldviews produce in terms of content and pedagogy—including a section that describes the central tendencies of worldview as a heuristic framework. Understanding worldview as the central tendencies of a culture or world region counters eurocratic concerns about essentializing culture that serve to further marginalize the worldviews of cultures outside the Anglosphere. To exemplify the pedagogical practices that African worldview can produce, we provide a list of African cultural concepts—drawn from consistently held patterns of traditional African thought and practice—as alternatives to the cultural concepts that have shaped current mainstream school practices. While the Afrocentric praxis of Teaching *for* Freedom is a model based on African worldview, philosophies, cosmologies, and cultural concepts, this does not exclude other worldviews and cultural concepts as seen in our example of Vietnamese language and Buddhist philosophy. By including diverse worldview elements and cultural concepts—and therefore all students, teachers, and families in the school experience—Teaching *for* Freedom models how to produce cultural continuity and agency for all groups of students who learn either by expanding their heritage knowledge or by gaining cultural knowledge.

In the next and final chapter, we present several Diasporan topics and show how Ms. Singleton and Ms. Hart teach one of the topics by "re-membering" several African cultural concepts with democratized content and emancipatory pedagogies. By using the Afrocentric praxis of Teaching *for* Freedom, they prepare students to engage differently with knowledge of the past and to grapple with the challenging exigencies that they and their families identify in their community.

References

Abímbólá, W. (1976a). *Ifá will mend our broken world: Thoughts on Yoruba religion and culture in Africa and the Diaspora.* Roxbury, MA: Aim Books.

Abímbólá, W. (1976b). *Ifá: An exposition of the Ifá literary corpus.* Ibadan, Nigeria: Oxford University Press Nigeria.

Akbar, N. (1984). Africentric social sciences for human liberation. *Journal of Black Studies, 14*(4), 395–414.

Alexander, M. (2012). *The new Jim Crow: Mass incarceration in the age of color blindness.* New York, NY: New Press.

Allwood, C. M. (2011). On the foundation of the Indigenous psychologies. *Social Epistemology: A Journal of Knowledge, Culture and Policy, 25*(1), 3–14.

Anyanwu, K. C. (1981a). The African world-view and theory knowledge. In E. A. Ruch & K. C. Anyanwu (Authors), *African philosophy: An introduction to the main philosophical trends in contemporary Africa* (pp. 77–99). Rome: Catholic Book Agency.

Anyanwu, K. C. (1981b). Artistic and aesthetic experience. In E. A. Ruch & K. C. Anyanwu (Authors), *African philosophy: An introduction to the main philosophical trends in contemporary Africa* (pp. 270–282). Rome: Catholic Book Agency.

Aptheker, H. (1951/1969). *A documentary history of the Negro people in the United States: From colonial times through the Civil War* (Vol. I). New York, NY: The Citadel Press.

Asante, M. K. (2007). *An Afrocentric manifesto.* Malden, MA: Polity Press.

Asante, M. K. (2009). *Maulana Karenga: An intellectual portrait.* Malden, MA: Polity Press.

Au, W. (2009). *Unequal by design: High-stakes testing and the standardization of inequality.* New York, NY: Routledge.

Ayers, J. (2014). *David Bronner gives $1 million to fight Big Ag in GMO labeling vote.* Retrieved from http://readersupportednews.org/news-section2/318-66/26743-focus-david-bronner-gives-1-million-to-fight-big-ag-in-gmo-labeling-vote.

Baldwin, J. A., & Hopkins, R. (1990). African-American and European-American cultural differences as assessed by the worldviews paradigm: An empirical analysis. *The Western Journal of Black Studies, 14*(1), 38–52.

Bennett, L., Jr. (1975). *The shaping of Black America.* Chicago, IL: Johnson Publishing Company.

Berliner, D. C., & Biddle, B. J. (1995). *The manufactured crisis, myths, fraud, and the attack on America's public schools.* Reading, MA: Perseus Books.

Bernal, M. (1987). *Black Athena, Vol. I.* New Brunswick, NJ: Rutgers University Press.

Berrigan, D., & Nhat Hanh, T. (1975). *The raft is not the shore. Conversations toward a Buddhist/Christian awareness.* Boston, MA: Beacon Press.

Bittman, M. (2012) *Sustainable farming: A simple fix, zero cost.* Retrieved at http://reader-supportednews.org/opinion2/271-38/14155-sustainable-farming-a-simple-fix-zero-cost.

Blaut, J. M. (1993). *The colonizer's model of the world: Geographical diffusionism and Eurocentric history.* New York, NY: The Guilford Press.

Boakye-Boaten, A. (2010). Changes in the concept of childhood: Implications on children in Ghana. *The Journal of International Social Research, 3*(10), 104–115.

Bohm, D. J. (1980). *Wholeness and the implicate order.* London: Routledge & Kegan Paul.

Bohm, D. J. (1989). *Interview with David Bohm.* Retrieved from www.youtube.com/watch?v=QI66ZglzcO0.

Bohm, D. J. (1990). *David Bohm speaks about wholeness and fragmentation from "Art meets science and spirituality in a changing economy—from fragmentation to wholeness."* Retrieved from www.youtube.com/watch?v=mDKB7GcHNac.

Bohm, D. J., & Hiley, B. J. (1975). On the intuitive understanding of nonlocality as implied by quantum theory. *Foundations of Physics, 5*(1), 93–109.

Boykin, A. W. (1986). The triple quandary and the schooling of Afro-American children. In U. Neisser (Ed.), *The school achievement of minority children* (pp. 57–92). Hillsdale, NJ: Lawrence Erlbaum.

Bullard, R. D., & Wright, B. (2012). *The wrong complexion for protection: How the government response to disaster endangers African American communities*. New York, NY: New York University Press.

Cajete, G. (1994). *Look to the mountain: An ecology of Indigenous education*. Durango, CO: Kivaki Press.

Capra, F. (1996). *The web of life: A new scientific understanding of living systems*. New York, NY: Anchor Books/Doubleday.

Capra, F. (2007). *The systems view of life*. Retrieved from www.youtube.com/watch?v=o_MDRI-Q76o.

Chomsky, N. (2013a). *A roadmap to a just world: People reanimating democracy*. Retrieved from www.chomsky.info/talks/20130617.htm.

Chomsky, N. (2013b). *Can civilization survive capitalism?* Retrieved from www.alternet.org/noam-chomsky-can-civilization-survive-capitalism.

Clarke, J. H. (1994). *Christopher Columbus and the Afrikan holocaust: Slavery and the rise of European capitalism*. Brooklyn, NY: A & B Publishers Group.

Darwin, C. R. (1859). *Origin of the species by means of natural selection, or the preservation of favoured races in the struggle for life* (1st ed.). Retrieved from http://darwin-online.org.uk/converted/pdf/1859_Origin_F373.pdf.

Darwin, C. R. (1869). *On the origin of species by means of natural selection, or the preservation of favoured races in the struggle for life* (5th ed.). Retrieved from http://darwin-online.org.uk/content/frameset?viewtype=side&itemID=F387&pageseq=121.

Davidheiser, M. (2008). Race, worldviews, and conflict mediation: Black and White styles of conflict revisited. *Peace & Change, 33*(1), 60–89.

Davis, B. (2014). *America's summer of white supremacy: A postmortem*. Retrieved from http://readersupportednews.org/opinion2/277-75/26127-americas-summer-of-white-supremacy-a-postmortem.

Diop, C. A. (1967). *Anteriority of Negro civilizations*. Paris: Presence Africaine.

Diop, C. A. (1985). Africa's contribution to world civilization: The exact sciences. In I. Van Sertima (Ed.), *Nile Valley civilizations* (pp. 69–83). New Brunswick, NJ: Journal of African Civilizations.

Dixon, V. J. (1971). African-oriented and Euro-American-oriented world views: Research methodologies and economics. *The Review of Black Political Economy, 7*(2), 119–156.

Dixon, V. J. (1976). World views and research methodology. In L. M. King, V. J. Dixon, and W. W. Nobles (Eds.), *African philosophy: Assumptions and paradigms for research on Black persons* (pp. 51–102). Los Angeles, CA: Fanon Research and Development Center.

Engelhardt, T. (2015). *A self-perpetuating machine for American insecurity*. Retrieved from http://readersupportednews.org/opinion2/277-75/27908-a-self-perpetuating-machine-for-american-insecurity.

Fayemi, A. K. (2009). Human personality and the Yoruba worldview: An ethico-sociological interpretation. *The Journal of Pan African Studies, 2*(9), 166–176.

Fendler, L., & Muzaffar, I. (2008). The history of the bell curve: Sorting and the idea of normal. *Educational Theory, 58*(1), 63–82.

Freeman, K. (2005). Black populations globally: The cost of the underutilization of Blacks in education. In J. E. King (Ed.), *Black education: A transformative research and action agenda for the new century* (pp. 135–156). Mahwah, NJ: Lawrence Erlbaum Associates for the American Educational Research Association.

Fu-Kiau, K. K. B. (2001). *African cosmology of the Bântu-Kôngo, tying the spiritual knot: Principles of life and living*. New York, NY: Athelia Henrietta Press.

Gould, S. J. (1981). *The mismeasure of man.* New York, NY: Norton.

Grande, S. (2004). *Red pedagogy: Native American social and political thought.* Lanham, MD: Rowman & Littlefield Publishers.

Gyekye, K. (1987). *An essay on African philosophical thought: The Akan conceptual scheme.* Cambridge, MA: Cambridge University Press.

Gyekye, K. (1997). *Tradition and modernity: Philosophical reflections on the African experience.* New York, NY: Oxford University Press.

Gyekye, K. (1998). Person and community in African thought. In P. H. Coetzee & A. P. J. Roux (Eds.), *The African philosophy reader* (pp. 317–336). New York, NY: Routledge.

Hall, G. M. (2005). *Slavery and African ethnicities in the Americas: Restoring the links.* Chapel Hill, NC: University of North Carolina Press.

Hall, K. (1994). Impacts of the energy industry on the Navajo and Hopi. In R. D. Bullard (Ed.), *Unequal protection: Environmental justice and communities of color* (pp. 130–154). San Francisco, CA: Sierra Club Books.

Hayes, F. W. III (2008). *The African presence in America before Columbus.* Retrieved from www.nathanielturner.com/africanpresenceinamericabeforecolumbus.htm.

Hedges, C. (2014). *Driving American politics underground.* Retrieved from www.truthdig.com/report/item/driving_american_politics_underground_20140907.

Hilliard, A. G. III (1989). Teachers and cultural styles in a pluralistic society. *NEA Today, 7*(6), 65–69.

Hilliard, A. G. III (1995). Bringing Maat, destroying Isfet: The African and African Diasporan presence in the study of ancient KMT. In I. Van Sertima (Ed.), *Egypt, child of Africa* (pp. 127–147). New Brunswick, NJ: Transaction Publishers.

Hilliard, A. G. III (1997). *SBA: The reawakening of the African mind.* Gainesville, FL: Makare Publishing Company.

Horne, D. (2014). *The counter-revolution of 1776: Slave resistance and the origins of the United States of America.* New York, NY: NYU Press.

Hwang, K-K. (2011). Reification of culture in indigenous psychologies: Merit or mistake? *Social Epistemology: A Journal of Knowledge, Culture and Policy, 25*(2), 125–131.

Ikuenobe, P. (2006). *Philosophical perspectives on communalism and morality in African traditions.* Lanham, MD: Lexington Books.

Johnson, D. W., & Johnson, R. T. (1985). The internal dynamics of cooperative learning groups. In R. Slavin, S. Sharan, S. Kagan, R. Hertz-Lazarowitz, C. Webb, & R. Schmuck (Eds.), *Learning to cooperate, cooperating to learn* (pp. 103–124). New York, NY: Plenum Press.

Karenga, M. (1999). *Odù Ifá: The ethical teachings.* Los Angeles, CA: University of Sankore Press.

Karenga, M. (2005). Odù Ifá. In M. K. Asanta & A. Mazama (Eds.), *Encyclopedia of Black studies* (pp. 388–390). Thousand Oaks, CA: Sage Publications.

Karenga, M. (2006a). *Maat, the moral ideal of ancient Egypt: A study in classical African ethics.* New York, NY: Routledge.

Karenga, M. (2006b). Philosophy in the African tradition of resistance: Issues of human freedom and human flourishing. In L. R. Gordon & J. A. Gordon (Eds.), *Not only the master's tools: African American studies in theory and practice* (pp. 243–271). Boulder, CO: Paradigm Publishers.

King, J. E. (1991). Dysconscious racism: Ideology, identity, and the miseducation of teachers. *Journal of Negro Education, 60*(2), 133–146.

King, J. E. (2006). "If justice is our objective": Diaspora literacy, heritage knowledge and the praxis of critical studyin' for human freedom. *Yearbook of the National Society for the Study of Education, 105*(2), 337–360.

King, J. E., & Akua, C. (2012). Dysconscious racism and teacher education. In J. A. Banks (Ed.), *Encyclopedia of diversity in education* (pp. 724–727). Thousand Oaks, CA: Sage Publications.

King, J. E., Swartz, E. E., with Campbell, L., Lemons-Smith, S. & López, E. (2014). *"Re-membering" history in student and teacher learning: An Afrocentric culturally informed praxis.* New York, NY: Routledge.

Klein, N. (2010). A hole in the world: The BP disaster reveals the risks in imagining that we have complete command over nature. *The Nation, 291*(2), 14–15, 17–18, 20.

Klein, N. (2014). A people's shock. *The Nation, 299*(14), 12–15, 17–18, 20–21.

Kliewer, C., & Fitzgerald, L. M. (2001). Disability, schooling, and the artifacts of colonialism. *Teachers College Record, 103*(3), 450–470.

Kumashiro, K. K. (2008). *The seduction of common sense: How the right has framed the debate on America's schools.* New York, NY: Teachers College Press.

Liliuokalani (1898). *Hawaii's story by Hawaii's Queen Liliuokalani.* Boston, MA: Lee and Shepard Publishers.

Mbiti, J. S. (1990). *African religions and philosophy* (2nd ed.). Portsmouth, NH: Heinemann Educational Books.

Meier, T. (1994). Why standardized tests are bad. In B. Bigelow, L. Christensen, S. Karp, B. Miner, & B. Peterson (Eds.), *Rethinking our classrooms: Teaching for equity and justice* (pp. 171–175). Milwaukee, WI: Rethinking Schools.

Mills, C. W. (1997). *The racial contract.* Ithaca, NY: Cornell University Press.

Mohawk, J. (1993). Coming to wholeness: Native culture as safe place. *Akwe:kon, A Journal of Indigenous Issues, X*(4), 31–36.

Nguyễn Vũ Hoàng, Vân (2009). *Contrasting of English and Vietnamese addressing forms.* Retrieved from http://khoaanh.net/_upload/CA2009/CqBT05_Nguyen_Vu_Hoang_Van_Contrasting_of_English_and_Vietnamese_addressing_forms.docx.

Nhat Hanh, T. (2001). *Thich Nhat Hanh essential writings.* Maryknoll, NY: Orbis Books.

Nhat Hanh, T. (2008). The environment is you: A talk by Thich Nhat Hanh—Denver, Colorado, August 29, 2007. *Human Architecture: Journal of the Sociology of Self-Knowledge, VI*(3), 15–20.

Nkulu-N'Sengha, M. (2005). African epistemology. In M. K. Asante & A. Mazama (Eds.), *Encyclopedia of Black studies* (pp. 39–44). Thousand Oaks, CA: Sage Publications.

Nobles, W. W. (1976). Extended self: Rethinking the so-called Negro self-concept. *The Journal of Black Psychology, 2*(2), 15–24.

NYS Board of Regents (2006, June). *Regents in U.S. History and Government.* Albany, NY: Regents of the State of New York.

NYS Board of Regents (2014, January). *Regents in U.S. History and Government.* Albany, NY: Regents of the State of New York.

Oakes, J. (1985). *Keeping track: How schools structure inequality.* New Haven, CT: Yale Press.

Oakes, J., Wells, A. S., Jones, M., & Datnow, A. (1997). Detracking: The social construction of ability, cultural politics, and resistance to reform. *Teachers College Record, 98*(3), 482–510.

Parry, R. (2014). *The State Department's Ukraine fiasco.* Retrieved from http://reader supportednews.org/opinion2/277-75/23858-focus-the-state-departments-ukraine-fiasco.

Pierce, C. (2014). *The body in the street.* Retrieved from http://readersupportednews.org/opinion2/277-75/25470-the-body-in-the-street.

Ravitch, D. (2013). *Reign of error: The hoax of the privatization movement and the danger to America's public schools.* New York, NY: Alfred A. Knopf.

Rodney, W. (1982). *How Europe underdeveloped Africa.* Washington, DC: Howard University Press.

Schamel, W., & Schamel, C. E. (1999). The 1897 petition against the annexation of Hawaii. *Social Education, 63*(7), 402–408.

Senghor, L. S. (1964). *On African socialism* (Mercer Cook, Trans.). New York, NY: Frederick A. Praeger. (Original work published 1961.)

Shenandoah, A. (1988). Everything has to be in balance. *Northeast Indian Quarterly, IV*(4) & *V*(1), 4–7.

Shields, C. M. (2004). Dialogic leadership for social justice: Overcoming pathologies of silence. *Educational Administration Quarterly, 40*(1), 109–132.

Simpson, L. (2011). *Dancing on our turtle's back: Stories of Nishnaabeg re-creation, resurgence and a new emergence.* Winnipeg, Manitoba: Arbeiter Ring Publishing.

Slavin, R. E. (1983). *Cooperative learning.* New York, NY: Longman.

Slavin, R. E. (1987). Cooperative learning and the education of Black students. In D. S. Strickland & E. J. Cooper (Eds.), *Educating Black children: America's challenge* (pp. 63–67). Washington, DC: Bureau of Educational Research, School of Education, Howard University.

Spencer, H. (1864). *The principles of biology* (vol. 1). Retrieved from http://books.google.com/books?id=SRkRAAAAYAAJ&printsec=frontcover&source=gbs_ge_summary_r&cad=0#v=onepage&q&f=false.

Swartz, E. E. (2007). Stepping outside the master script: Re-connecting the history of American education. *The Journal of Negro Education, 76*(2), 173–186.

Swartz, E. E. (2012). Distinguishing themes of cultural responsiveness: A study of document-based learning. *The Journal of Social Studies Research, 36*(2), 179–211.

Tedla, E. (1995). *Sankofa: African thought and education.* New York, NY: Peter Lang.

Van Sertima, I. (1976). *They came before Columbus: The African presence in ancient America.* New York, NY: Random House.

Von Sydow, M. (2014). "Survival of the fittest" in Darwinian metaphysics: Tautology or testable theory? In E. Voigts, B. Schaff, & M. Pietrzak-Franger (Eds.), *Reflecting on Darwin* (pp. 199–222). Farnham, London: Ashgate.

Waghid, Y. (2014). *African philosophy of education reconsidered: On being human.* New York, NY: Routledge.

Waln, V. (2014). *The Keystone XL's Senate failure isn't the end of the pipeline as an act of war.* Retrieved from http://readersupportednews.org/opinion2/271-38/27048-the-keystone-xls-senate-failure-isnt-the-end-of-the-pipeline-as-an-act-of-war.

Wiener, L. (1922). *Africa and the discovery of America, 3 Volumes.* Philadelphia, PA: Innes and Sons.

Wilder, C. S. (2013). *Ebony and ivy: Race, slavery and the troubled history of America's universities.* New York, NY: Bloombury Press.

Williams, P. J. (1991). *The alchemy of race and rights: Diary of a law professor.* Cambridge, MA: Harvard University Press.

Williams, R. (2000). Social Darwinism. In J. Offer (Ed.), *Herbert Spencer: Critical assessments of leading sociologists* (pp. 186–199). New York, NY: Routledge.

Williams, W. A. (2007/1980). *Empire as a way of life.* Brooklyn, NY: Ig Publishing.

Wolf, F. A. (1981/1989). *Taking the quantum leap: The new physics for nonscientists*. New York, NY: Harper & Row.

Wolf, F. A. (2011). *Part 1, complete shamanic physics, with Jeffrey Mishlove*. Retrieved from www.youtube.com/watch?v=yufAa4oFyug.

6

PRACTICING CULTURAL CONCEPTS AND CONTINUITY

> In an emancipatory approach, teachers and students arrive at answers; we create and construct answers by thinking together. There are no scripts because you can't script thinking.... [H]aving to contemplate questions and construct answers through interaction is already a part of an African American and Indigenous American cultural base. When children come to school and are told the answers, there is no purposeful work to do.
>
> Susan Goodwin, "Emancipatory pedagogy," 2004, in Goodwin & Swartz,
> *Teaching Children of Color: Seven Constructs of Effective Teaching in Urban Schools*,
> pp. 38–39

> Contemporary examples of traditional African educational and socialization beliefs and practices survive and thrive in Africa and the African diaspora. Only through study can we come to know, understand and utilize those practices. Only through study can we live up to the quality of the master teachers of the past.
>
> Asa G. Hilliard, III, *SBA: The Reawakening of the African Mind.* 1997, p. 78

This final chapter looks at cultural concepts in practice—how they were used in their original historical contexts and how we can use them in the classroom today. We present several African Diasporan topics, identify the cultural concepts that shaped these topics, and show how two practitioners of Teaching *for* Freedom use African cultural concepts and emancipatory pedagogies to deepen students' understanding of content and of themselves. You will also observe how these teachers provide learning experiences that include families in sustaining cultural continuity—a continuity that is visible in the African Diasporan topics themselves. For example, the same cultural concepts exhibited today by African American advocates of environmental justice were exhibited by African men and women who liberated themselves from enslavement 300 to 400 years ago, by the Jeanes teachers in rural schools and communities 100 years ago, and by participants in the Montgomery Bus Boycott 60 years ago. In other words, the cultural concepts that shaped these occurrences and gave them meaning have endured across time and place.

Identifying Cultural Concepts

In our view, understanding the meanings of past events—which is found in a culture's worldview and cultural concepts—and drawing lessons from those meanings in the present is the primary purpose of learning history. Established historical organizations claim learning history is for the purpose of fostering engaged citizenship, understanding how change shaped the world as we know it, expanding critical thinking, and inspiring through example (NCSS, 2013, 2014; AHA, 2013). While these reasons have merit, they are not primary, since they provide no direction for connecting events to the contexts in which they occurred. It is as if history, in this established view of its purpose, happened outside of culture—outside of the contexts where we can find the meanings of past events. We propose that meanings reside in the heritage knowledge (group memory) of each culture and that these meanings are identifiable in the cultural concepts that shape what people do and how they live their lives. For example, when environmental justice advocates of African ancestry act to protect their communities from industrial contamination, their actions are influenced by African cultural concepts such as *sharing responsibility for communal well-being and belonging, demonstrating concern for human welfare through actions based on community mindedness and service to others*, and *protecting childhood as a collective responsibility*. These concepts explain what the actions of these advocates mean—that in an African worldview, everyone shares the responsibility to protect the well-being of the community through service to others. These and other African cultural concepts also explain what the actions of the Jeanes teachers, the Montgomery Bus Boycott participants, and other African Diasporan people and events mean. Later in this chapter, we step back into the classroom to see how Ms. Singleton and Ms. Hart use the praxis of Teaching *for* Freedom to teach a lesson on the environmental justice movement. They engage students and families in learning not only about this movement, but about what it means—shared responsibility and service to others—in order to enact these meanings in their own community.

Below are descriptions of three African Diasporan topics. Throughout each description, we identify a number of cultural concepts that shaped the topic. As you read these accounts, notice that *sharing responsibility for communal well-being and belonging*—which is the first African cultural concept listed in Table 5.1 in Chapter 5—is present in each topic. This is such a fundamental cultural concept—one that is informed by all of the elements in an African worldview as discussed in Chapter 1—that it can be used to shape the teaching of any topic that locates African people as subjects and substantive participants in the socio-political, economic, and cultural phenomena of their time. Our first topic is the formation of early African Diasporan communities in the Americas whose members chose freedom and cultural preservation over enslavement and subjugation. Note that the number of each African cultural concept identified in the description of a topic is placed in parentheses and corresponds to the numbered cultural concepts listed in Table 5.1 in Chapter 5.

Freedom and Cultural Sovereignty

Beginning in the 16th century, the people from diverse Nations in Africa who were enslaved in the Americas brought their worldview, philosophies, cosmologies, and cultural concepts and practices with them. Thus, they embodied cultural concepts such as *the inherent right of freedom, pursuing freedom and justice as communal responsibilities*, and *knowing that cultural sovereignty* (or the maintenance of culture) *is the right of all Peoples* (see #3, #6, and #12 respectively in Table 5.1). These cultural concepts were manifested in varied forms of resistance, including self-liberation and the building of self-sustaining free African communities (Fick, 1990; Hart, 1985/2002). Thousands of men and women—some of royal ancestry—liberated themselves and formed organized hidden communities throughout the Americas beginning in the 16th century. Through self-determination, they chose freedom not only from enslavement, but freedom to maintain culture on their own terms as a common right and responsibility (Hilliard, 1995; Piersen, 1993). In Jamaica and the United States, these liberationists were called Maroons (Hart, 1985/2002). For over 200 years, there were Maroon communities in South and North Carolina, Virginia, Louisiana, Florida, Georgia, Mississippi, and Alabama (Hilliard, 1995). One such Maroon community was composed of several settlements located in the bayous surrounding New Orleans. Juan St. Maló, who was the well-supported 18th century African leader of these Maroons, inspired enough resistance to threaten the stability of the local plantocracy (Hall, 1992). While Maroon communities like the one named after St Maló were typically under assault by plantation owners and colonial military forces, free and enslaved Africans who viewed *sharing freedom as a human entitlement* formed networks of information and supplies in support of these free communities (see #16 in Table 5.1).

In Puerto Rico and Panama, self-liberated men and women were called *Cimarrones*; in Colombia and Cuba, *Palenques*; and in Brazil, *Quilombolas* (Hilliard, 1995). *Palmares*, begun in the late 16th century, was the name of a fortified *Quilombo* community of over 15,000 people in Pernambuco, Brazil, that governed itself for almost 100 years (Gomez, 2004; Kent, 1965). Bantu-speaking Angolans established *Palmares*, and their descendants lived there along with other people of African descent—both free and self-liberated, poor immigrants of diverse cultural origins, and Indigenous people (Anderson, 1996; Kent, 1965). *Zumbi Dos Palmares*—an Angolan leader of this African state from 1675–1694—continuously resisted Portuguese military attempts to destroy *Palmares*. Similarly, François Makandal, of the Kôngo—who was enslaved in Saint Domingue in the early decades of the 18th century—organized and led a massive uprising of thousands of Maroons and free Africans in 1757. Known as an excellent herbalist, doctor, and orator, his vision of emancipation encouraged his fellow freedom seekers to fight the French in an effort to overthrow them 40 years prior to the Haitian Revolution of 1791 (Fick, 1990). The men and women who liberated themselves and formed—or were born into—re-created African societies throughout the Americas were standard bearers of cultural sovereignty. They were communally oriented, meaning that their self-determination to live free was not individually focused. Rather they *exhibited self-determination that considered the needs of the collective* (see #13 in Table 5.1). In addition to self-sustaining free communities being an important form of resistance to the system of slavery, they also exemplify cultural continuity through their demonstration of the African cultural concept of *sharing responsibility for communal well-being and belonging* (see #1 in Table 5.1).

Isabella Dorsey: Each Child is Everyone's Child

Every community can name women and men who exemplify the values, principles, and virtues held in common by community members. Such is the case in the Black community of Rochester, New York, where a woman named Isabella Dorsey lived in the early 20th century. Ms. Dorsey was known as a woman who made sure that no child was without a home. In this way, she exemplified her African ancestors who viewed each child in the community as everyone's child (Swartz, 2012). Her practice of the African cultural concept of *protecting childhood as a collective responsibility* indicates the cultural continuity between her African ancestry and her life in the Diaspora (see #17 in Table 5.1).

While most children in Isabella Dorsey's community lived with and were cared for by their parents, grandparents, or other relatives, some children's parents or family members were either too sick to care for their children or had passed on. When this happened, Ms. Dorsey, with the support of her husband, Thomas Dorsey, took these children into her home. Soon the Dorsey home near downtown Rochester was not large enough to accommodate their growing family, and they moved to a larger home in the country. Their stay in this new home near Lake Ontario was short lived, since Rochester and surrounding communities were no exception in terms of the presence of white supremacy racism (Swartz, 2012). Segregation and severely limited housing, job, and educational opportunities were regularly experienced by Black residents. These unjust and unethical practices were either supported by law or by custom, and by the attitudes and actions of most White people. As a result, the Dorsey family was forced to move from their country home to another home closer to the city (Du Bois, 1994). With the help of people in the Black community and a few White supporters, the Dorsey family found and purchased this new home.

Black community support for the Dorsey home was very strong. Community members such as Reverend Dr. James E. Rose, pastor of the well-known Mt. Olivet church, supervised the Dorsey home, and in addition to his own medical practice, Dr. Charles T. Lunsford took care of the medical needs of the Dorsey children (Dorsey, n.d.). These men embodied the African cultural concept of *demonstrating concern for human welfare through actions based on community mindedness and service to others* (see #15 in Table 5.1). They, along with the Dorseys, also enacted the African cultural concept of *sharing responsibility for communal well-being and belonging* through their collective efforts to create opportunities for children to know that they belong—that they are loved and cared for by their community (see #1 in Table 5.1). Their actions indicate their awareness that the well-being of children makes the future health of a community possible.

These residents of Rochester's Black community also *exhibited self-determination that considers the needs of the collective* (see #13 in Table 5.1). For example, Dr. Lunsford was a self-determined man as he pursued a medical degree and later a practice in Rochester, but his self-determination also considered the needs of the community as he spoke out about the lack of justice for Black people in Rochester (Du Bois, 1994; Jacobson, 1985). In the 1920s and 1930s, no hospitals in Rochester would hire Black doctors or nurses, and the University of Rochester Medical School would not admit Black students. Dr. Lunsford met numerous times with medical school officials, but they would not agree to make any changes. Yet, he persisted and, due to his efforts, Edwin A. Robinson was eventually accepted as a student and became the first Black person to graduate from the University of Rochester Medical School in 1943 (Lunsford, n.d.). As a man of African ancestry, Dr. Lunsford's consistent actions—and the manner in which he pursued them—reflected his heritage knowledge. He knew that people are *responsible to bring good into the world through actions that are ethical, just, generous, compassionate, and peaceable* (see #5 in Table 5.1).

Over the years, many children lived at the Dorsey home, which functioned like a small community. Children learned about caring for each other, and everyone did something to add to the well-being of this large family. Thus, Isabella Dorsey taught her children about *sharing responsibility for communal well-being and belonging* (see #1 in Table 5.1). She also modeled *love, dignity, and decency as shared by all* (see #8 in Table 5.1). In these ways, Ms. Dorsey followed in the tradition of her African ancestors, who made sure that no child was ever without a home and that each child was everyone's child.

African American Leadership in the Environmental Justice Movement

Who lives in a community where one in five households has someone suffering from a respiratory illness (Stephenson, 2014)? This is your reality if you live in Port Arthur, Texas, a historically Black community surrounded by four oil refineries, six chemical plants, one international incineration facility, and one pet coke plant (Hunt, 2014). These industries stretch for miles—a "petrochemical landscape" that constantly emits poisons into the air, earth, and water (Stephenson, 2014, p. 25). While the Environmental Protection Agency (EPA) finally acknowledged that the toxins released into the air in Port Arthur are dangerous, this was only due to efforts by local residents and leaders like Hilton Kelley, who founded the Port Arthur Community In-Power Development Association in 2000. Kelley and other community members used the courts to force the EPA to upgrade its rules for petroleum refineries (Stephenson, 2014). Like other people in communities across the country who have responded to the disproportionate pollution that exists in urban and rural communities of color, the commitment of Port Arthur's residents to environmental justice demonstrates the African cultural concept of *sharing responsibility for communal well-being and belonging* (see #1 in Table 5.1) (Bullard, 1994, 2005; Ferris, 1994; Hunt, 2014; Russell, 2011; Stephenson, 2014).

For more than three decades, similar conditions have been documented and environmental justice efforts have occurred in places like Richmond, California, Gainesville, Georgia, Dearborn, Michigan, Northeast Philadelphia, Pennsylvania, Northeast Houston, Texas, West Dallas, Texas, East and South Central Los Angeles, California, South Tucson, Arizona, Alsen and Mossville, Louisiana, Chicago's South Side, Illinois, and Southwest Detroit, Michigan, where residents have come together to protect their families and communities (Bullard, 1990; 1994; Gomez, Shafiei, & Johnson, 2011; Hayoun, 2015; Gutiérrez, 1994; Hunt, 2014; Shabazz, 2013; Solnit, 2014; UCC Commission for Racial Justice, 1987). Many of these communities are called fence-line communities since they share a fence line with the industries that poison them (Gomez et al., 2011; Stephenson, 2014).

Theresa Landrum has always lived in Southwest Detroit since being a small child in the 1960s. Steady expansion of petroleum, recycling, and other industries in her Black community has resulted in her neighborhood being the most polluted in all of Michigan, with high rates of cancer and respiratory illnesses (Hunt, 2014). Landrum's parents died of cancer, she is a cancer survivor, and many of her neighbors are sick. Expansion of these unwanted industries in Black communities is due to victories of the mainstream environmental movement to keep them out of White middle- and lower-income communities (Bullard, 1990). In fact, the mainstream environmental movement has shown little interest in the particular conditions faced by urban communities (Collin

& Collin, 2005). In the face of these realities, Landrum is one among many women of color in the country who are leaders and participants in the movement to end environmental injustice (Gomez et al., 2011). She speaks out at community meetings and testifies at EPA hearings about the non-enforcement of environmental regulations by local officials, several who have been involved in scandals related to their dealings with the corporations responsible for the pollution (Bukowski, 2010). As a community leader, Theresa Landrum works to change not only environmental injustice, but the environmental racism that attempts to define her community. This form of racism results in the official sanctioning of contamination in communities of color through the failure to enforce regulations and laws that would remove life-threatening poisons from the environment (Chavis, 1993). By resisting environmental racism, Landrum embodies the African cultural concept of *demonstrating concern for human welfare through actions based on community mindedness and service to others* (see #15 in Table 5.1).

Academic/activist Robert D. Bullard (1990) provided early direction for the environmental justice movement by documenting landfill sitings, lead smelters, garbage incinerators, and other toxic chemical facilities that contaminate the air, soil and waterways in the South. He continues to work with local leaders and communities to document how protection from environmental abuse unequally impacts the life chances of people of color. Their actions reflect such African cultural concepts as *sharing responsibility for community well-being and belonging, exhibiting self-determination that considers the needs of the collective, demonstrating concern for human welfare through actions based on community mindedness and service to others, and knowing that cultural sovereignty* (in the form of environmental integrity) *is the common right of all Peoples* (see #1, #13, #15, and #12 respectively in Table 5.1).

Segregated housing patterns that result in the geographic proximity of poor, working class, and more affluent Black people mean that race more than class predicts harmful exposure to combined pollutants in the sections of towns, cities, and suburbs where Black people live (Bullard & Wright, 2012; Moffat, 1995). Case study research offers extensive data that detail this environmental racism (Bullard, 1994, 2005). Actually, current environmental practices provide more protection to industries that pollute African American, Native American, and Latino communities than to their residents (Bullard & Wright, 2012). While these communities are less responsible for environmental contamination, they experience more outcomes from this contamination than other communities. According to Bullard (1994), current environmental practices reflect

> the dominant environmental protection paradigm [that] 1) institutional-izes unequal enforcement [in communities of color compared to White communities]; 2) trades human health for profit; 3) places the burden of proof on the "victims," not on the polluting industry; 4) legitimates

human exposure to harmful chemicals, pesticides, and hazardous substances; 5) promotes "risky" technologies, such as incinerators; 6) exploits the vulnerability of economically and politically disenfranchised communities; 7) subsidizes ecological destruction; 8) creates an industry around risk assessment; 9) delays cleanup actions [which take longer in communities of color]; and 10) fails to develop pollution prevention as the overarching and dominant strategy.

(p. xvi)

These outcomes have literally defined an agenda for environmental justice activists in communities of color. This human rights agenda has been building over several decades to include educational programming, legal challenges, lobbying, and holding the EPA accountable for enforcement of its own policies, regulations, and initiatives; participation in local, state, and national policy making; inter-community networking and building coalitions with other civil rights organizations to defeat local legislation that would, for example, support building garbage incinerators in urban communities of color; and public protests and demonstrations that can raise awareness about environmental racism (Bullard, 1990; Gutiérrez, 1994; Hall, 1994). In terms of the long range, Bullard and colleagues are *pursuing freedom and justice as communal responsibilities* (see #6 in Table 5.1). To do this they are developing leadership for the protection of African American communities in the next generation of scholars/activists—students from HBCUs (Historically Black Colleges and Universities) who are participating in efforts to end environmental racism in their communities.

As a strong indicator of African Diasporan cultural continuity, participants in the environmental justice movement consistently embody several other cultural concepts practiced by their African ancestors: *perceiving the interconnectedness of all life; being responsible to bring good into the world through actions that are ethical, just, generous, compassionate, and peaceable;* and *protecting childhood as a collective responsibility* (see #2, #5, and #17 respectively in Table 5.1). These cultural concepts are evident in the actions of men and women from neighborhood organizations, civic clubs, and parent groups who have come together to protect the health and well-being of their children and families. They fully understand what is at stake if they don't.

"Re-membering" Cultural Concepts in the Classroom

As you know from Chapter 2, Ms. Hart is quite adept at connecting emancipatory pedagogies to democratized content due to years of mentoring by Ms. Singleton, who is a veteran colleague. As demonstrated in Ms. Hart's practice of emancipatory pedagogies such as Eldering, Locating Students, Question-Driven Pedagogy, and Culturally Authentic Assessment, she has learned that being knowledgeable—not only about a topic, but about the students she is teaching—

leads to asking open-ended questions, building upon students' cultural characteristics, co-creating curriculum with students, and engaging families in
developing assessments that include community-informed standards and expectations. Ms. Hart also learned how African cultural platforms, which carry
African worldview, philosophies, cosmologies, and related cultural concepts,
inform and support each of the emancipatory pedagogies she uses in her classroom. We have just learned that Ms. Hart and Ms. Singleton are planning a unit
that guides students to not only learn about past and current events, but to use
the cultural concepts that inform those events to act in the present.

Developing a Unit on the Environment

Toward the end of her unit on *Black Community Building*, Ms. Hart began to
discuss a possible unit on the environment with Ms. Singleton. Around the
same time, both teachers were reviewing and giving us feedback on sections of
our upcoming book, and after reading about the environmental justice movement, they decided to co-develop and co-teach an interdisciplinary unit on
environmental justice that would combine content and standards in social
studies, English Language Arts (ELA), and science. They were unable to find a
grade-level text that provided the information they were looking for, so they
adapted content from our manuscript and the sources we cited to write a
student text at grade level and to develop lesson plans. The two teachers framed
their text for students with Afrocentric concepts and wrote it using culturally
informed principles (see Tables 1.1 and 1.2 in Chapter 1). They also discussed
how to connect several African cultural concepts to the content and emancipatory pedagogies they would be using. They wanted students to experience
African Diasporan continuity in the actions of African American men and
women who have been advocating for environmental justice. They also
sketched out some assignments that could involve students and families in using
African cultural concepts in their own lives. We asked if we could observe one
of their lessons and share our observations with readers. Ms. Singleton and Ms.
Hart agreed, but suggested that we first ask our readers to consider what a unit
on this topic might look like.

Your Unit on Environmental Justice

Ms. Hart and Ms. Singleton offered several suggestions and questions to guide
your thinking about a unit on environmental justice. Ms. Singleton suggested
that you review this chapter's account of African American Leadership in the
Environmental Justice Movement (above) in preparation for finding or writing
text for students that is framed with Afrocentric concepts and written with
culturally informed principles. She explained how important it is to have "re-
membered" (democratized) student materials, how they fit with emancipatory

pedagogies, and how together they enhance students' sense of belonging through either building on and expanding their heritage knowledge or facilitating their acquisition of cultural knowledge. While the experience of writing content to grade level is good preparation for planning a unit, she emphasized that you will not always have time to do this, so first see if culturally informed materials are available. If you do need to write student text, Ms. Hart suggested that you work with a partner or in small groups to share the writing. She explained that this is a good time to discuss and take notes about which emancipatory pedagogies you might use with each section of text you are writing. Ms. Singleton agreed and offered the following questions:

> When you are writing or reviewing the student materials you will be using, what do you need to know, be able to do, and be like to use the emancipatory pedagogy called Eldering? Where might you use the emancipatory pedagogy called Locating Students to build upon students' cultural characteristics? [If you aren't sure what these characteristics are, re-read the section titled "Locating Students—an Emancipatory Pedagogy" in Chapter 2 as well as explore some of the citations in that section.] For example, how might you connect *Nguzo Saba* Principles such as Unity and Collective Work and Responsibility to Hilton Kelley and the Port Arthur Community In-Power Development Association's use of the courts to force the EPA to strengthen its rules for petroleum refineries? How can connecting *Nguzo Saba* Principles to content center students? What kinds of open-ended questions might you ask students so you can build on what they know [Question-Driven Pedagogy]? An example could be something like, "What might people in fence-line communities be thinking when they decide to confront powerful industries that are poisoning their communities?" All students will have thoughts about this that you can build on during instruction. Also, in what ways can you encourage students to draw upon their heritage knowledge or cultural knowledge as they are learning new information [Multiple Ways of Knowing]? What ideas do you have for engaging parents and family members in authentically assessing what students have learned [Culturally Authentic Assessment]? Since this unit is interdisciplinary, what curricular topics, materials, and standards might you select for each subject area?

As you are thinking about what a unit on environmental justice might look like, Ms. Hart suggested that you review the list of African cultural concepts in Table 5.1 in Chapter 5. She would like you to consider the following questions after you explain—to yourself and someone else—how you see several of these concepts being embodied in the actions of African American environmental justice leaders like Hilton Kelley, Theresa Landrum, and Robert D. Bullard:

How would you use several African cultural concepts to show that the actions of environmental leaders of African ancestry represent African Diasporan continuity? Since we're not trying to be teachers who just tell students what to think, which emancipatory pedagogies can you use to guide students to "discover" these examples of African Diasporan continuity? How might you involve students and families in using several African cultural concepts to shape responses to environmental or other injustices that might be occurring in their own communities? And how can families be part of developing authentic assessments that include community-informed ideals and standards?

If, as you are writing your student text and responding to the above suggestions, you have any questions, you can send them to omnicentricpress@gmail.com. With input from Ms. Singleton and Ms. Hart, we will provide feedback.

Classroom Observation

We decided to observe the lesson in which Ms. Singleton and Ms. Hart planned to introduce the unit's final assessment. For the previous two weeks—in ELA, social studies, and science—students had been learning about the environment and the environmental justice movement. The student text written by Ms. Singleton and Ms. Hart served as the primary text for ELA and social studies. For science lessons, they identified a few online sources and trade books about the effects of toxic waste sites, industrial emissions, fracking, and radiation on the air we breathe, the water we drink, and the soil in which our food is grown; and what can happen to organs in our bodies when we are exposed to these toxins (Bryan, 2004; Kukreja, 2015; Food and Water Watch, 2014; UCC Commission for Racial Justice, 1987). Students examined evidence of greater exposure to environmental contamination in communities of color, and discussed how environmental racism is a civil rights issue. They also learned about the actions of African American leaders and community members throughout the country who have been challenging industrial contamination in the courts, building coalitions across communities and with civil rights organizations, and engaging in public protests and demonstrations to raise awareness about environmental injustice. Ms. Singleton and Ms. Hart presented these actions to students as expressions of African cultural concepts such as *sharing responsibility for communal well-being and belonging, perceiving the interconnectedness of all life*, and *demonstrating concern for human welfare through actions based on community mindedness and service to others*. By learning that African cultural concepts are expressed in the actions of environmental leaders and community members, students gained access to what these actions mean. In particular, they learned that all life is interconnected and that we are collectively responsible to serve and care for each other.

TABLE 6.1 African Cultural Concepts and Environmental Justice

- *sharing responsibility for communal well-being and belonging* (1)
- *perceiving the interconnectedness of all life including the unseen world* (2)
- *being responsible to bring good into the world through actions that are ethical, just, generous, compassionate, and peaceable* (5)
- *pursuing freedom and justice as communal responsibilities* (6)
- *knowing that cultural sovereignty is a common right of all Peoples* (12)
- *exhibiting self-determination that considers the needs of the collective* (13)
- *demonstrating concern for human welfare through actions based on community mindedness and service to others* (15)
- *protecting childhood as a collective responsibility (each child is everyone's child)* (17)

While the irrefutable evidence of unequal protection of communities of color was troubling to everyone, learning how African cultural concepts shaped the practices of African American leaders and community members—and how these concepts had been practiced for centuries—made change seem possible. Table 6.1 above lists eight African cultural concepts that were manifested in the actions of environmental justice leaders and community residents. (Note that the numbers following each concept refer to its placement in the original list of 18 African cultural concepts in Table 5.1 in Chapter 5.)

Throughout the unit, Ms. Singleton and Ms. Hart shaped their pedagogy with other African cultural concepts, such as *pursuing knowledge as inseparable from pursuing wisdom, inquiring as a source of true knowledge,* and *gaining knowledge for the purpose of bringing goodness, harmony, and balance into the world.* The two teachers also designed a culminating project to involve students and families in *demonstrating concern for human welfare through actions based on community mindedness and service to others*—that is, in using what some of their new knowledge means in community-enhancing ways. They were introducing this final project to their combined classes as we arrived. Vignette 6.1 describes what occurred.

VIGNETTE 6.1

Observing the "Re-membering" of African Cultural Concepts in the Classroom

Ms. Singleton

Class, we'd like you to meet Dr. King and Dr. Swartz, who have come to observe our class today.

Class (in unison)

Good afternoon, Dr. King and Dr. Swartz.

Dr. King

Good afternoon, everyone! We want to thank your teachers for inviting us into your classroom. We have heard so many good things about what you are doing and we've been looking forward to this visit.

Ms. Hart

Welcome! We're so glad to have you. Our two classes have been working together on a unit about environmental justice, and today we are talking about our final project. This project will be a way for students to continue learning as they show each other, their families, and us what they have already learned.

Ms. Singleton

We have been studying about the environment and how industries and government practices are responsible for polluting Black, Native American, and Latino communities. We've learned what African American residents and leaders have done to end this abuse, and how their actions are shaped by cultural concepts that are centuries old. (Turning to the students) Let's share some of this with our visitors. What are a few examples of African cultural concepts that we have seen in the actions of African American leaders and community members in the environmental justice movement?

Terrel

They think everyone deserves a good place to live, a place where you don't get sick from breathing the air.

Andrea

They work hard to make things good and decent for everyone, not just for some people.

Jada

People thought that children should be safe, and to do that people should work together.

Larissa

The people we learned about, they try to do the right things. They care about people and want things to be fair.

Ms. Hart

Yes, and how do we know that these concepts are African—that they are African cultural concepts?

Rob

I think because as African people we have a way of looking at things like everyone should have justice. Then we make a plan like Mr. Kelley did so it can happen.

Marcos

I know Latino people that think like that—maybe because we have African ancestors.

Ms. Singleton

Yes, Marcos, what you are saying is true. There are many examples all over the world of people of African ancestry who have worked for freedom and justice, and still do.

Christine

What I read said that Mr. Kelley went to court to have better air because he thought all people deserved it, and that was a way of looking at things that African people had.

Ms. Singleton

Yes, Christine, you can know that these cultural concepts are African by reading about it.

Kanokwan

In my neighborhood at home* we try to make sure that everyone is OK. If someone isn't OK, then we try to make things better. This is like one of the African ideas we learned about.

Ms. Hart

Yes, so how do cultural concepts get from one part of the world to another?

Rodney

People bring it with them. It's part of who they are.

Zaki

I agree. My family is from another part of the world and we brought our ideas about things to this country.** Since we are here, our ancestors are here with us too. We think that people should be the ones to say what goes on in their own town. Other people shouldn't come in and try to take over and change things.

Ms. Hart

Yes, cultural concepts shape how people think and what they do. And wherever people move, they bring those concepts with them. It is the African cultural concepts you have all described that give people like Hilton Kelley, Theresa Landrum, and Robert Bullard the strength to challenge big industries and the government agencies that protect them.

Ms. Singleton

As I listen to this conversation, I realize that in talking about what we know we are also talking about who we are. So how can we show that we care about the well-being of our community? How can we use African cultural concepts to make some change that is needed in our community?

Sharesse

We should do something to take care of children who maybe don't have a home or food to eat.

Rob

We could try to find out if the air and water in this city are polluted. Then we could tell the EPA like Ms. Landrum did.

Terrel

Yeah, but the EPA doesn't always help. Mr. Bullard said that sometimes the EPA doesn't make industries follow their regulations.

Tiffany

That's true but we could write a petition or maybe speak at a City Council meeting. If we find out that a company or the city is poisoning the air or water, we could organize a march and get our parents and people they know and some of our teachers and lots of kids to come.

Ms. Hart

I really like the way you are using what you have learned about environmental injustice to think about what we can do in our own community. (Pointing to the *Nguzo Saba* poster) I'm seeing the Principles of *Umoja* [Unity], *Kujichagulia* [Self-Determination], and *Nia* [Purpose] at work here.

Elena

And if we do some kind of project we'd be using *Ujima* [Collective Work and Responsibility] too.

Ms. Singleton

That's right, and using *Nguzo Saba* Principles about how to conduct ourselves will help us to put the very old African cultural concepts we have been talking about into practice.

Ms. Hart

So, let's say we followed up on Rob's idea about seeing if the air and water in our city are polluted. Which African cultural concepts would we be putting into practice? (Ms. Hart points to another poster that lists the African cultural concepts related to the unit on environmental justice and waits as students take time to review the list). [See Table 6.1 above.]

Several students

Most of them. Every one of them. All of them.

Ms. Singleton

Yes! So if we're going to use any of these ideas—and maybe some other ones—we're going to need help from our families. They all know about the environmental justice unit we're doing, and many family members have already participated in homework assignments and in-class activities. We also have copies of the survey results that some of Ms. Hart's students and parents conducted as a final project for their unit on *Black Community Building*. They asked residents what they thought were the most pressing needs in our community.

Ms. Hart

Well, we have a lot to work with. So let's get into small groups to talk about how we can work together to make some change that is needed in this community. If your group has ideas that are not in the list of survey results, add them to the list. See if your group can agree on one or two ideas and then we'll get back together to come up with a list of possible projects. We want you to take that list home tonight and get some input from your family. They might have other ideas or some suggestions about ideas on the list. Then tomorrow, we'll use the Principle of *Kuumba* [Creativity] to figure out what we're going to do so that our community is "more beautiful and beneficial than we inherited it." That's how Maulana Karenga—the man who developed the *Nguzo Saba* Principles and *Kwanzaa*—describes *Kuumba*.

Ms. Singleton

Yes, and whatever we decide to do, it will be a way for us to bring good into the world through community-minded service to others and to show how all life is interconnected. In that way we'll be using African cultural concepts just like the people we learned about.

* Home for Kanokwan is a town in southern Thailand called Phang Nga.
** Zaki's family is Hausa from the town of Bwi in Kebbi State, Nigeria.

In this demonstration of the praxis of Teaching *for* Freedom, Ms. Singleton and Ms. Hart used several emancipatory pedagogies to engage students in learning. Can you identify where the pedagogies of Eldering, Locating Students, Multiple Ways of Knowing, and Question-Driven Pedagogy were used? (See Table 1.2 in Chapter 1 to review descriptions of these pedagogies.) Can you see how African cultural concepts—which are part of the African cultural platforms described in Chapter 2—shaped and support these emancipatory pedagogies? For example, *inquiring (the acknowledgment of not knowing) as a source of true knowledge* is a cultural concept in the philosophy of the Baluba People (a Bantu People of Central Africa), which is part of the African cultural platform that supports Question-Driven Pedagogy. As seen in this vignette, the demonstrated knowledge and expertise of Ms. Singleton and Ms. Hart (Eldering), their open-ended questions that invited everyone to contribute (Question-Driven Pedagogy), their centering of students culturally and individually (Locating Students), and their encouragement of heritage knowledge and cultural knowledge (Multiple Ways of Knowing) created ways for students to deepen their understanding of other African cultural concepts related to being community minded and to justice being a communal responsibility. It was also clear in our observation of this lesson and lessons in Chapter 2 that these teachers take every opportunity to connect families to curriculum and assessment. Practitioners of Teaching *for* Freedom know that families "hold" and convey culture in the form of heritage knowledge (group memory), including worldview, cultural concepts, and community-informed ideals and standards. By connecting the heritage knowledge of families with "re-membered" content and emancipatory pedagogies, these practitioners create learning contexts in which African Diasporan cultural continuity can be experienced and sustained. In addition to these observations, we noticed how Ms. Singleton and Ms. Hart manifested an African cultural concept at the heart of Teaching *for* Freedom: *pursuing knowledge as inseparable from pursuing wisdom.* They kept the knowledge these students were gaining about threats to community well-being linked to their development of good sense about how to use that knowledge, that is, how to discern the relationship between what is and what can be.

Conclusion

The Afrocentric praxis of Teaching *for* Freedom is an educational model in which teaching and learning occur in the context of culture. Practitioners of this praxis view themselves as connected to the cultural communities to which their students belong. They consciously locate all students—and the cultures and groups they represent—as subjects in the curriculum and pedagogy of schooling. In so doing, these practitioners teach students not only how to read, write, compute, and become informed citizens, but how to speak for and define themselves, identify meaning in the cultural concepts that have shaped events in the past and present, and recognize cultural continuity across time and place. Throughout this volume, we have invited you to learn about:

- the elements of African worldview and the philosophies, cosmologies, and cultural concepts that people with this worldview have developed and maintained (Chapters 1, 2, and 5);
- African cultural platforms that support emancipatory pedagogies (Chapter 2);
- replacing standard instructional content with "re-membered" (democratized) content that is framed with Afrocentric theoretical concepts and written with culturally responsive principles (Chapters 1 and 3);
- how the central tendencies of diverse worldviews—and their related cultural concepts—shape school and other social practices (Chapter 5);
- using African cultural concepts to transform mainstream school practices when they are "re-membered" with democratized content and emancipatory pedagogies (Chapter 5);
- how African cultural concepts shape numerous African Diasporan topics (Chapters 3, 4, and 6); and

- how cultural concepts carry meaning and sustain cultural continuity across time and place (Chapters 4, 5, and 6).

You can use the knowledge you have learned to become practitioners of Teaching *for* Freedom—to build upon and expand students' heritage knowledge and support students in gaining cultural knowledge by learning about the cultures of others. As you learn to Teach *for* Freedom, you will prepare students, with the support of their families, to gain and use knowledge that can build community in the classroom and in neighborhoods by *sharing responsibility for well-being and belonging, demonstrating concern for human welfare through actions based on community mindedness and service to others,* and *gaining knowledge for the purpose of bringing goodness, harmony, and balance into the world.*

Encore

The following culminating activity asks you to use many of the concepts, culturally informed principles, and emancipatory pedagogies presented throughout this volume. We provide a vignette of "re-membered" student text about segregation and the Montgomery Bus Boycott as a context for using these concepts, principles, and pedagogies. This two-page excerpt is located in a chapter from a "re-membered" middle school U.S. history textbook (in conceptualization) that represents a rethinking and rewriting of content about the Civil Rights movement of the mid-20th century. The vignette is printed below in black and white. For information about receiving one or more color copies of these two pages, write to omnicentricpress@gmail.com. After reading the text in Vignette 6.1, we invite you to work with a partner, in small groups, or by yourself to do the following:

1   Locate where at least three Afrocentric theoretical concepts were used to frame the student text (see Table 1.1 in Chapter 1).
2   Locate where at least three culturally informed principles were used to write the text (see Table 1.2 in Chapter 1).
3   Identify at least three African cultural concepts you see represented in the text and where (refer to Table 5.1 in Chapter 5 for a list of these concepts).
4   Select which emancipatory pedagogies you would use to teach the text (see Table 1.2 in Chapter 1 and Ms. Hart's use of these six pedagogies in Chapter 2). How would you explain these selections to a colleague?

Following Vignette 6.2 is a template for this activity (Table 6.2) that you can enlarge or redraw. Examining a "re-membered" text in this way is an authentic assessment that can help to clarify many of the concepts, principles, and pedagogies presented in this volume. It is this volume's encore, and we ask you to perform it.

VIGNETTE 6.2

The Unjust System of Segregation

Segregation is a violent system that has dominated life in the United States. As you read in chapter 14, Black people gained legal rights after the Civil War through Amendments to the U.S. Constitution. This period of time was called Reconstruction. However, by the end of this period, white plantation owners and former Confederate leaders had taken back power in Southern States. They established segregation in order to take away the rights that Black people had gained. Even though slavery was legally ended, these White men did everything they could to maintain white supremacy.

Until the mid-20th century, schools, restrooms, libraries, restaurants, transportation, and all public places were segregated. For example, segregation laws made Black people sit in the back section of all buses in the South. If a bus was crowded, Black people had to get out of their seats and stand so that white people could sit down. To pay, they had to get on the bus at the front door and then get off the bus and board at the back door. If they refused to follow these unjust rules, they were thrown off the bus or arrested.

Segregation was unethical because it denied Black people their civil and human rights. This system separated Black and White people by law and custom in every area of life. As you will read in chapter 23, its effects are still with us today.

Working to End Bus Segregation

Like their African ancestors, Black leaders in Montgomery, Alabama knew that everyone was entitled to justice, so they were working together to end segregation on the buses. Jo Ann Robinson, a teacher at Alabama State College, led a group called the Women's Political Council (WPC). In 1949 the WPC began planning a bus boycott. Another group, the National Association for the Advancement of Colored People (NAACP) was also involved in

Inside of the bus that Rosa Parks was riding when she was arrested. Photograph by Derek KT W

planning to end bus segregation. Leaders were looking for just the right case. Over 42,000 Black people lived in Montgomery in the early 1950s and all had bad experiences riding the buses. They were disrespected by the bus company, bus drivers, White patrons, and the police.

At this time, Rosa Parks was the secretary of the Montgomery NAACP and leader of its youth division. She had been working for equal rights for Black people for many years. In 1943 a driver put her off a bus for refusing to board at the back. Ms. Parks also studied at the Highlander Folk School where she and other leaders learned methods of organizing for Civil Rights.

On December 1, 1955, Rosa Parks was riding a bus home from work. When the bus driver told her to give up her set to a white man, she refused. The driver called the police and Ms. Parks was arrested. Later she said, "When I made that decision, I knew that I had the strength of my ancestors with me."

The very next day Jo Ann Robinson and two of her students handed out 50,000 fliers calling for a boycott of the buses on December 5th—the day Ms. Parks went to trial. Other community leaders agreed to begin the bus boycott around the case of Rosa Parks. They knew that having justice was the responsibility of the whole community. They also knew that Rosa Parks was the right person, because she had the courage to stand up under pressure—even when threats were made on her life.

The Montgomery Bus Boycott

Dr. Martin Luther King, Jr. was a new minister in town. Once the boycott started, he agreed to lead it because community leaders chose him. With support from the WPC, the NAACP, and the Black community, the bus boycott lasted 381 days. Thousands of Black people walked to work every day in good and bad weather. Teachers, housekeepers, laborers, shop keepers, clerks, and students—people from all walks of life—took part. On the first day of the boycott there were almost no Black people on the buses. That night 7,000 Black people met and agreed to continue the boycott. They knew that segregation was wrong, and that everyone was entitled to dignity and decency. These were brave men and women. Many lost their jobs and were threatened with violence for participating in the boycott.

While the boycott was going on, Black leaders in Montgomery filed a court case against bus segregation. It went all the way to the Supreme Court of the United States. The Court finally ruled that bus segregation was unconstitutional. The boycott ended once the Court ruling was delivered to officials in Montgomery on December 20, 1956. The next day Black people rode the buses in Montgomery after more than a year. Acting for justice and being community minded brought an end to bus segregation in Montgomery and the nation.

Some White people responded with violence, shooting at buses and bombing Black leaders' homes and churches. But Dr. King, other African American leaders, and citizens continued to follow the practices of their African ancestors. They worked to build communities where everyone was entitled to justice and freedom and everyone belonged.

Ms. Rosa Parks and Dr. Martin Luther King, Jr. ca. 1955

This is a picture of the Dexter Avenue Baptist Church today. In 1954, Dr. Martin Luther King, Jr. was the full-time pastor of this Church in Montgomery, Alabama. On December 4, 1955—just a few days after Ms. Rosa Parks was arrested—Dr. King held a meeting in the basement of this Church. Leaders who were present agreed to go ahead with the bus boycott. They also formed the Montgomery Improvement Association (MIA) to plan and organize the boycott. This Church remained a planning site for future Civil Rights actions after the Montgomery Bus Boycott ended.

Photograph by Colin Mutzkler

TABLE 6.2 Activity Template: Identifying Concepts, Principles, and Pedagogies

Identifying Concepts, Principles, and Pedagogies
1   Locate where at least three Afrocentric theoretical concepts were used to frame the student text (see Table 1.1 in Chapter 1).
2   Locate where at least three culturally informed principles were used to write the text (see Table 1.2 in Chapter 1).
3   Identify at least three African cultural concepts you see represented in the text and where (see Table 5.1 in Chapter 5).
4   Select which emancipatory pedagogies you would use to teach the text (see Table 1.2 in Chapter 1 and Ms. Hart's use of these six pedagogies in Chapter 2). How would you explain these selections to a colleague?

References

AHA (American Historical Association) (2013). *Why study history: Two views.* Retrieved from www.historians.org/teaching-and-learning/why-study-history.

Anderson, R. N. (1996). The Quilombo of Palmares: A new overview of a Maroon state in seventeenth-century Brazil. *Journal of Latin American Studies, 28*(3), 545–566.

Bryan, N. (2004). *Love Canal: Pollution crisis.* Milwaukee, WI: World Almanac Library.

Bukowski, D. (2010). *Southwest Detroit wins court victories against polluter.* Retrieved from http://voiceofdetroit.net/2010/12/08/southwest-detroit-wins-court-victories-against-polluter/.

Bullard, R. D. (1990). *Dumping in Dixie: Race, class, and environmental quality.* Boulder, CO: Westview Press.

Bullard, R. D. (Ed.) (1994). *Unequal protection: Environmental justice and communities of color.* San Francisco, CA: Sierra Club Books.

Bullard, R. D. (2005). *The quest for environmental justice: Human rights and the politics of pollution.* Berkeley, CA: Counterpoint Press.

Bullard, R. D., & Wright, B. (2012). *The wrong complexion for protection: How the government response to disaster endangers African American communities.* New York, NY: New York University Press.

Chavis, B. F. Jr. (1993). *Confronting environmental racism: Voices from the grassroots.* Boston, MA: South End Press.

Collin, R. M., & Collin, R. (2005). Environmental reparations. In Robert D. Bullard (Ed.), *The quest for environmental justice: Human rights and the politics of pollution* (pp. 209–221). San Francisco, CA: Sierra Club Books.

Dorsey, I. (n.d.). *Newspaper clipping file for Isabella Dorsey*. Rochester, NY: Local History Division of the Central Library of Rochester and Monroe County.

Du Bois, E. E. (1994). *The city of Frederick Douglass: Rochester's African-American people and places*. Rochester, NY: The Landmark Society of Western New York.

Ferris, D. (1994). A call for justice and equal environmental protection. In R. D. Bullard (Ed.), *Unequal protection: Environmental justice and communities of color* (pp. 298–319). San Francisco, CA: Sierra Club Books.

Fick, C. E. (1990). *The making of Haiti: The Saint Domingue revolution from below*. Knoxville, TN: The University of Tennessee Press.

Food and Water Watch (2014). *Fracking*. Retrieved from www.foodandwaterwatch.org/water/fracking/.

Gomez, A. M., Shafiei, F., & Johnson, G. S. (2011). Black women's involvement in the environmental justice movement: An analysis of three communities in Atlanta, Georgia. *Race, Gender & Class, 18*(1/2), 189–214.

Gomez, M. (2004). *Reversing sail: A history of the African Diaspora*. New York, NY: Cambridge University Press.

Goodwin, S. (2004). Emancipatory pedagogy. In S. Goodwin & E. E. Swartz (Eds.), *Teaching children of color: Seven constructs of effective teaching in urban schools* (pp. 37–48). Rochester, NY: RTA Press.

Gutiérrez, G. (1994). Mothers of East Los Angeles strike back. In R. D. Bullard (Ed.), *Unequal protection: Environmental justice and communities of color* (pp. 220–233). San Francisco, CA: Sierra Club Books.

Hall, G. M. (1992). *Africans in colonial Louisiana: The development of Afro-Creole culture in the eighteenth century*. Baton Rouge, LA: Louisiana State University Press.

Hall, K. (1994). Impacts of the energy industry on the Navajo and Hopi. In R. D. Bullard (Ed.), *Unequal protection: Environmental justice and communities of color* (pp. 130–154). San Francisco, CA: Sierra Club Books.

Hart, R. (1985/2002). *Slaves who abolished slavery: Blacks in rebellion*. Kingston, Jamaica: University of the West Indies Press.

Hayoun, Massoud (2015). *China's Louisiana purchase: Toxic concerns in "Cancer Alley."* Retrieved from http://readersupportednews.org/news-section2/312-16/28314-chinas-louisiana-purchase-toxic-concerns-in-cancer-alley.

Hilliard, A. G., III (1995). *The Maroon within us: Selected essays on African American community socialization*. Baltimore, MD: Black Classic Press.

Hilliard, A. G., III (1997). *SBA: The reawakening of the African mind*. Gainesville, FL: Makare Publishing Company.

Hunt, J. (2014). *EPA to require air pollution measurements in Black communities*. Retrieved from www.blackpressusa.com/epa-to-require-air-pollution-measurements-in-black-communities/#sthash.6nPnfuhR.dpbs

Jacobson, S. (February 22, 1985). Dr. Charles Lunsford dies: Rochester's first Black physician fought bias, disease. *Times Union*, Rochester, NY (Local History Division of the Central Library of Rochester and Monroe County, newspaper clipping file, Dr. Lunsford).

Kent, R. K. (1965). Palmares: An African state in Brazil. *The Journal of African History, 6*(2), 161–175.

Kukreja, R. (2015). *Conserve energy future*. Retrieved from www.conserve-energy-future.com/AboutUs.php.

Lunsford, C. T. (n.d.). *Newspaper clipping file for Dr. Charles T. Lunsford*. Rochester, NY: Local History Division of the Central Library of Rochester and Monroe County.

Moffat, S. (1995). *Minorities found more likely to live near toxic sites: Environment: Study finds race is more important than income in determining whether a neighborhood has such a hazard*. Retrieved from http://articles.latimes.com/1995-08-30/local/me-40344_1_ hazardous-waste.

NCSS (National Council for the Social Studies) (2013). *Revitalizing civic learning in our schools: A position statement of National Council for the Social Studies*. Retrieved from www.socialstudies.org/positions/revitalizing_civic_learning.

NCSS (National Council for the Social Studies) (2014). Developing state and local social studies standards. *Social Education, 78*(4), 199–201.

Piersen, W. D. (1993). *Black legacy: America's hidden heritage*. Amherst, MA: University of Massachusetts Press.

Russell, L. M. (2011). *Reducing disparities in life expectancy: What factors matter?* Retrieved from www.iom.edu/~/media/Files/Activity%20Files/SelectPops/HealthDisparities/2011-FEB-24/Commissioned%20Paper%20by%20Lesley%20Russell.pdf.

Shabazz, Saeed (2013). *Black Louisiana town latest victim of "environmental racism."* Retrieved from www.finalcall.com/artman/publish/health_amp_fitness_11/article_100643.shtml.

Solnit, R. (2014). *Welcome to year one of the climate revolution*. Retrieved from http://readersupportednews.org/opinion2/277-75/27705-welcome-to-year-one-of-the-climate-revolution.

Stephenson, W. (2014). Ground zero in the fight for climate justice. *The Nation, 298*(26), 16–17, 19–20, 22–25.

Swartz, E. E. (2012). *Remembering our ancestors*. Rochester, NY: Rochester City School District.

United Church of Christ (UCC) Commission for Racial Justice (1987). *Toxic wastes and race in the United States: A national report on the racial and socio-economic characteristics of communities with hazardous waste sites*. Retrieved from www.ucc.org/about-us/archives/pdfs/toxwrace87.pdf.

ABOUT THE AUTHORS

Joyce E. King, Ph.D., holds the Benjamin E. Mays Endowed Chair for Urban Teaching Learning and Leadership at Georgia State University and is Professor of Educational Policy Studies and affiliated faculty in the Department of African American Studies. Her research and publications address a transformative role for culture in teaching and teacher preparation, Black Studies curriculum theorizing, community-mediated research, and dysconscious racism, the term she coined. King has international experience teaching, lecturing, and providing professional development in Brazil, Canada, China, England, Jamaica, Japan, Kenya, Mali, New Zealand, and Senegal. She is the 2014–2015 president of AERA.

Ellen E. Swartz, Ph.D., is an independent scholar and education consultant in curriculum development and the construction of culturally informed instructional materials for K-12 teachers and students. As the former Frontier Chair in Urban Education at Nazareth College, Dr. Swartz conducted research on the knowledge base of preservice teachers in urban education as part of identifying how teacher educators can more effectively prepare teachers for urban schools. She has also published in the areas of education history, emancipatory pedagogy, and the concept of "re-membering" as an approach to achieving more comprehensive accounts of the past.

INDEX

Page numbers in *italics* denote tables, those in **bold** denote figures or vignettes.